UNHCR as a Surrogate State

International organizations (IOs) that focus on refugees are finding themselves spread increasingly thin. As the scale of displacement reaches historic levels—protracted refugee situations now average 26 years—organizations are staying for years on end, often working well beyond their original mandates. In some cases, IOs may even act as a substitute for the state. This book considers the conditions under which surrogacy occurs and what it means for the organization's influence on the state. It looks specifically at the United Nations High Commissioner for Refugees (UNHCR) as a surrogate state in protracted refugee situations in Kenya, Tanzania, and Uganda.

Drawing on international relations literature and empirical studies of UNHCR, Miller asks how and when UNHCR takes on surrogacy, and what effect this has on its ability to influence how a host state treats refugees. The book develops a framework for understanding IOs at the domestic level and presents a counterintuitive finding: IO surrogacy actually leads to less influence on the state. In other words, where UNHCR behaves like a state, it is less able to influence a host state's refugee policies.

UNHCR provides an excellent example of an IO working on multiple levels, making this book of great interest to practitioners and policymakers working on refugee-related issues, and scholars of forced migration, international relations, international organizations, and UNHCR.

Sarah Deardorff Miller teaches international relations and refugee-focused courses with Columbia University, American University and the University of London. She previously worked, and continues to consult, with NGOs, and think tanks and recently released a book on Syrian displacement.

Routledge Global Institutions Series

Edited by Thomas G. Weiss
The CUNY Graduate Center, New York, USA
and Rorden Wilkinson
University of Sussex, Brighton, UK

About the series

The "Global Institutions Series" provides cutting-edge books about many aspects of what we know as "global governance." It emerges from our shared frustrations with the state of available knowledge—electronic and print-wise, for research and teaching—in the area. The series is designed as a resource for those interested in exploring issues of international organization and global governance. And since the first volumes appeared in 2005, we have taken significant strides toward filling conceptual gaps.

The series consists of three related "streams" distinguished by their blue, red, and green covers. The blue volumes, comprising the majority of the books in the series, provide user-friendly and short (usually no more than 50,000 words) but authoritative guides to major global and regional organizations, as well as key issues in the global governance of security, the environment, human rights, poverty, and humanitarian action among others. The books with red covers are designed to present original research and serve as extended and more specialized treatments of issues pertinent for advancing understanding about global governance. And the volumes with green covers—the most recent departure in the series—are comprehensive and accessible accounts of the major theoretical approaches to global governance and international organization.

The books in each of the streams are written by experts in the field, ranging from the most senior and respected authors to first-rate scholars at the beginning of their careers. In combination, the three components of the series—blue, red, and green—serve as key resources for faculty, students, and practitioners alike. The works in the blue and green streams have value as core and complementary readings in courses on, among other things, international organization, global governance, international law, international relations, and international political economy; the red volumes allow further reflection and investigation in these and related areas.

The books in the series also provide a segue to the foundation volume that offers the most comprehensive textbook treatment available dealing with all the major issues, approaches, institutions, and actors in contemporary global governance—our edited work *International Organization and Global Governance* (2014)—a volume to which many of the authors in the series have contributed essays.

Understanding global governance—past, present, and future—is far from a finished journey. The books in this series nonetheless represent significant steps toward a better way of conceiving contemporary problems and issues as well as, hopefully, doing something to improve world order. We value the feedback from our readers and their role in helping shape the on-going development of the series.

A complete list of titles can be viewed online here: www.routledge.com/Global-Institutions/book-series/GI.

Global Governance and China (2018)
edited by Scott Kennedy

The League of Nations (2018)
by M. Patrick Cottrell

The British Media and the Rwandan Genocide (2018)
by John Nathaniel Clarke

The Millennium Development Goals (2018)
by Sakiko Fukuda-Parr

Sustainable Development Goals and the UN Goal-Setting (2017)
by Stephen Browne

Inside the United Nations (2017)
by Gert Rosenthal

International Institutions of the Middle East (2017)
by James Worrall

The Politics of Expertise in International Organizations (2017)
edited by Annabelle Littoz-Monnet

UNHCR as a Surrogate State

Protracted Refugee Situations

Sarah Deardorff Miller

Routledge
Taylor & Francis Group
LONDON AND NEW YORK

First published 2018
by Routledge
2 Park Square, Milton Park, Abingdon, Oxon OX14 4RN

and by Routledge
711 Third Avenue, New York, NY 10017

Routledge is an imprint of the Taylor & Francis Group, an informa business

British Library Cataloguing-in-Publication Data
A catalogue record for this book is available from the British Library

Library of Congress Cataloging-in-Publication Data
A catalog record for this book has been requested

ISBN: 978-1-138-20978-7 (hbk)
ISBN: 978-1-31545-681-2 (ebk)

Typeset in Times New Roman
by Apex CoVantage, LLC

Contents

List of illustrations

Figures

Tables

Acknowledgments

I am very grateful to the many people who made this research possible: all of the NGO, government, UN and civil society interviewees; refugees; fellow students; and faculty who gave their time to inform the book. A special thanks to former colleagues who helped host me during field research and helped to connect me to additional interviewees. I am especially grateful to my primary doctoral supervisor, Dr. Alexander Betts, for all of his feedback and comments that generated new insights and clarity throughout the process. I am also grateful to my secondary supervisor, Jennifer Welsh, for her support and guidance.

Most of all, I am thankful to my family: my two dogs who slept at my feet while most of this was written; my parents, who never tire of cheering me on; my children, who remind me of what is most important and keep me on my toes; and most of all, to my husband, Sean, who has always encouraged and supported me. It is my hope that this book will help to further inform important issues and debates that affect the lives of the displaced.

Abbreviations

C&M	care and maintenance (UNHCR)
CSR51	1951 Convention Relating to the Status of Refugees
DAR	Development Assistance to Refugees (Uganda)
DRA	Department of Refugee Affairs (Kenya)
DRC	Democratic Republic of the Congo
DV	dependent variable
EAC	East African Community
IDP	internally displaced person
GoK	government of Kenya
GoT	government of Tanzania
GoU	government of Uganda
ICC	International Criminal Court
ICRC	International Committee of the Red Cross
IO	international organization
IP	implementing partner
IR	international relations
IV	independent variable
LI	local integration
MHA	Ministry of Home Affairs (Tanzania)
MNC	multinational corporation
MNOC	multinational oil corporation
NEP	Northeastern Province (Kenya)
NGO	nongovernmental organization
NNT	newly naturalized Tanzanian
OAU	Organisation of African Unity
OPM	Office of the Prime Minister (Uganda)
PRS	protracted refugee situation
RSD	Refugee Status Determination
SP	Settlement Policy (Uganda)

SRS/DAR	Self-Reliance Strategy (Uganda)
TCRS	Tanganyika Christian Refugee Service (Tanzania)
UN	United Nations
UNDP	United Nations Development Programme
UNHCR	United Nations High Commissioner for Refugees
USG	US Government
WFP	World Food Programme

Introduction

- **Introducing the puzzle**
- **Situating the puzzle in international relations**
- **Overview of the framework**
- **Applying the framework to UNHCR, methods of inquiry**
- **Why the empirical work is important**
- **Structure of the book**

International organizations that focus on humanitarian relief and refugees in particular are working in nearly every corner of the world and face greater and greater demands as forced displacement continues on a massive scale. Likewise, as displacement lasts for longer periods of time—the average length of displacement is 17 years[1]—these organizations may find themselves staying in a given area for years on end, in most cases far longer than ever anticipated at the beginning of the crisis. Many of these organizations feel demands to do more and more for displaced persons who are often ignored by host governments that are unable or unwilling to respond. At the same time, they are often working well beyond their original mandates, appearing to be victims to "mission creep" at best and greedy for "humanitarian territory" at worst. For example, in some cases, refugee protection may span into paving roads, paying police salaries or settling land disputes—activities seemingly far outside the original mandate to assist the displaced. Organizations may even take on "surrogate state" properties where the state has little presence among the displaced. For example, Jeff Crisp and Amy Slaughter (2008) write that the United Nations High Commissioner for Refugees (UNHCR)

> created a widespread perception that the organization was a surrogate state, complete with its own territory (refugee camps), citizens (refugees), public services (education, health care, water, sanitation, etc.), and even ideology (community participation, gender equality).[2]

This book examines the role of UNHCR as a surrogate state in protracted refugee situations (PRS) in Kenya, Tanzania and Uganda. It asks how and when it takes on surrogacy and what effect this has on its ability to improve protection for refugees. The topic is timely: in 2016 the United Nations (UN) General Assembly adopted the New York Declaration for Refugees and Migrants, which aims to improve refugee and migrant protections and to address large-scale movements with greater responsibility sharing by 2018. UNHCR, which is already spread very thin across the globe, welcomed this commitment in hopes that states will commit more to protecting refugees. But it is also unclear what it will mean for UNHCR's work—namely, whether it will require even greater expansion into new issue areas and situations. Thus, considering UNHCR's role in PRS is highly relevant to understanding its potential expansion in the near future.

Situating the puzzle in international relations

International relations (IR) theory is a natural home for debating what UNHCR's surrogacy might look like and mean. IR understands the role of international organizations (IOs) in a variety of ways, ranging from mere instruments through which states act, created for the sole purpose of serving state interests (e.g. rationalist, realist and neorealist approaches); to views that see IOs as affecting state behavior by promoting cooperation (e.g. liberal institutionalists); and to views of IOs as authoritative, autonomous actors with their own political agency (e.g. some constructivists). Amidst this wide array of approaches to IOs, most of the debate remains focused on IOs working at the global level, despite many also having a domestic-level "field" presence. Those that do look locally tend to focus on norm diffusion and institutionalization, often thinking of IO domestic behavior through networks, domestic actors or partners, but seldom by looking at the IO itself working *within* the state.[3] Comparative politics and other disciplines also offer some insight into IOs working domestically, but tend to lose sight of the ways organizations act "as simultaneously domestic and international actors."[4] None of this literature theorizes specifically about the domestic-level role of an IO with an "on the ground" presence, how such a role may differ from the IO's international roles and what this means for the IO's relationship with the state in which it is working.

In response, this research responds to a gap in the literature that neglects to consider IO roles at the domestic level, and subsequently what that role means for the IO's relationship with the state. This encompasses the unique component of an IO's physical presence on the ground and the ways in which it takes on roles at the domestic level that are different from its roles at the global level.

These questions thus speak to larger, unanswered scholarly debates about the ways in which IOs work on multiple levels (ranging from "on the ground" to internationally) and how domestic-level IO roles can shift with the passing of time. They relate to the broader question in IR: "how do international institutions 'matter'?" or influence state behavior. Furthermore, the focus on IOs operating domestically expands IR literature on IOs, to consider not just how it is working from a global level, but also in a given locale. In some cases, the IO's local presence morphs into something far different than originally intended in its international form. In many relief and development settings, for example, IOs headquartered in Geneva or New York with a very specific mandate may find themselves taking on different roles in the context of remote, impoverished areas with little state presence or capacity. These IOs may perform their traditional activities, may work in partnership with the state, may act as an instrument of the state or may take on responsibilities far beyond their mandates, in some cases becoming surrogate states of their own. The IO may be reluctantly filling a void left by the state's absence, or it may be grabbing power more directly. This phenomenon can most easily be seen where the IO takes on governance functions or service provision responsibilities. How this happens and what it means for state behavior are questions that have been largely neglected in IR literature.

IOs focused on humanitarian relief, development, or human rights often work on multiple levels, having headquarters in one place, in addition to an "on the ground" presence. UNHCR in particular provides an excellent example of an IO working on multiple levels, from the commonly studied global level, to an extended domestic presence through its work in long-term refugee camps. Indeed, its history since the mid-twentieth century is marked with expansion, from an organization working at the international level, to one that is now largely operational in the field. What started as a small office in the 1950s as a response to refugee movements in Europe now has a budget of over US$3.5 billion and more than 7,600 staff in more than 125 countries, of which some 85 percent work in the field.[5] And while UNHCR still remains a predominantly hierarchical, top-down organization headquartered in Geneva, a number of forced migration scholars have outlined the complexities of this multileveled role, including the ways in which UNHCR's operational role at the domestic level can morph into other things, including a surrogate state.[6] This is especially evident in PRS, where it may begin its involvement with the expectation that it is there for temporary emergency relief and immediate refugee protection, but as the emergency drags on and years pass, it may absorb more responsibility and permanence through a care and maintenance (C&M) model that can lead to substitution for the state, or surrogacy.

How can IR account for examples such as this? Despite an expansive literature on IOs, it struggles to explain how and when an IO like UNHCR takes on a domestic-level role like surrogate statehood over time, how this role differs from the international role it simultaneously holds and what the broader implications are for the IO's relationship with the state in which it is working. With respect to the latter question, it is unclear as to whether an IO's increased presence and responsibility positively affects its ability to influence the state. Indeed, intuitive logic would seem to imply that an actor with a large presence that takes on responsibility and provides services and funds would have greater political leverage. In many states, for example, large companies, organizations or political constituencies are more powerful because of their expansive presence. However, a closer look at the phenomenon of IOs engaging in surrogate statehood questions this logic, demonstrating that influence is not as clear-cut.

The concept of "domestication" helps explain these dynamic roles that IOs assume when working in a given locale. The concept shows the range of roles an IO can assume, from having a small role to working as a surrogate state. Thus far, there is no IR literature on IO surrogacy, and only a small number of studies within forced migration literature consider UNHCR as a surrogate state.[7]

The book engages with international relations, comparative and empirical literature on UNHCR and international organizations in East Africa. It thus seeks to understand how an IO's role (particularly a surrogate state role) at the domestic level—with a physical presence in a given locale—can affect state behavior. The questions posed in this research are also relevant to a range of issues in international relations today, not least the relationship between international, domestic and local actors, as well as questions of sovereignty, norms, human rights, humanitarian intervention (especially in "failed" or "weak" states), international law, globalization, global governance, the politics of citizenship, the locus of power and transnational actors.

Overview of the framework

This book is guided by two central questions, one descriptive and one explanatory: *how and when does an IO take on surrogate state properties? And if they do, how does this affect its ability to influence the state ("so what?")?*

The framework employs the concept of "domestication" to provide a broad spectrum of roles that IOs can take on at the domestic level, ranging from working on a small scale to working as a surrogate state. It then homes in on surrogacy, addressing theoretical and empirical questions on two levels:

Level 1 (broader IO-theory level): When and how do IOs take on surrogate state roles, and how does this affect their relationship with the states in which they work?

Level 2 (empirical UNHCR-focused level): When and how does UNHCR take on surrogate statehood, and how does this affect its relationship with the state vis-à-vis the refugees with whom it is working (or, put simply, how does it affect state behavior toward refugees)?

In light of these questions, two different, but related, arguments are at play in each level of the framework. The first is descriptive, demonstrating that IOs can take on surrogate statehood at the domestic level—one of a range of domestic roles IOs can take—and exploring under what conditions this is likely to occur. This can be in contrast to, or complementary to, its global roles, which are already well documented within IR. This is a unique contribution to IR literature in and of itself, as no previous studies have focused on this. The second rests on affirmation of the first (that an IO takes on surrogacy) and analyzes the implications: what difference does it make if an IO takes on surrogacy? It examines this question by looking at the IO's ability to influence the state. Thus, the latter question is only considered upon demonstration that the former occurs. Both questions speak to IO influence domestically (from within), contributing more broadly to IR's understanding of the role and influence of IOs.[8]

Empirically, then, this research is more about how UNHCR's domestic, surrogate state role affects (or has no effect on) the state's behavior toward refugees. This is not to say that its surrogacy is the sole factor dictating how much a state will be influenced on refugee matters by UNHCR—certainly state behavior toward refugees is affected by a range of variables, many of which are outlined in the case studies. Indeed, with so many factors playing a role in a state's policy decisions toward refugees, it would be naïve to assert one cause amidst so many variables and contexts; it would also be very difficult to control for and test the variables as separate units. Consequently, this research does not propose an exact causal "recipe" for why one state treats refugees one way and another treats them in a different way but rather seeks to engage with the full context, carefully tracing the relevant variables in order to gauge the relationship between UNHCR's role "on the ground" and its influence on the state's behavior toward refugees. In this respect, the research is more focused on process and the ways in which surrogacy can play a role in a broader causal story—not as the sole cause, but in conjunction with other variables. Thus, a parsimonious causal explanation—one where the research proclaims with certainty that "x causes y" is not the intention (or within the scope) of this research. Rather a descriptive account of what surrogacy looks like, when and how it occurs and how to identify it, followed by a discussion of its effects on the IO's relationship with the state (thus demonstrating some of the effects of IO surrogacy on the relationship of influence between the IO and the state) is the goal. Causation is part of the discussion, but this book seeks to add to the picture of influence, rather than negate the many other explanations of influence.

To engage with these questions, this book develops a framework for understanding IOs working domestically. It considers the concept of "domestication" to understand the range of roles IOs take at the domestic level, before homing in on one particular domestic-level IO role: surrogate statehood. The framework outlines indicators of IO surrogacy, conditions under which it is likely to occur and factors that sustain IO surrogate state roles over long periods of time. It then describes the various types of relationships that can emerge from IO surrogacy, including states that engage in partnership with the IO versus states that engage in abdication of the situation in which the IO is working. Finally, it presents a counterintuitive claim: *IOs that take on more surrogate state properties tend to have less influence on the states in which they work.* Such findings are certainly surprising. Indeed, at first glance, one might expect an IO that has taken on surrogacy to translate to greater influence on the state. After all, if the IO is funding and carrying out a range of projects—in some cases administering entire regions, perhaps paving roads, providing water, education and health resources, as well as being perceived as an authority by locals—this would seem to render it more leverage. In reality, the opposite seems to be true. An IO that takes on surrogacy tends to have *less* influence on the state.

The framework applies several mechanisms (drawn from scholars like Monica Kathina Juma and Astri Suhrke 2002, Chris Dolan and Lucy Hovil 2006, and Loren Landau 2008) to help unpack why this is the case, including responsibility shifting and marginalization of the state (also discussed in Chapter 1). It does not claim that surrogacy alone affects an IO's influence on the state—certainly, a number of variables determine this, as discussed further in Chapter 1. However, recognizing that surrogacy does not necessarily lead to greater IO influence is in and of itself an interesting and useful contribution to IR, given that no other literature has fully assessed the ramifications of IO surrogacy. Thus, this study considers whether and how the dependent variable (DV), IO influence over state behavior, is affected by the independent variable (IV), IO surrogate statehood.

Applying the framework to UNHCR, methods of inquiry

To bring the framework from the theoretical to the empirical, this study examines the role of UNHCR as a surrogate state in PRS, looking at case studies of Kenya, Tanzania and Uganda. These cases offer variation in UNHCR's surrogacy and its ability to influence the state and demonstrate a spectrum of state behavior toward refugees, with different attitudes and policies ranging from open to restrictive. The framework is applied to each case by first demonstrating when and how UNHCR takes on surrogate state properties over time and, second, by considering how this surrogacy affects its ability to influence state behavior. Chapter 1 discusses how to measure these variables. While this study will focus only on UNHCR in PRS, the potential for further studies of this nature within IR literature on IOs is expansive. For example, one might examine development actors or nongovernmental organizations (NGOs) with similar "on the ground" roles.

Proving that UNHCR takes on surrogate state roles, then, is only the first step of this research. The second, more challenging question is what this means in terms of influence on the state. In other words, an IO like UNHCR might take on a surrogate state role, but it is not clear how, if at all, this affects its ability to influence the state on issues it cares about, such as refugees. Moreover, it is not clear how the surrogate state properties of UNHCR morph over time in PRS, giving UNHCR a reach and scope it otherwise might not possess, and for which current IR theories on international organizations do not account. Thus, the framework has broader implications for IR literature on IOs, including new ways of thinking about IO influence and power.

The book draws on qualitative methods. In addition to a thorough literature review of academic, humanitarian and policy sources, semistructured interviews with UNHCR, government and NGO officials at local, national and international levels were conducted. These interviews provided first-hand accounts of how UNHCR functioned "on the ground," how it was perceived by other actors (including refugees and locals) and the ways in which surrogacy affected its relationship with the state. The book thus builds a framework via heuristic case studies, drawing on material and non-material indicators to help identify and measure IO influence on the state—empirically taken as UNHCR's influence on state treatment of refugees. To understand the causal relationship between IO surrogate statehood and influence over state decisions, two main mechanisms are employed: marginalization of the state and responsibility shifting.[9] These mechanisms help demonstrate how—across the range of interwoven variables at work—IO surrogacy relates to influence over state behavior.

UNHCR was selected as the IO to study because it exemplifies an IO that has taken on a host of roles at domestic and global levels. Indeed, Chapter 2 outlines its historical trajectory, demonstrating the different roles it takes and its "toolbox" of ways to influence states, including through moral authority, persuasion between individual leaders or "naming and shaming" states. There is also extensive literature written on UNHCR's role, including some of the only scholarship on surrogate statehood, which makes it a good IO to study. Finally, as discussed later in this chapter, studying the role of UNHCR at the domestic level is not only academically interesting but speaks to an important set of issues for practitioners and policymakers alike. Shedding light on its role and its ability to influence states, therefore, might better inform the policies pertaining to some of the world's most challenging political, economic and humanitarian situations.

This research narrows its focus to UNHCR's involvement in PRS. Examining protracted cases (as opposed to newer refugee crises) makes inherent sense, given that IO surrogacy tends to occur with the passing of time as an IO like UNHCR accrues more and more responsibility. PRS are also very different from emergency situations where states and IOs may take on temporary roles to respond to a crisis but would not have enough time to assume the duties and responsibilities of a surrogate state. Moreover, what is most needed during the immediate crisis phase of an initial influx is very different many years into a refugee camp. The rights denied over longer periods of time and the choices and wishes of those in exile also differ greatly from the first months in a camp to, say, 10 years in. Thus, looking at an emergency situation would not provide the timeframe or context relevant to study UNHCR's surrogacy. In contrast, PRS provide adequate windows of time to trace the historical presence of UNHCR, tracking how and under what conditions it assumed surrogacy and how that affected its influence on the state. In other words, looking at longer-term cases enables the study of observable variance, the evolution of surrogacy and the conditions that bring about surrogacy.

While the study of PRS has gained traction among forced migration scholars in the last decade, most PRS receive less and less international attention as years pass and new emergencies take precedence. UNHCR and most scholars define a PRS as a situation where "a refugee population of 25,000 persons or more has been living in exile for five years or longer in a developing country."[10] It is a situation where:

> refugees find themselves in a long-lasting and intractable state of limbo. Their lives may not be at risk, but their basic rights and essential economic, social and psychological needs remain unfulfilled after years in exile. A refugee in this situation is often unable to break free from enforced reliance on external assistance.[11]

According to this definition, nearly two-thirds of refugees in 2015—some 12 million—are considered to be in a protracted situation.[12] The average PRS has lasted 26 years, and the states hosting the largest populations tend to be the least capable, themselves facing poverty and insecurity.[13]

The 10 largest PRS as of 2015 were: [14]

- Palestinians in Lebanon, Jordan and Syria;
- Afghans in Iran and Pakistan;
- Somalis in Yemen, Ethiopia and Kenya;
- Burmese in Bangladesh, Malaysia and Thailand;
- Colombians in Ecuador and Venezuela;
- Congolese from the Democratic Republic of the Congo (DRC) in Uganda, Rwanda, Tanzania and Burundi;
- Sudanese in Chad, South Sudan and Ethiopia;
- Vietnamese in China;
- Central Africans in Chad and Cameroon; and
- Rwandans in Democratic Republic of the Congo.

The oldest PRS as of 2015 were:[15]

- Palestinians (since 1948);
- Sudanese in Ethiopia (since 1968);
- Burundians in Tanzania (since 1971);
- Sahrawis from Western Sahara in Algeria (since 1975);
- Rwandans in DRC (since 1978);
- Afghans in Iran and Pakistan (since 1979);
- Vietnamese in China (since 1979);
- Iraqis in Iran (since 1979);
- Congolese (DRC) in Burundi and Tanzania (since 1980); and
- Chadians in Sudan (since 1984).

For further reference, Table I.1 shows major PRS as of 2008.

The case studies of Kenya, Tanzania and Uganda thus provide a natural grouping of PRS to study UNHCR's role. How generalizable the findings in these cases are to other contexts (and other IOs, for that matter), however, is dealt with carefully. The book holds that the framework and claims of UNHCR's surrogacy do apply to UNHCR elsewhere. While thorough investigation into new cases would be needed to unpack UNHCR's varied involvement, its top-down approach to its work makes it relatively uniform in its procedures around the world.[16] Likewise, many UNHCR interviewees that have worked in Tanzania, Uganda and Kenya have also worked in Thailand, Eastern Europe, Nepal or Latin America, for example, and thus spoke

Table I.1 Major PRS as of January 2008, according to UNHCR Statistics from the end of 2006[17]

Country of asylum	*Origin*	*Refugee numbers (as of end of 2004)*
Algeria	Western Sahara	90,000
Armenia	Azerbaijan	113,200
Azerbaijan	Armenia	188,400
Burundi	Dem. Rep. of Congo	12,600
Cameroon	Chad	7,100
Central African Rep.	Sudan	7,900
China	Vietnam	300,900
Congo	Dem. Rep. of Congo	46,300
Côte d'Ivoire	Liberia	25,600
Croatia	Bosnia and Herzegovina	2,100
Dem. Rep. of Congo	Angola	132,300
Dem. Rep. of Congo	Rwanda	37,300
Dem. Rep. of Congo	Sudan	6,200
Egypt	Occupied Palestinian Territory	70,200
Ethiopia	Somalia	16,600
Ethiopia	Sudan	67,000
Ghana	Liberia	35,700
Guinea	Liberia	21,800
Guinea	Sierra Leone	5,300
India	China	77,200
India	Sri Lanka	69,600
Iraq	Islamic Rep. of Iran	11,800
Iraq	Occupied Palestinian Territory	15,000
Islamic Rep. of Iran	Afghanistan	914,300
Islamic Rep. of Iran	Iraq	54,000
Kenya	Somalia	173,700
Kenya	Sudan	73,000
Liberia	Sierra Leone	3,600
Malaysia	Philippines	45,100
Mexico	Guatemala	1,200
Nepal	Bhutan	107,800
Pakistan	Afghanistan	1,044,000
Rwanda	Dem. Rep. of Congo	46,300
Saudi Arabia	Occupied Palestinian Territory	240,000
Senegal	Mauritania	19,600
Serbia	Bosnia and Herzegovina	27,400
Serbia	Croatia	71,100
Sierra Leone	Liberia	27,300
Sudan	Eritrea	157,200
Sudan	Ethiopia	11,000
Thailand	Myanmar	132,200
Uganda	Sudan	215,700
Uganda	Dem. Rep. of Congo	113,290[18]
United Rep. of Tanzania	Burundi	352,600

Country of asylum	*Origin*	*Refugee numbers (as of end of 2004)*
United Rep. of Tanzania	Dem. Rep. of Congo	128,000
Uzbekistan	Tajikistan	39,200
Yemen	Somalia	91,600
Zambia	Angola	42,700
Zambia	Dem. Rep. of Congo	60,900

from this rich trove of experience. Moreover, many of the most acclaimed studies on UNHCR take a similar route: basing generalizations off of a smaller number of case studies about UNHCR because UNHCR works so uniformly on the global scale.[19] Jeff Crisp and Amy Slaughter (2008) also discuss UNHCR's surrogacy across the board, drawing on a range of cases from different time periods and around the globe to demonstrate the ways in which UNHCR's behavior in certain cases is representative of its behavior more broadly. The broader layer of how well this study on UNHCR is representative of other IOs is discussed in greater detail in the conclusion. Indeed, the study raises important questions about the role and effects of IOs on state behavior.

Why the empirical work is important

On an empirical level, one does not have to look far to see why this study is important. Protracted refugee situations are linked to some of the most devastating conflicts in the world. Not only are they indicative of ongoing political strife and states' inability to solve both intra- and interstate crises, but they are often both a result and a cause of these conflicts. Refugees are key elements to many of the world's most highly complex puzzles of war and peace. Likewise, PRS represent some of the direst humanitarian situations, with generations of some refugee populations growing up in confinement with little access to many of their most basic human rights. Generally these situations become protracted as political conflicts continue, and one of the three "durable solutions" (return, local integration (LI) or resettlement) has failed.[20] In most PRS, return is seen as the most desirable solution, and thus refugees remain in camps and wait for decades in hopes that conditions for return will emerge. At the core of this research, then, is a very pressing issue that goes beyond intellectual interest: how states react to refugees matters and how states interact with the IOs that serve refugee populations, like UNHCR, matters a great deal to refugees. In addition to human suffering that takes place in refugee camps, there are security, economic and social concerns, and thus, understanding the role of an IO like UNHCR is both timely and important.

Protracted exile has taken center stage in many state, UN and NGO migration initiatives, including the recent summits in 2016 alongside the UN General Assembly. Studies on PRS have become more prevalent over the last decade, depicting them as unique and deserving individual attention. While this research will not advocate for specific policies or assert a specific viewpoint, it is undeniable that the subject matter of refugees has ethical implications.[21] After all, studying why and how refugees might obtain better access to their basic human rights, including freedom of movement and the right to work, is important, just as states seeking better, safer responses to refugee populations is also a pressing question. This therefore hopes to help policymakers, practitioners and refugees to better understand the broader relations between states and IOs like UNHCR, perhaps generating insights on how states can find better policies for their refugee populations and ultimately improve conditions for refugees while also alleviating host state concerns.

Structure of the book

The next chapter introduces the theoretical framework proposed, explaining the relationships, variables and mechanisms at work. Chapter 2 applies the framework to the empirical case of UNHCR, introducing the relevant forced migration literature on UNHCR's surrogate statehood and providing some background to UNHCR's history, its "toolbox" of influence over states and its operational presence. Chapters 3, 4 and 5 provide case studies of UNHCR's surrogacy, looking at its role and varied levels of influence in Kenya, Tanzania and Uganda. The final chapter concludes the study by pulling together overarching themes, considering the findings in light of the framework and drawing out areas for further research.

Notes

1 US Department of State, "Protracted Refugee Situations." Available from www.state.gov/j/prm/policyissues/issues/protracted/.

2 Jeff Crisp and Amy Slaughter, "A Surrogate State? The Role of UNHCR in Protracted Refugee Situations," in *Protracted Refugee Situations: Political, Human Rights and Security Implications*, ed. Gil Loescher, James Milner, Edward Newman and Gary Troeller, 123–140 (New York: United Nations University Press, 2008), 131–132.

3 E.g. Acharya 2004; Cortell and Davis 1996; Keck and Sikkink 1998; Thomas Risse, Stephen C. Ropp and Kathryn Sikkink, *The Power of Human Rights: International Norms and Domestic Change* (Cambridge: Cambridge University Press, 1999); Grace Skogstad, ed., *Policy Paradigms, Transnationalism, and Domestic Politics* (Toronto: University of Toronto Press, 1999).

4 Margaret E. Keck and Kathryn Sikkink, *Activists beyond Borders: Advocacy Networks in International Politics* (Ithaca, NY: Cornell University Press, 1998), 6.

5 United Nations High Commissioner for Refugees, "Displacement: The New 21st Century Challenge," *UNHCR Global Trends 2012* (2012). Available from www.unhcr.org/51bacb0f9.html.

6 Michael Kagan, "We Live in a Country of UNHCR: The UN Surrogate State and Refugee Policy in the Middle East," *New Issues in Refugee Research*, Paper No. 201 (2011), UNHCR Policy Development and Evaluation Service.

Jeff Crisp and Amy Slaughter, "A Surrogate State? The Role of UNHCR in Protracted Refugee Situations," *New Issues in Refugee Research*, Research Paper No. 168 (2009), UNHCR.

Barbara Harrell-Bond, *Imposing Aid: Emergency Assistance to Refugees* (Oxford: Oxford University Press, 1986).

Simon Turner, *Politics of Innocence: Hutu Identity, Conflict and Camp Life* (New York: Berghahn Books, 2010).

Jacob Stevens, "Prisons of the Stateless: The Derelictions of UNHCR," *New Left Review* 42 (2006) (November–December).

7 Kagan, "We Live in a Country of UNHCR"; Stevens, "Prisons of the Stateless."

Jeff Crisp and Amy Slaughter, "A Surrogate State? The Role of UNHCR in Protracted Refugee Situations," in *Protracted Refugee Situations: Political, Human Rights and Security Implications*, ed. Gil Loescher, James Milner, Edward Newman and Gary Troeller (New York: United Nations University Press, 2008), 123–140.

8 IOs can be defined in a range of ways. Scholars like Pease (2012) take a broad approach, understanding IOs to potentially encompass IGOs, NGOs, regimes and MNCs. This book does not refute that a broad understanding of IOs could be applicable here—indeed, the theoretical framework could apply to MNCs, NGOs and regimes, though further testing would be needed to confirm this. However, this book takes a more cautious route and focuses solely on IGOs as IOs, drawing on Dai (2007), Hurd (2011) and Abbott and Snidal (1998) for definitional reference. This has direct implications for how far generalizations are taken: conclusions about UNHCR drawn here can be translated, albeit with caution, to other IGOs like UNDP, ICRC, IOM or WFP. It should not be applied to NGOs, MNCs or regimes without a much deeper and rigorous analysis.

9 Monica Kathina Juma and Astri Suhrke, "Introduction," in *Eroding Local Capacity: International Humanitarian Action in Africa*, ed. Monica Kathina Juma and Astri Suhrke (Uppsala: Nordiska AfrikaInstitutet, 2002), 5–18.

Bonaventure Rutinwa, "The Marginalisation of Local Relief Capacity in Tanzania," in *Eroding Local Capacity: International Humanitarian Action in Africa*, ed. Monica Kathina Juma and Astri Suhrke (Uppsala: Nordiska AfrikaInstitutet, 2002), 73–93.

Loren B. Landau, *The Humanitarian Hangover: Displacement, Aid and Transformation in Western Tanzania* (Johannesburg: Wits University Press, 2008).

10 UNHCR, "Protracted Refugee Situations: High Commissioner's Initiative," (2008): 5. Available from www.unhcr.org/4937de6f2.pdf.

11 UNHCR, "Protracted Refugee Situations," 5. This definition does not include Palestinian refugees, internally displaced people or urban self-settled refugees.

12 US Department of State, Humanitarian Information Unit, "Global Protracted Refugee Situations." Available from www.state.gov/documents/organization/266018.pdf.

13 US Department of State, "Protracted Refugee Situations." Available from www.state.gov/j/prm/policyissues/issues/protracted/.

14 US Department of State, Humanitarian Information Unit, "Global Protracted Refugee Situations." Available from www.state.gov/documents/organization/266018.pdf.

Some of these refugee numbers have increased since this data was compiled (case studies reflect the most recent data, but this at least provides an overview). Likewise, new crises, including that of Syria, can now be included as protracted cases. Note: not all of these are in camps, and UNHCR's presence varies in each.

15 US Department of State, Humanitarian Information Unit, "Global Protracted Refugee Situations." Available from www.state.gov/documents/organization/266018.pdf.

16 Gilbert Loescher, *The UNHCR and World Politics: A Perilous Path* (Oxford: Oxford University Press, 2001).

17 Forced Migration Online, "Protracted Displacement" (2011). Available from www.forcedmigration.org/research-resources/thematic/protracted-displacement-situations.

Their data does not include internally displaced people or urban self-settled refugees.

18 This number was inserted from UNHCR's current 2013 statistics.

19 E.g. Harrell-Bond, *Imposing Aid*; Loescher, *The UNHCR and World Politics*.

Gilbert Loescher and James Milner, "Protracted Refugee Situations: The Search for Practical Solutions," in UNHCR, *The State of the World's Refugees* (Oxford: Oxford University Press and UNHCR, 2006), 105–127.

Gilbert Loescher and James Milner, *Protracted Refugee Situations: Domestic and International Security Implications*. Adelphi Paper 375 (Oxford: Routledge, 2005).

Gilbert Loescher and James Milner, "Protracted Refugee Situations: Causes, Consequences, and Trends," Paper presented to RSC 25th Anniversary Conference, Oxford University, Oxford, United Kingdom, 2007.

Gilbert Loescher, Alexander Betts and James Milner, *The United Nations High Commissioner for Refugees (UNHCR): The Politics and Practise of Refugee Protection in the Twenty-First Century* (Routledge: New York, 2008).

More relevant here, see, for example, Grabska (2008) in Michael Kagan, "We Live in a Country of UNHCR: The UN Surrogate State and Refugee Policy in the Middle East," *New Issues in Refugee Research*, Paper No. 201, UNHCR Policy Development and Evaluation Service (2011).

20 According to the 1951 United Nations Convention Relating to the Status of Refugees, a refugee is a person who (according to the formal definition in article 1A of this Convention) "owing to a well-founded fear of being persecuted for reasons of race, religion, nationality, membership of a particular social group or political opinion, is outside the country of his nationality, and is unable to or, owing to such fear, is unwilling to avail himself of the protection of that country" (United Nations High Commissioner for Refugees, *Convention Relating to the Status of Refugees*, United Nations, 1951. Available from www.unhcr.org/pages/49da0e466.html. The definition goes hand-in-hand with the principle of *non-refoulement*, or the notion in international law that one cannot be forced back to a place where their life or freedoms may be threatened.

21 David Turton, for example, writes,

> I cannot see any justification for conducting research into situations of extreme human suffering if one does not have the alleviation of suffering as

> an explicit objective of one's research. For the academic this means attempting to influence the behavior and thinking of policy-makers and practitioners so that their interventions are more likely to improve than worsen the situation of those whom they wish to help. (1996, 96)

David Turton, "Migrants and Refugees: A Mursi Case Study," in *In Search of Cool Ground: War, Flight and Homecoming in Northeast Africa*, ed. Tim Allen (London/Trenton: James Currey/Africa World Press, 1996), 96–110.

1 The framework

- **Introducing the framework**
- **Domestication and IO surrogacy**
- **Measuring surrogacy and influence**
- **Relations and causality in the framework: less is more**
- **The mechanisms**
- **Conclusion**

This book was guided by two overarching questions: first, how can IR understand IOs working at the domestic level and in particular those that appear to be surrogate states? And second, how does surrogacy affect the IO's ability to influence the state? Many IOs working operationally "on the ground" now carry out activities far beyond their original mandates, doing everything from providing social services and security, to paying police salaries and settling land disputes. In some developing countries, populations may see an IO, not the central state, as the authority governing in their given locale.

This chapter introduces a theoretic framework on IOs at the domestic level, focusing specifically on IO surrogacy. Building on IR literature on IOs, it presents a spectrum of IO roles at the domestic level, explained by a concept called "domestication," which describes both properties of and processes through which IOs take on different roles at the domestic level. The framework then focuses on a more extreme end of the spectrum: IOs as surrogate states. It outlines the ways in which an IO takes on surrogacy, including conditions and indicators and the ways in which states tend to react (by abdicating responsibilities to the surrogate state IO or partnering with it). The framework then considers how IO surrogacy affects its ability to influence the state in which the IO is working. It presents the counterintuitive claim that IO surrogate statehood works inversely to its influence over the state: the more an IO takes on surrogate statehood, the less capable it is to influence state behavior. Finally, the chapter seeks to understand this relationship by setting out two mechanisms: marginalization of the state and responsibility/blame shifting.

Domestication and IO surrogacy

The previous section outlined some of the shortcomings of IR's understanding of IOs at the domestic level. While there any number of IOs working domestically, most IO literature looks at IO behavior and influence from a global level, and the IO literature that does engage with the domestic level tends to be focused on norm diffusion and institutionalization, not the domestic role of the IO itself. Thus, there is a gap in the literature addressing IOs at the domestic level—what roles they take and what these roles mean for relations with the state.

This framework responds to this gap by suggesting that IOs can "domesticate," or take on various roles at the domestic level (e.g. instrument of the state, autonomous actor in its own right, transterritorial deployment, surrogate state), and that states react in a range of ways (e.g. abdicationist or partnership-oriented). Of these domesticated types, this book focuses on the most extreme end of the spectrum: surrogate statehood. The framework considers what it means for the IO's relationship with the state, namely, the extent to which IOs as surrogate states can exert influence over state behavior. It does not purport that IO surrogate statehood is the only factor influencing the policy decisions states make—certainly, a number of variables influence these decisions—but nonetheless traces its role in the relationship. Thus, two interrelated questions are at play in the framework. First, how and under what conditions can IOs become surrogate states? When they do, the second question addresses what this means for the relationship between IOs operating domestically and the states in which they work.

The findings lead to a counterintuitive claim that has interesting theoretical implications. At first glance, one might initially expect an actor with a large presence, lots of funding and responsibility for a large number of people to have more political influence. This would be a natural assumption: actors that take on state-like properties (surrogate statehood) at the domestic level garner greater influence. Instead, the framework suggests that IO surrogacy has an inverse relationship to influence over state policy decisions; the closer to surrogacy an IO gets, the less influence it tends to have over the state in which it is working. This "less is more" outcome can be explained via two primary mechanisms—marginalization of the state and responsibility shifting—both of which are explored on p. 31. Thus, besides contributing to understandings of IOs working domestically, focusing specifically on surrogate statehood reveals, not only that IOs can and do work domestically as surrogate states, but that surrogate statehood does not necessarily increase influence over the state.

The sections in this chapter unpack what is meant by surrogate statehood and some of the characteristics attributed to an IO assuming surrogate statehood. However, it is important to begin the analysis by noting that surrogate statehood is not binary but rather falls along a spectrum. Surrogacy is measured via both material things (e.g. the IO provides services that the state would normally provide; it may pay policy salaries or pave roads; it may even administer or adjudicate, such as helping to broker land deals) and nonmaterial things (e.g. the IO is perceived by local communities to be an authority; rhetoric may indicate that it is seen as having state-like power). Influence, also discussed further on p. 27, is defined as the ability to affect outcomes; to sway decisions that might otherwise take a different direction; and even to pressure, impact and hold some level of authority.

Before moving forward, however, it should be mentioned that, while the scope of the framework is generalizable to other IOs, it does not apply to IOs working in emergency situations such as war, famine or natural disasters, which in turn would exhibit an entirely different set of political variables, different actors and different roles for the state and emergency response IOs. Rather, the focus on surrogacy is by definition something that evolves with the passing of time and therefore should not be examined in emergency settings. In addition, the framework helps unpack one aspect of IOs working at the domestic level: the way in which an IO can take on surrogate state characteristics and what that means for its relationship with the host state. Thus, it is important to stress that the framework and the causal relationships are narrow in scope: they are not meant to explain all of the different variables that go into policy processes and decisions on the part of states. Finally, the framework cannot be generalized to imply that less IO involvement from an international standpoint would have the same effects (more or less influence) as less involvement from a domestic standpoint—in other words, the "domestic" IO claims offered here do not necessarily translate to "international" IO behavior.

"Domestication" of an IO: a spectrum of IO roles at the domestic level

The literature discussed earlier outlines some of the ways IOs are viewed by IR scholars, including as an instrument of states, as an autonomous actor, as a network or transnational actor, as a forum for debate and discussion, as an interlocutor, as a norms-setter, as a creator and generator of knowledge, and any number of other roles (see Ian Hurd 2011, 16).[1] This study argues that IO literature lacks an understanding of how IOs act at the domestic level—not simply through the diffusion of norms or through other domestic actors, but as an actor in its own right at the domestic level. Zooming in from the global to the domestic level, then, this section sketches a spectrum of roles IOs may take at the domestic level, using the concept of "domestication."

Domestication points to the ways in which an IO becomes embedded into a given locale in a way that is unique to its otherwise international status. It thus describes different degrees to which an IO can be involved domestically and furthermore the different labels and characteristics it might assume. Being mindful of Michael Barnett's (2001) argument on avoiding analytical entrapment from the rigid categories of "local," "national," "global" and "international" (see p. 34), domestication helps uncover the processes by which an IO's role can be altered from its international roles when it works operationally on the ground. Working within the domestic level does not mean that the IO ceases to be "international" and becomes a domestic actor entirely, but it does imply that an IO can straddle multiple identities at once. Ronald Kassimir's (2001) depiction of the Catholic Church as a multileveled institution parallels the concept: just as the Catholic Church maintains an international presence, with the Pope in Rome, it also works domestically through local parishes, in a sense holding multiple identities at once. Numerous IOs, from the International Committee of the Red Cross (ICRC) to UNHCR, can be described this way.

Domestication is therefore a descriptive concept relating to IO behavior. Operationalization or having a field presence is not the same as domestication—indeed they are part of it, but there are also deeper implications relating to responsibility, authority and status, as described on p. 23.[2] In contrast to other uses of the word, it is not meant to imply that the IO is somehow "tamed" but rather points to the process by which it takes on properties at the domestic level. These properties may or may not differ from all of its international properties and could include a range of behaviors (e.g. participating in local politics, hiring local staff and conducting business according to local customs[3] or governing a given locale). All require a physical presence on the ground—not through partners or networks, but of the IO itself (though this book does have some discussion of working through subcontracted organizations, which is quite common). As Figure 1.1 shows, an IO at the domestic level can take on a range of roles from working undercover in a small capacity to being a surrogate state, all while maintaining its international identity and global role.

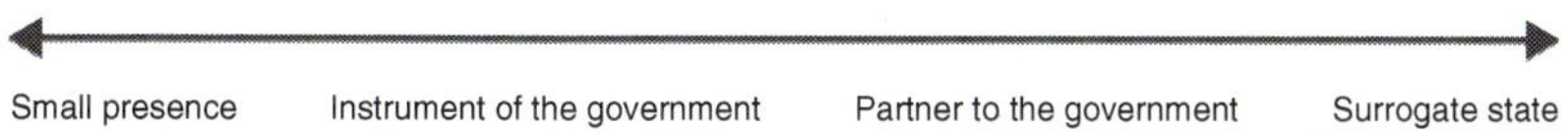

Figure 1.1 Spectrum of "domesticated IOs" with examples

Each type of "domesticated IO" could be the subject of its own book, harboring its own nuances and complexities. IOs can move in any direction along the spectrum or remain static. Moreover, IO surrogate statehood is not the automatic outcome (and may in fact be the rarest of outcomes). Furthermore, it should be noted that all IOs do not necessarily domesticate. Indeed, many work solely through domestic partners, which is well documented in the literature and not the focus here.

Looking at the spectrum of domestication helps unpack how an IO becomes a surrogate state. Although few scholars have employed the term, Cyril Obi (2001), for example, uses "domesticated" to describe how some multinational oil companies (MNOCs) in Nigeria act in partnership with the state but operate directly in the community.[4] He argues that some MNOCs actually "govern" local communities by exercising power and allocating resources and by influencing local and national decisions. These MNOCs may work in conjunction with the central authorities or may overshadow them completely. Similarly, Onishi (1999) writes how MNOCs can carry out state-like roles, including the provision of services and facilities of education, agriculture, health and water.[5] Other scholars within forced migration literature (e.g. Jeff Crisp and Amy Slaughter 2009; Michael Kagan 2011) have hinted at the concept, as will be examined in the next chapter, but none has related their findings to IR theory on IOs.[6]

Perhaps the most relevant scholarship to the concept of domestication considered here is Robert Latham's (2001) research on transterritorial deployments. He looks specifically at where international, global and transnational actors bump up against political and social life "on the ground."[7] According to Latham, transterritorial deployments are "hinges joining global and local forces around the exercise of power and responsibility and the pursuit of political projects across boundaries."[8] Transterritorial deployments are externally based, meaning they have "relatively thick organic links back to some outside point of origin" and usually involve "the purposeful forward placement of a unit, division, or representative of an organization or institution in some local context."[9] By definition, they are specialized in relation to any local social order they enter "since they rest on the forward placement of a defined and delimited organization from outside. . . . [T]hey move along relatively narrow bands of intervention or engagement with local order."[10] Organizations working via transterritorial deployment, therefore, have a "dual face" as they interact on multiple levels, representing identities and interests to authoritative institutions (the state, IOs and other "local" organizations), and govern their own members through internal politics of legitimation, resource allocation and social control, influenced by extralocal connections.[11] Even when there is technically political authority in a municipal administration over a local polity, transterritorial deployments can take responsibility, carrying out their own systems of order. This is related to how "domestication" is used here. Latham even uses the term "domestication" at one point:

> A deployment such as a church mission, a transnational oil corporation installation, or an international NGO office can also become a node in a translocal network. The organizational form in this case is no longer simply an external entity: a mission becomes a diocese, a company affiliate becomes '*domesticated*' . . . and a factory becomes a town. Connections to platforms such as headquarters may take on both network and deployment qualities.[12]

Transterritorial deployments do not, however, go so far as to be surrogate states, nor does the literature on them consider some of the nuances of governance, power/influence and service provision as examined in this study.

Domestication also helps explain varied levels of influence and authority that IO surrogate states acquire over time. Indeed, surrogate statehood does not occur immediately upon an IO's arrival in a country but rather happens with the passing of time. Latham's transterritorial deployments offer some clarity here as well. The passing of time can transform an IO that is initially a transterritorial deployment into a surrogate state with some semblance of authority, governance and power. Latham looks at authority in terms of whether the transterritorial deployment is seen as temporary or permanent.[13] This relates to the status and scope of their specialization on the ground. Latham writes, "Status, like scope, has a bearing on the question of responsibility for local order. It also serves as a marker for what an outside agent thinks it has a right to do in some place."[14] With temporary status, the transterritorial deployment is not expected to be the "ultimate and lasting authority over local order," and it is certainly still susceptible to pressures from other state and nonstate actors.[15] However, local actors are less likely to cooperate with international efforts if they know a withdrawal will happen soon.[16] In a similar way, domesticated IOs, particularly those that become surrogate states, need others—be it local populations, civil society groups or local government officials—to recognize their authority. Domestication looks further, however, in accounting for the "domino effect" over time—cases where an IO may unintentionally move along the spectrum, taking on more and more responsibility with the passing of time, heading toward surrogacy (or vice versa).

How an IO domesticates certainly depends upon other important facets of IOs, including their nature and characteristics. How "top-down," hierarchical and bureaucratic it is or what type of leadership it has (and the power of individuals), for example, can all have influence. Whether it is a normative organization and the nature of its partners—especially NGOs that are its implementing partners (IPs) on the ground—are others in a long list of variables that explain when and how domestication might occur. These are not directly analyzed here but are discussed in the context of the case studies. In addition, domesticated IOs may subcontract some work to domestic actors (e.g. NGOs), which give the IO a local presence (though working through partners alone does not constitute domestication; as noted earlier, a physical, local presence of the IO must be necessary).

Measuring surrogacy and influence

As highlighted in the introduction, IOs work in a range of ways at the domestic level, some with minimal involvement, some as instruments of the state and others taking on expansive operations. In order to begin to understand how IOs work domestically, this book narrows the scope to the most extreme, focusing on one type of domestic IO role: surrogate statehood. It not only identifies and describes IO surrogacy but also considers its effects.

Measuring surrogacy

The framework seeks to explain the nature and effects of IOs acting domestically. Building on the literature discussed earlier, this research has demonstrated that IOs can take on a number of roles, one extreme being a surrogate state, which is the focus here. It does not understand surrogate statehood as binary but rather as a general category occupying the far end of the spectrum; IOs approaching surrogacy can be "more" or "less" in the direction of surrogacy, but it is not a clean-cut category with an exact cut-off. However, there are some helpful indicators that help reveal the extent to which an IO is approaching surrogate statehood, thus giving some semblance of a threshold for the category. These are described further in this section. Moreover, as the previous section indicates, surrogacy is not automatically the outcome that occurs with domestication. Many IOs work domestically and never approach surrogacy.

To describe an IO as a "surrogate state" first requires a working understanding of what a state is. This is, of course, a subject of extensive literature within IR and beyond. This book will not rehash the debate in detail but draws from James Milner (2009) in conceiving of a state as consisting of a "territory, a population that inhabits that territory, and an authority that governs that population and which has a monopoly over the use of force to exercise its authority."[17] He also adds that recognition by other states and sovereignty is important and draws on Barry Buzan (1991) to understand a state via three components: physical (population, territory, resources);

institutional expression ("the machinery of government, including its executive, legislative, administrative and judicial bodies, and the laws, procedures and norms by which they operate");[18] and the "idea of the state, rooted both in the nation . . . and in organizing ideologies."[19] He differentiates it from "regime," which refers to the ruling elites (citing Job 1992, 15), noting that they can be the same, but are not always. Buzan's first component, the physical protection and security of the territory and population, tends to be the first priority.

While surrogate statehood has not been written on within IR, a few forced migration scholars have examined it.[20] Building on their analyses, this study proffers that IO surrogate statehood is best understood in relation to state functions of service provision, security and governance functions in a given territory. Crisp and Slaughter (2008), for example, discuss surrogate statehood in terms of "territory (refugee camps), citizens (refugees); public services (education, health care, water, sanitation, etc.); and ideology (community participation, gender equality)."[21] Other scholars have described the same idea with different terms (e.g. Lund's "local shadow government").[22] Surrogate statehood also requires a higher level of local responsibility than other IOs assume, which may or may not translate into authority, autonomy, governance or power, as examined on p. 29. Thus, key indicators (necessary, but not sufficient on their own) of IO surrogate statehood include:

- *Service provision:* The IO may take on total or partial service provision, often services normally expected to be provided by the government (e.g. health, education, infrastructure, water etc.);
- *Forms of governance:* The IO may take on functions of governance usually carried out by the state, including administrative or adjudicatory functions (relates to power/authority);
- *Perception of legitimacy:* The IO is visible, perceived as a legitimate authority, perhaps because of its presence or resources; and
- *Territory:* The IO has a physical presence "on the ground," in a given locale.

First, one indicator of IO surrogate statehood is the provision of services, particularly substituting for services often expected to be fulfilled by the state.[23] This might range from services relating to health, education, infrastructure, water or other public goods often expected from state authorities. Examples of IOs providing services are not hard to find. In Africa, for example, "the provision of services is not simply a domestic affair" but one that commonly includes international humanitarian actors.[24] Indeed, the provision of services in Africa by IOs has grown in the context of decolonization and globalization, which have led the international aid community to concern itself with more conflicts and disasters than ever before.[25] As a result, IOs "developed into large, professional institutions with stable bureaucratic procedures," many becoming "reliable welfare providers in what Mark Duffield (1994) has called an international safety net."[26] Moreover, cases where states abdicate responsibilities for service provision and turn them over to IOs, or where IOs take over state responsibilities without the state's consent, can also point to IO surrogate statehood. In the cases here, this is generally seen via an IO filling a void where the state is lacking, rather than a power grab (however, some, like Harrell-Bond (1986), see the latter as the more likely story; Chapter 3 addresses this further).

Finally, when the international community deems a state as "failed," "weak" or as having low capacity, it might not even consider drawing on that state to provide humanitarian aid, instead preferring an IO to provide service and thus opening the door to surrogate statehood. Surhke writes, "In some semi-permanent emergencies, the international aid community *de facto* took over social service and welfare functions normally provided by states."[27]

However, providing services alone does not mean an IO is a surrogate state. There are cases where some services may be provided to portions of the population, but the IO is not a surrogate state. Additional key components of IO surrogate statehood are in the form of adjudication and administration, or governance, and the perception that the IO is a legitimate authority. For example, Semboja and Therkildsen write that an IO's legitimacy as a political actor could be seen in the behavior of some political candidates who sought popularity based on their perceived ability to assuage an IO—not government authorities—to provide local services.[28]

This type of legitimacy to govern also requires that an IO have a physical presence in a given locale. Kassimir, for example, discusses how organizations govern and gain legitimacy by taking on the role of both *representing* a portion of the population and being recognized as one that represents.[29] Latham's (2001) "transterritorial deployments" also provide an example of how an IO can produce the necessary physical presence in a locale, and "intentionally or not, these non-state organizations often become bound up in local processes of governance."[30] In reference to the Catholic Church in Uganda, for example, Kassimir points out the multileveled parts at work in this representation:

> Its permanent presence allows it to be seen both as an international organization with local branches and as a local organization 'networked' globally. The Ugandan Church is thus a local 'representative' both *of* and *to* a global institution, its bishops appointed by the Vatican, its administrative structure and its doctrine provided externally by a model

> that is formally similar everywhere, its funding largely provided by overseas agencies, even some of its personnel provided from outside.[31]

One might draw similar conclusions to the role of an IO at the domestic level, both representing a particular group to the state and the world and representing the response of the world to that group (the next chapter, for example, applies this to UNHCR, which both represents refugees to the world/host state, and the world to refugees).[32] Thus, varied representation on different levels helps unpack IO authority domestically, further informing surrogate statehood at the domestic level and differentiating it from other roles at the international level.

An IO surrogate state exercises its "statehood" over a specific population (as would an actual state), but this population does not have to be a specific group. In the refugee/UNHCR example discussed in Chapter 2, the population over which UNHCR has surrogate statehood is refugees. In theory, the state should be responsible for all people within its borders, including refugees, but in this example, the IO assumes some forms of statehood in the absence of the state's presence. Thus, the IO surrogate state may only extend over a specific group of people (in some cases, a group that appears not to "belong to anyone") and might not affect the daily lives of other citizens. In other cases, particularly where the national authorities are absent, both citizens and refugees (in the UNHCR example, at least) may see UNHCR behaving as their surrogate state. Nonrefugee examples may include examples where an IO working on development in a remote area where there is little state presence may assume surrogacy. It may not be uniform to the UNHCR example but may have enough semblance to still be explained by the framework.

IO surrogate states tend to occur when several conditions are present. First, they are more likely to occur when there is some type of void left by the state or other actor. This may occur because the state requests the IO to assist because it lacks the capacity or will to carry out activities in this area, or in response to a critical juncture event such as an enormous refugee influx. It may also occur because the IO feels morally responsible to act in an area where the state cannot. Likewise, the IO may expand responsibilities into a void left by the state because it is a means to carry out other tasks. For example, in cases where a state is unable or unwilling to pave roads in rural areas, UNHCR may take on the task in order to get its supplies to refugees that it seeks to serve. In other cases, the IO may actually crowd out the state in a certain area,[33] grabbing power or responsibility for its own interests (see the next chapter for more on this). The fact that surrogacy tends to occur over long periods of time—it is not a one-off event that happens overnight—also demonstrates how IO surrogacy can occur with "mission creep" or domino responsibilities: an IO wants to carry out one project, which is related to another, and another, until it takes on responsibilities far beyond its original intent.

Other conditions that can set the stage for IO surrogacy include broader trends, such as shifts in the perception of sovereignty (Landau 2008) which describe how IOs in the humanitarian sphere view intervention differently (literature on the responsibility to protect is also relevant here); the privatization of social services (Semboja and Ole 1995); and the desire of donor states to channel funds through IOs rather than through governments, either as foreign policy or because of distrust (Rutinwa 2002). Each of these trends represents important shifts in how states interact with other states and IOs and help create conditions whereby an IO might develop into a surrogate state. The next chapter outlines specific conditions that can contribute to IO surrogacy, particularly in Africa, including how centralized a state is or how well it can broadcast power to remote areas.[34]

In addition to conditions that make IO surrogacy more likely, there are also factors, which tend to *sustain* surrogacy. As the case studies show, one reason IOs may remain surrogates for long periods of time is that once an IO becomes a surrogate state, it is hard to go back to a nonsurrogate existence. This might be rooted in institutional design of the IO or individuals who simply do not want to scale back their work or "put themselves out of a job" once the IO has expanded to take on surrogacy. IO staff may also make a moral argument, noting that if they were to leave after years of doing "x," it would be disastrous. There is also financial incentive to maintain surrogacy; one interviewee for this study stated that substitution for the government is more profitable than simply supporting the government. Another stated that donors are less interested in giving to projects that do not involve surrogacy. This is in part due to donor governments continuing to give funds for certain projects and not others or the IO wanting to continue to raise money for certain projects it has taken on as a substitute for the government. Finally, an IO may sustain surrogacy because the government may become further and further removed from carrying out tasks the IO has taken over, and thus, it may not have the expertise or capability to take over if an IO were to pull back from surrogacy.

IO surrogate statehood is thus not easily measured or defined, but these indicators and conditions help to unpack what is meant by the concept. Indeed, it is less about the label and more about the underlying ideas. As Kassimir writes, "Whether or not one characterizes the activities of non-state entities as 'state-like,' these organizations are, in some sense, 'politics' that engage in 'governing.'"[35] These indicators and conditions are not purely scientific, but they do outline some of the ways an IO approaches surrogacy in more extreme or less extreme ways, and thus maintaining a view of the spectrum helps understand this variable, and the concept, more broadly. To recap, the first step is showing how IOs can take on surrogacy (just one of a range of domestic roles an IO may take on); this is relatively descriptive in nature. The second step is understanding what this means for its relations with the state (measured in terms of influence, as outlined in the next section). While the case study chapters are focused on measuring variation in DV influence, it is also important to recognize that there is some variation among surrogacy as well.

Measuring IO influence on the state

After identifying and describing IO surrogacy, the next step is understanding how it affects behavior—namely, state behavior. This book is not making the sweeping generalization that IO surrogacy is the sole cause of certain policies nor is it implying that the causal relationship works in both directions (for example, more surrogacy paired with less influence does not necessarily imply that less surrogacy always means more influence; obviously an IO with no presence or activity in a state would not have influence—rather, there is likely a balance where an IO has maximum influence—something worth further research). The challenge, then, is teasing out the ways in which IO surrogacy may or may not have an effect. Careful process tracing of each case's history of decision-making toward refugees was followed up with interviews in order to understand the relationship.

At the core of measuring influence lies a long-standing IR debate over power and authority, with power often being measured in terms of a relationship of influence.[36] Given that this research draws on constructivist understandings of power via social relations between actors, it understands an IO's ascension to surrogacy (moving along the spectrum with the passing of time) as a result of two processes: socialization[37] and a shift in social identity.[38] This view of power (and by extension influence) is in contrast to other views of power, which might only view it in terms of tangible, material things.[39] It builds on the notion that there is a "distinction between potential versus actual power in which actual power was a 'type of causation' rooted in the capacity of actor A to get actor B to do what it would otherwise not do."[40] This means that nonmaterial factors, like the scope and norms of states' relationships matter as well. Janice Bially Mattern writes that this has brought about understandings of power as relationships of influence—as examined here.[41] It is not necessarily thought of as zero-sum (though in some cases it may be), nor is surrogacy viewed as inherently implying some form of power or influence (though this may be the case); these are both topics that are discussed in greater detail throughout the book. Michael Barnett and Raymond Duvall's (2005) research on power creates a typology of power, viewing it ultimately as "the production, in and through social relations, of effects that shape the capacities of actors to determine their own circumstances and fate."[42] This is useful for mirroring the multiple forms of power (or relationships of influence) that are used here.[43]

In light of this, measuring influence in a qualitative study such as this is crucial to understanding how well the theory describes the realities within the cases. And yet it is elusive and complex. On the one hand, the easiest way to see influence is through concrete policy decisions—a direct material result. Indeed, the case studies do spend significant amounts of time considering if and how an IO has had direct policy influence over the state and if its role as a surrogate state increases or decreases its ability to influence the state. However, only looking at material influence would miss the many nonmaterial aspects of influence, and thus this study does not argue that a concrete policy decision is the sole measure of influence. Rather, considering ideas, beliefs, norms, expectations and social relationships between actors provides a fuller picture of influence. Indicators of IO surrogate state influence on a state are outlined in Table 1.1.

Table 1.1 Potential indicators of IO surrogate state influence

Indicator of influence	*How it might be measured*
Change in perception	Perception (by local populations and other authorities) of who is in authority. Perception of authority may translate into direct or indirect influence.
Shifts in responsibility, blame and expectations	The IO might not directly change states' decisions but may reshape the way responsibility, accountability or blame are attributed.
Material shift	Adjustment or change in policy—either an outright about-face in policy decision, stated clearly as a result of the IO's involvement, or a visible shift in some other way.
Change in individual leaders' demeanor	Influencing individual policymakers via one-on-one relationships, who in turn may influence state policy choices.
Change in rhetoric	Rhetorical influence, such as the way the IO may change the terms or language of the debate, possibly symbolically.
Change in other actors' behavior	Influencing other actors (e.g. NGOs, IPs, donor governments or civil society) to apply pressure in a certain direction and thus having an indirect means of influence.
Carrying out governance functions	Administration and adjudication of specific territories or locales (also an indicator of surrogate statehood) may show influence.
Directly writing policy	Helping to negotiate and write policy by being "in the room" (writing it up, meeting with leaders, lobbying).

These are not necessarily the only indicators of influence but demonstrate some of the ways of measuring IO influence vis-à-vis its surrogacy.

Relationships and causality in the framework: less is more

Thus far, this chapter has outlined the gap in IR literature on IOs, noting how it neglects to understand how IOs act at the domestic level. In response, the chapter offered a spectrum of IO behavior at the domestic level, explained by the concept of "domestication." This concept demonstrated a range of IO domestic roles, stretching from an IO with a very small presence, to one that is acting as a surrogate state. It then zeroed in on one of these roles, IO surrogacy, and how it influenced state behavior.

The rest of this chapter focuses on the two relationships—one descriptive and one causal—that emerge from the framework: 1) IO surrogate states tend to be paired with abdicationist states (and inversely IOs that are not surrogate states are more likely to be working in partnership with the state), and 2) IO surrogacy results in less influence on the state than other relationships between IOs and states. The framework shows that states tend to have different relationships with IOs across the surrogacy spectrum, ranging from "partnership" models (working in partnership with the IO) to "abdicationist" (ignoring the IO and letting it do everything). As shown on p. 31, the framework ultimately suggests that the relationship is, surprisingly, inverse: the more an IO takes on surrogate state properties, the less it is able to influence the state.

1) IO surrogacy and state role

The first relationship of the framework describes the link between IO surrogate statehood and state reaction to the IO. This is important to the overall question because how the state reacts to the IO is indicative of how much influence the IO is likely to have on the state. The framework holds that IOs that have taken on less of a surrogate state role tend to work in greater partnership with the state, and conversely IOs that have taken on a more expansive surrogate state role see greater state abdication. Caution should be used, however, in inserting causal arrows in this relationship. It is difficult to generalize which causes which, and further research would be necessary to confirm, for example, whether IOs take on more surrogate state roles in the face of state abdication, whether states move toward abdication in response to IO surrogate statehood or whether a combination produces such relationships. For the purposes of this framework, however, simply recognizing that the two are paired, as demonstrated in the case studies, is enough for moving forward with the questions posed here.

Future studies may be able to incorporate all types of domesticated IOs into one study, but this study focuses only on surrogate state IOs, honing in on the right half of the spectrum because it is among the most under-researched parts of IO literature. In addition, those working with a smaller presence are less likely to reveal influence on the state, which is the core question here. This book argues that those approaching surrogacy tend to be more likely to be paired with an abdicationist state, as shown in Figure 1.2.

These relationships are important because they set the context for the relationship of influence. States that engage in partnership work more directly with the IO, facilitating its work, even as the IO may approach surrogacy as it pays the bills, carries out its own projects and bears much of the responsibility. This tends to occur when the IO has fewer surrogate state properties. In contrast, when an IO is on the more extreme end of surrogacy, the state is more likely to be abdicationist, completely ignoring and avoiding the IO, letting it carry out its work with little interference or government oversight.

Again, there are cases where state abdication brings about IO surrogacy, and cases where IO surrogacy encourages state abdication, so causal arrows may not be in one direction. There are also cases where the two may emerge simultaneously. Moreover, a state's reasons for abdication or partnership are far beyond IO surrogacy and relate to capacity, resources, motives and context. For example, in the case study of Kenya, the state was happy to abdicate refugee responsibility in Dadaab to a surrogate state, UNHCR, in large part because Dadaab's geographic location is a remote, undesirable location that the government preferred to ignore for political and historical reasons. Moreover, these relationships are mere labels that help structure the analysis; they are not meant to simplify highly complex relationships between the state and the IO. The relationships are not fixed, and amidst partnership or abdication, the state may still use the IO, restrict the IO or try to manipulate the IO. What they do help uncover, however, is the nature of the relationship and, most importantly, build context for how the IO might be able to influence the state.

Figure 1.2 Subview of the "surrogate state" end of the spectrum paired with state disposition

Figure 1.3 Relationship between IO surrogacy and influence on the state

2) The relationship between IO surrogacy and influence on the state

The second causal relationship advanced by the framework is between IO surrogate statehood and level of influence on state behavior. This study argues that an IO's ability to influence state behavior is inversely related to its level of surrogate statehood. In other words, the more an IO acts like a surrogate state, the less influence it is likely to have over a state. The case studies confirm this counterintuitive suggestion, and the mechanisms shown in Figure 1.3 explain why this result occurs.

Caution should be used when extending this relationship too far beyond the issue area relating to the IO. In other words, if, for example, UNHCR (the IO studied in this book) works on refugee protection, it would not be relevant to try to measure the IO's influence over the state via a completely unrelated issue area, such as banking regulations. And again, further research should also examine where a point of highest influence occurs (as noted earlier, it is not likely that an IO with no presence has the most influence—this would be a false dichotomy—but rather that the place of highest influence is somewhere else on the spectrum, not at either extreme end).

The mechanisms

Returning to the causal relationship outlined earlier in this chapter, the framework presents a counterintuitive finding for IOs working domestically: the more an IO approaches surrogate statehood, the less influence it is likely to have over state policy decisions. Why? Process tracing within the case studies helps to uncover mechanisms that explain why greater surrogacy leads to less influence. At first glance, it would seem enough to simply attribute it to the fact that states generally wish to retain all of the power and none of the responsibility, thus making a state happy to let an IO do all the work and pay the bills. However, a closer look reveals that this is only part of the story and that two mechanisms account for the inverse causal relationship: 1) marginalization of the state and 2) responsibility/blame shifting. These mechanisms are drawn from studies by Landau (2008), Juma and Suhrke (2002) and Rutinwa (2002).

First, marginalization of the state[44] occurs with IO surrogate statehood. For example, in reference to humanitarian aid, Suhrke (2002) notes that IOs often assume that there is no relevant local aid capacity and that state institutions are corrupt and thus unable to be trusted with aid resources.[45] Juma argues that this has resulted in an isolation of the state's existing local capacity, whereby "local aid structures were overwhelmed, diminished or destroyed" and "the horde of international agencies overwhelmed the local scene and went about their activities in disregard of any prior experience or knowledge about emergency response."[46] In addition to marginalizing local actors and continuing in the example of humanitarian aid in Africa, Juma and Surhke write that many states in East Africa have been "systematically sidestepped by the international aid agencies."[47] This has also been compounded by the creation of parallel humanitarian structures, where accountability for humanitarian aid is shifted from the host state to the IO.[48] They argue that this has solidified links between humanitarian actors on the ground and donors, in clear disregard of host states, thus leaving the state and local community both unaccountable and without benefit or responsibility for humanitarian assistance.[49]

Marginalization of the state leads to a number of outcomes that suggest an inverse causal relationship between IO surrogate statehood and influence over state behavior. To begin, when the state is marginalized, leaders may feel that their authority and the state's sovereignty are challenged. This sentiment can result in a desire to overcompensate or overdemonstrate power and authority.[50] This scenario only further develops when authorities see the IO with authority over local actors that they (the state authorities) have struggled to control or an area where they have struggled to broadcast power. When leaders of a state are anxious to show their power and authority (wanting to give the appearance of "ruling toughly"), they are less likely to be less open to input or influence from an IO. Marginalization of the state can also lead to state authorities not knowing what is going on—not having the knowledge, skills or capacity to deal with a certain issue in a certain area within the state's borders while the IO holds specialized knowledge and expertise.[51] This in turn can make them less willing to listen to the IO working on those issues, either because they do not care or do not understand.

In addition, marginalization of the state may lead to the state decision-makers to be content with the status quo—happy to let the IO do everything and pay for everything—and thus to have little reason to listen to anything that might change the status quo. Marginalization of the state may also leave the IO surrogate state with less influence because it might position the IO in such a way such that it needs to stay on the good side of the state; trading moral authority to speak out against the state for access granted by the state. Indeed, IOs with surrogate state roles can become beholden to the states in which they work because their work (and hence their reputation among donors and other international actors) relies on access, which only the state—even a weak state—can provide. Thus, they can be hesitant to criticize the very state that provides them with access to their work—work that they must continue in order to uphold their reputation in the eyes of their donors.[52] As one interviewee put it, IOs carrying out service provision often attributed with the state not only accept blame for the state's shortcomings but lose their ability to "responsibilize" the government or force it to take responsibility for its obligations, including refugee protection. By substituting for government services at the domestic level and embedding/entwining itself within the state, the IO can lose its ability to be an external arbitrator of the state's behavior. This weakens some of the tools it would normally use to influence a state, including the ability to "name and shame."

The second mechanism of responsibility shifting builds on Loren Landau's (2008) research on UNHCR in western Tanzania and is related to marginalization of the state. Landau finds that many Tanzanians, over the course of the Burundian PRS, shifted to seeing UNHCR as responsible for service provision. Thus, rather than blaming the state when services are lacking, they blame UNHCR and the international community. He asserts that this enables the population to maintain a surprisingly positive view of their national authorities.[53] He writes,

> By blurring lines of responsibilities, officials and politicians were provided with additional mechanisms and incentives for "shirking." Both local and national officials rarely missed an opportunity to publicly blame international actors for the district's problems and the administration's own weaknesses.[54]

The unexpected result that Landau uncovers, then, is that Tanzanians have a "heightened loyalty to their nation, territory and political leadership, while expectations of and material interactions with the state have declined."[55]

This mechanism again shows how the state has less incentive to listen to the IO regarding any policy change, as it continues to benefit from the status quo. By inadvertently propping up or benefiting a state that should be held accountable and lobbied to change its behavior, the IO finds itself in a weaker position of influence. Instead of using its moral authority to call the state out, it is on the receiving end of public criticism and blame for any shortcomings in services, governance or resources. This leaves it in a weaker bargaining position to advocate for specific policies and can leave it with an unsure footing on how to influence a government that has no incentive to change this relationship. After all, the state receives the benefits without having to do any of the work or foot the bill and thus has little reason to be influenced in any way that would change the status quo. While one might think the IO's inadvertent propping up of authorities might grant it some leverage, the responsibility shifting instead seems to leave it in a weak, less-influential position. As one interviewee said in reference to UNHCR, the position that grants them the least amount of bargaining power is when they are seen as responsible for everything and pay for the government's work.

IO substitution for the state (and thus responsibility shifting) also potentially weakens the state in its ability and attitude (possibly, though not necessarily, zero-sum power dynamics) toward the work the IO may be doing,[56] further making it less open to policy change. For example, in being absent from the work that the IO surrogate is doing in its given issue area (e.g. refugee protection) and other issue areas (e.g. water provision), the state does not build its own capacity and staff in these issue areas. As with marginalization, not only are they less likely to care because it is not an issue area in which they are working (the IO surrogate state is doing it), but they do not develop the expertise and roster of professionals who might encourage policy changes. Instead, the IO may cultivate all the expertise and staff knowledge needed, in some cases even drawing highly skilled, highly educated and quality staff away from government positions.[57] In the end, this, too, can contribute to the IO surrogate state having less influence over the state because the state is so far removed from the issue areas at stake.

A note on the levels of analysis (international, national, domestic)

The next chapter considers the framework in light of the main empirical actor of this book: UNHCR. Before moving on, however, it is important to clarify the way certain terms, concepts and ideas are used in the framework. While scholarly literature (and this book, for that matter) tends to use the terms "international," "global," "domestic," "local" and "national" as if they are rigid categories that can be easily delineated, this is not the case. In reality, they are fluid and often overlapping categories of analysis.

Nevertheless, for analytical purposes, this study understands the terms in the following ways. The term "local" is essentially drawing on a territorial understanding of space, referring to politics that take place on a smaller scale at the village, town, or city level.[58] "Local" is generally not autonomous (it is shaped from the outside) but rather relates to a higher authority.[59] Moreover, "local" interacts with other factors of influence and is "a political arena where order and disorder are constructed and spheres of authority are forged and intersect."[60] Similarly, this research follows Krasner when understanding "domestic" as "authoritative institutional arrangements of any given polity," and domestic politics are a contestation among actors within that polity.[61]

Likewise, "national" can be understood as politics taking place at the state level, generally in the capital, involving state leaders. "Domestic" therefore encompasses both "national" and "local" and everything in between.

"International" is a term more frequently used and refers to politics occurring beyond the borders of the state, either between states or other actors. The term "global" is related but is broader, referring to something that is everywhere and anywhere, grounded in institutions and the relations that define them.[62] Callaghy, Kassimir and Latham's conception of "shadow networks" helps to uncover some of this ambiguity via an analysis of power. They see power as transformative and recognize that "the global" can only be produced in action, and action is by definition localized.[63] Definitions for transnational networks, policies, international organizations and international institutions, are also quite fluid, and this book will draw on Margaret Keck and Kathryn Sikkink (1998) and Xinyuan Dai (2007) for definitions of transnational networks, norms, international organizations, international institutions and policy. Some of these were discussed earlier in this chapter.

Most notably, as Barnett writes, IR theory often falls prey to the "territorial trap" whereby it maintains a narrow view of rigid, separate understandings of "domestic" and "international" according to borders on the map and sees the state as the sole authoritative actor.[64] He argues that IR's attempts to integrate the domestic and global reflect this territorial trap and that more recent scholarship on globalization and the ways in which transnational actors and NGOs can shape outcomes without having their own material bases of power (but rather through persuasion, communication and information) all demonstrate ways of breaking away from the territorial trap.[65] He further argues that critiques of neorealism and statist approaches have advanced IR away from this blunder but that it is still a common problem. He writes that in being forced to consider theories of globalization, which move away from the state's authority, autonomy and sovereignty, IR scholars "have been forced to address . . . new connections and networks that structure interactions between state and non-state actors and generate new spheres of authority."[66] This is certainly relevant to this study's understanding of IO surrogate state roles.

Thus, while various IR theories have moved away from a sole focus on the state, IR in general remains largely statist, even when considering domestic and international relations interwoven together. However, thinking through IO-state power relations when there are weak states, "shadow states" or "shell states,"[67] and particularly where international actors assume state-like functions in a local capacity, is especially relevant in Africa, where many states are deemed "weak." As Barnett writes by way of an introduction:

> [P]olitics and exchange take place outside the state's purview and transcend its highly porous borders. The scholars in this volume also climb

> through the window of the weak African state to consider alternative ontological grids, the networks of actors that congregate and span those grids, and the overlapping and complex relationship between the various "levels" of politics that mock the neat categories of the "global" and the "local." The territorial trap is easily eluded for these scholars.[68]

It is the goal here to also elude the pitfalls of this trap, even though some discussion of these categories is necessary to have some frame of reference, and much of the discussion is still state-focused, looking at influence on the state. The concluding chapter will also highlight some of the similarities and differences between IO behavior "internationally" versus "domestically" thus making some use of the labels necessary. Therefore, while this research will discuss "global" and "local" as general categories, it is important to recall that these labels are far more fluid and overlapping.[69]

Conclusion

This chapter presented the theoretical framework of this book. It employed the concept of "domestication" to unpack the various roles IOs take at the domestic level, before homing in on one particular role: surrogate statehood. It outlined the ways in which IOs take on surrogacy, conditions for surrogacy and indicators of surrogacy, before turning to the main variable in question: IO influence on the state. Thus, the first part of the framework is descriptive (understanding if and when IOs take on surrogacy) and the second asks a causal question: when IOs do take on surrogacy, what does this mean for their ability to influence the state? The framework posits that there is a surprising relationship that emerges: IOs that take on more surrogate state properties are less influential over the states in which they work. Two mechanisms—marginalization of the state and responsibility shifting—help explain this, amidst an array of additional explanations that fill in the context and also influence the outcomes in state behavior. The next chapter operationalizes the framework to the empirical level, looking at the main IO of study in this book: UNHCR.

Notes

1 See Ian Hurd, *International Organisations: Politics, Law, Practise* (Cambridge, Cambridge UP, 2011), 16. "IOs can be actors in their own right, or tools in the hands of other actors (presumably states), or places where states come to hold meetings with other states," or in other words, an actor, resource or forum (Hurd 2011, 16).

2 On the flip side, one might instead consider "internationalization of a locality" rather than domestication of the IO. For example, Latham writes that in Africa

in particular, supralocal rule (making claims of responsibility over one or more locales) is considered weak, as are many African states, and thus "merchants, missionaries, and humanitarians, in their transterritorial deployments, could confront *Africans as subjects of international order rather than guardians of their own robust national projects*" (2001, 89, emphasis added). Robert Latham, "Identifying the Contours of Transboundary Political Life," in *Intervention and Transnationalism in Africa: Global-Local Networks of Power*, ed. Thomas Callaghy, Ronald Kassimir and Robert Latham (Cambridge: Cambridge University Press, 2001), 89.

Treating Africa as "one big internal frontier" many IOs have therefore deployed and are "directly intervening in local contexts" where "African rulers must share their *internationally constituted national territories*—or claims on the locales within—with organizational platforms ranging from NGOs and IOs to states in the West" (2001, 89, emphasis added).

3 Though this is certainly not always the case. Juma, for example, discusses how many international humanitarian actors, including UNHCR, impose Western ways of operating in local contexts, further dwarfing local relief structures (2002, 160). Monica Kathina Juma, "The Political Economy of Building Local Capacity," in *Eroding Local Capacity: International Humanitarian Action in Africa*, ed. Monica Kathina Juma and Astri Suhrke (Uppsala: Nordiska AfrikaInstitutet, 2002), 160.

4 While this book does not extend the framework to MNOCs, it is a useful parallel that provides context. Cyril I. Obi, "Global, State, and Local Intersections: Power, Authority and Conflict in the Niger Delta Oil Communities," in *Intervention and Transnationalism in Africa: Global-Local Networks of Power*, ed. Thomas Callaghy, Ronald Kassimir and Robert Latham (Cambridge: Cambridge University Press, 2001), 176.

5 Obi, "Global, State, and Local Intersections: Power, Authority and Conflict in the Niger Delta Oil Communities," 175.

Monica Kathina Juma and Astri Suhrke, "Introduction," in *Eroding Local Capacity: International Humanitarian Action in Africa*, ed. Monica Kathina Juma and Astri Suhrke, 5–18 (Uppsala: Nordiska AfrikaInstitutet, 2002), 9.

Further research might look to literature on "domesticated" MNOCs as a conceptual model for IO domestication or surrogate statehood.

6 As the next chapter will show, forced migration literature offers some of the only research on an IO (UNHCR) as a "surrogate state" (Crisp and Slaughter, "A Surrogate State? The Role of UNHCR in Protracted Refugee Situations"; Barbara Harrell-Bond, *Imposing Aid: Emergency Assistance to Refugees* (Oxford: Oxford University Press, 1986); Barbara Harrell-Bond and Guglielmo Verdirame, *Rights in Exile: Janus-Faced Humanitarianism* (New York: Berghahn Books, 2005). Again, however, this is not in relation to IR, nor does they discuss broader implications for state behavior.

7 Latham, "Identifying the Contours of Transboundary Political Life," 69.

8 Latham, "Identifying the Contours of Transboundary Political Life," 71.

9 Latham, "Identifying the Contours of Transboundary Political Life," 76.

10 Latham, "Identifying the Contours of Transboundary Political Life," 76. The most extreme versions of this would be when a transterritorial deployment is "extraterritorial," carrying out its own culture, laws and juridical authority (e.g. military or consular). Extraterritorial status is mirrored today in the near immunity possessed by some humanitarian workers who increasingly employ their own security forces

(de Waal 1997, 190)" (2001, 76). He goes on to mention "camp havens" for traders profiting from war and extraterritoriality emerging from some African rulers operating in zones outside formal state boundaries (2001, 76).

11 Ronald Kassimir, "Producing Local Politics: Governance, Representation, and Non State Organisations in Africa," in *Intervention and Transnationalism in Africa: Global-Local Networks of Power*, ed. Thomas Callaghy, Ronald Kassimir and Robert Latham, 93–114 (Cambridge: Cambridge University Press, 2001), 96.

12 Latham, "Identifying the Contours of Transboundary Political Life," 80, emphasis added.

13 In thinking about authority and power, Latham refers to expanded understandings of power under Foucault, moving away from understanding power in terms of Weberian definitions ("power over another's choices" versus via structures that constitute social existence).

14 Latham, "Identifying the Contours of Transboundary Political Life," 77.

15 Latham, "Identifying the Contours of Transboundary Political Life," 77.

16 Latham, "Identifying the Contours of Transboundary Political Life," 77.

17 James Milner, *Refugees, the State and the Politics of Asylum in Africa* (Basingstoke, UK: Palgrave Macmillan, 2009) (citing on p. 9, Gibney 2004, 198–201).

Joel S. Migdal, *Strong Societies and Weak States: State-Society Relations and State Capabilities in the Third World* (Princeton, NJ: Princeton University Press, 1988).

Max Weber, "The Profession and Vocation of Politics," in *Weber: Political Writings*, ed. Peter Lassman and Ronald Speirs (Cambridge: Cambridge University Press, 1994), 309–369.

18 Barry Buzan, *People, States and Fear: An Agenda for International Security Studies in the Post-Cold War Era, Second Edition* (London: Longman, 1991), 83.

19 Milner, *Refugees, the State and the Politics of Asylum in Africa*, 9.

20 Kagan, "We Live in a Country of UNHCR: The UN Surrogate State and Refugee Policy in the Middle East"; Crisp and Slaughter, "A Surrogate State? The Role of UNHCR in Protracted Refugee Situations."

21 Crisp and Slaughter, "A Surrogate State? The Role of UNHCR in Protracted Refugee Situations," 131–132.

22 Christian Lund, ed., *Twilight Institutions: Public Authority and Local Politics in Africa* (London: Wiley-Blackwell Publishing, 2007).

Or see Monica Kathina Juma, "The Political Economy of Building Local Capacity," in *Eroding Local Capacity: International Humanitarian Action in Africa*, ed. Monica Kathina Juma and Astri Suhrke, 159–196 (Uppsala: Nordiska AfrikaInstitutet, 2002), 8–9.

23 Ronald Kassimir, "Producing Local Politics: Governance, Representation, and Non-State Organisations in Africa," 99.

24 Joseph Semboja and Ole Therkildsen, ed., *Service Provision under Stress in East Africa: The State, NGOs and People's Organisations in Kenya, Tanzania and Uganda* (Copenhagen: Centre for Development Research, 1995), 18.

25 Juma and Suhrke, *Eroding Local Capacity: International Humanitarian Action in Africa*, 6.

26 Juma and Suhrke, *Eroding Local Capacity: International Humanitarian Action in Africa*, 6–7.

27 Astri Suhrke, "From Relief to Social Services: An International Humanitarian Regime Takes Form," in *Eroding Local Capacity: International Humanitarian Action in Africa*, ed. Monica Kathina Juma and Astri Suhrke, 19–34 (Uppsala: Nordiska AfrikaInstitutet, 2002), 29.

28 Semboja and Therkildsen, *Service Provision under Stress in East Africa: The State, NGOs and People's Organisations in Kenya, Tanzania and Uganda*, 207.
29 Kassimir, "Producing Local Politics: Governance, Representation, and Non-State Organisations in Africa," 102.
30 Kassimir, "Producing Local Politics: Governance, Representation, and Non-State Organisations in Africa," 105.
31 Kassimir, "Producing Local Politics: Governance, Representation, and Non-State Organisations in Africa," 105.
32 Other parallels might be drawn with transnational oil companies vis-à-vis national governments and local communities (see Kassimir, "Producing Local Politics: Governance, Representation, and Non-State Organisations in Africa," 107ff for more on how INGOs have altered local politics).
33 Rutinwa, "The Marginalisation of Local Relief Capacity in Tanzania"; Juma and Suhrke, *Eroding Local Capacity: International Humanitarian Action in Africa*.
34 Jeffrey Herbst, "The Role of Citizenship Laws in Multiethnic Societies: Evidence from Africa," in *State, Conflict, and Democracy in Africa*, ed. Richard Joseph (Boulder, CO: Lynne Rienner Publishers), 267-–296; Christopher Clapham, *Africa in the International System: The Politics of State Survival* (Cambridge: Cambridge UP, 1996).
35 Kassimir, "Producing Local Politics: Governance, Representation, and Non-State Organisations in Africa," 94.
36 Janice Bially Mattern, "The Concept of Power and the (Un)discipline of International Relations," in *The Oxford Handbook of International Relations*, eds. Christian Reus-Smit and Duncan Snidal (New York: Oxford UP), 694–695.
37 Jeffrey T. Checkel 2005 in Michael Barnett and Kathryn Sikkink, "From International Relations to Global Society," in *The Oxford Handbook of International Relations*, eds. Christian Reus-Smit and Duncan Snidal (New York: Oxford UP), 71.
38 Wendt 1992, 397 in Ian Hurd, "Constructivism," in *The Oxford Handbook of International Relations*, eds. Christian Reus-Smit and Duncan Snidal (New York: Oxford UP), 303.
39 E.g. realists like Mearsheimer, "The False Promise of International Institutions"; Morgenthau, *Politics Among Nations: The Struggle for Power and Peace*, and Waltz, *Theory of International Politics*; Bially Mattern, "The Concept of Power and the (Un)discipline of International Relations," 692.
40 Baldwin 2000, 178 in Bially Mattern, "The Concept of Power and the (Un) discipline of International Relations," 692.
41 Bially Mattern, "The Concept of Power and the (Un)discipline of International Relations," 692. See Hurd, "Constructivism," 692ff to read about the four faces of power, which move from materiality, institutionality, social structures (markets and class, rather than relations between states) and finally discourses that create social meaning.
42 In Bially Mattern, "The Concept of Power and the (Un)discipline of International Relations," 695.
43 More specific to IO power and the role of IOs in global governance (at international and local levels), see Barnett and Finnemore's ("The Politics, Power, and Pathologies of International Organisations") understanding of "constitutive" and "regulative" power.
44 Juma and Suhrke, *Eroding Local Capacity: International Humanitarian Action in Africa*; Rutinwa, "The Marginalisation of Local Relief Capacity in Tanzania";

Lund, *Twilight Institutions: Public Authority and Local Politics in Africa*; Chris Dolan and Lucy Hovil, "Humanitarian Protection in Uganda? A Trojan Horse?" in Humanitarian Policy Group Background Paper, Overseas Development Institute.

45 See also Landau, *The Humanitarian Hangover: Displacement, Aid and Transformation in Western Tanzania*; Harrell-Bond and Verdirame, *Rights in Exile: Janus-Faced Humanitarianism*; Juma and Suhrke, *Eroding Local Capacity: International Humanitarian Action in Africa.*

46 Juma, "The Political Economy of Building Local Capacity," 169–171.

47 Juma and Suhrke *Eroding Local Capacity: International Humanitarian Action in Africa*, 15–16; Juma, "The Political Economy of Building Local Capacity," 170.

48 Juma, "The Political Economy of Building Local Capacity," 174; Landau, *The Humanitarian Hangover: Displacement, Aid and Transformation in Western Tanzania.*

49 Juma and Suhrke, *Eroding Local Capacity: International Humanitarian Action in Africa*, 174. NGOs and IOs continue to seek greater influence, and donors often prefer to give to them instead of states, seeing them as "democratic, self-reliant, poverty-oriented and efficient organisations in contrast to the authoritarian, donor-dependent and inefficient state organisations involved in service provision" (Joseph Semboja and Ole Therkildsen, ed., *Service Provision under Stress in East Africa: The State, NGOs and People's Organisations in Kenya, Tanzania and Uganda* (Copenhagen: Centre for Development Research, 1995), 27.

50 Dolan and Hovil, "Humanitarian Protection in Uganda? A Trojan Horse?"

51 Michael Barnett and Martha Finnemore, "The Politics, Power, and Pathologies of International Organisations," *International Organization* 53(4): 699–732.

52 This can happen with surrogate state IOs or IOs with other roles at the domestic level. As noted later, Loescher, Betts and Milner write "In many instances, UNHCR has to engage with governments that are uncooperative, troublesome and even hostile to UNHCR. Given that the Office can only work in a country if it is invited to do so by the government, it ignores the importance of local politics at its peril. Governments have a range of mechanism[s] for frustrating the work of UNHCR, including preventing access to regions of the country, isolating UNHCR Representatives and denying entry for visiting missions from headquarters. An extreme consequence of ignoring these dynamics is the real danger of UNHCR being expelled from a country" (*The United Nations High Commissioner for Refugees (UNHCR): The politics and practice of refugee protection in the twenty-first century*, 82).

53 Landau, *The Humanitarian Hangover: Displacement, Aid and Transformation in Western Tanzania*, 141–148.

54 Landau, *The Humanitarian Hangover: Displacement, Aid and Transformation in Western Tanzania*, 141.

55 Landau, *The Humanitarian Hangover: Displacement, Aid and Transformation in Western Tanzania*, 145.

56 Dolan and Hovil, "Humanitarian Protection in Uganda? A Trojan Horse?"

57 Barnett and Finnemore, "The Politics, Power, and Pathologies of International Organisations"; Juma and Suhrke, *Eroding Local Capacity: International Humanitarian Action in Africa.*

58 Some scholars take a nonterritorial approach to understanding "local." For example, Hannerz, an anthropologist, writes that 'local' conjures up notions of everyday life (1996, 26 in Kassimir, "Producing Local Politics: Governance, Representation, and Non-State Organisations in Africa," 102).

59 Kassimir, "Producing Local Politics: Governance, Representation, and Non-State Organisations in Africa," 102ff.
60 Kassimir, "Producing Local Politics: Governance, Representation, and Non-State Organisations in Africa," 103.
61 Stephen D. Krasner, "Revisiting 'The Second Image Reversed'," Paper prepared for conference in honor of Peter Gourevitch, University of California, San Diego, 23–24 April, 2.
62 Carolyn Nordstrom, "Out of the Shadows," in *Intervention and Transnationalism in Africa: Global-Local Networks of Power*, ed. Thomas Callaghy, Ronald Kassimir and Robert Latham, 216–239 (Cambridge: Cambridge University Press, 2001), 218.
63 Thomas Callaghy, Ronald Kassimir and Robert Latham, ed., *Intervention and Transnationalism in Africa: Global-Local Networks of Power* (Cambridge: Cambridge University Press, 2001), 216. They write, "While shadow networks work both through and around states, they are distinct from them. . . . They form a different kind of power formation than the state does. . . . States and shadow networks exist simultaneously, each representing distinct kinds of authority and political-economic arrangements" (2001, 219).
64 Michael Barnett, "Authority, Intervention, and the Outer Limits on International Relations Theory," in *Intervention and Transnationalism in Africa: Global-Local Networks of Power*, ed. Thomas Callaghy, Ronald Kassimir and Robert Latham, 47–68 (Cambridge: Cambridge University Press, 2001), 52.
65 Barnett, "Authority, Intervention, and the Outer Limits on International Relations Theory," 54.
66 Barnett, "Authority, Intervention, and the Outer Limits on International Relations Theory," 54.
67 Barnett, "Authority, Intervention, and the Outer Limits on International Relations Theory," 55; Lund, *Twilight Institutions: Public Authority and Local Politics in Africa.*
68 Barnett, "Authority, Intervention, and the Outer Limits on International Relations Theory," 55.
69 See Lund (2007) for more on borders. Borders and maps are important to the nation-state, and territorial delimitation is equally important to twilight institutions (2007, 694). "The term 'local' often invokes an assumed spatial mapping of 'local' in contrast to 'global' and of 'below' in contrast to 'above'" (2007, 694). He writes, "Legitimation of public authority takes many forms, but it would seem that territorialization by delimitation and assertion of control over a geographic area offers a particularly potent language" (2007, 695). Lund, *Twilight Institutions: Public Authority and Local Politics in Africa.*

2 Applying the framework to UNHCR

- **UNHCR's background and "toolbox" of influence**
- **Domestication: UNHCR's varied domestic roles**
- **UNHCR's surrogacy and its ability to influence**
- **Conclusion**

This chapter applies the theoretical framework of "domestication" to the empirical level, focusing on one IO in particular: UNHCR. UNHCR provides a wealth of data for this research, given its long-term involvement in many PRS, its diverse relations with states and its commitment to refugee protection. Indeed, scholarship on UNHCR demonstrates that it has embraced a range of roles at the domestic level, including everything from an instrument of the state to an autonomous actor and surrogate state.[1] Moreover, its ability to influence states remains elusive: at times, it successfully lobbies states to respond to refugees in a specific way, and other times it is completely at the mercy of the refugee-hosting state. Understanding how and why its role "on the ground" affects its ability to influence the state not only has interesting theoretical implications for this book but is also a real world puzzle that practitioners and policymakers seeking better solutions stand to benefit from solving.

This chapter first provides context and background to UNHCR's history vis-à-vis its ability to influence states. It then draws on forced migration literature to trace the extent of its power and influence in light of the various roles it has taken on at the domestic level, including ways it acts as an instrument of states, an autonomous political actor, a transnational/multileveled actor and finally as a surrogate state. It focuses most heavily on UNHCR acting as a surrogate state after years of involvement in a PRS. In applying the framework—examining the relationship between the surrogate state IO (UNHCR) and state behavior (the host state's treatment of refugees) and exploring the relationship through the mechanisms—it provides analysis on UNHCR's varied domestic roles and subsequent influence more broadly.

UNHCR's background and "toolbox" of influence

UNHCR has been the subject of extensive study by historians, political scientists, anthropologists, sociologists, legal scholars and others. A number of studies have been carried out on its evolution in the field and at the headquarter level, and healthy debate continues about its role and relationship with donors, host states and refugees. Gil Loescher's *The UNHCR and World Politics: A Perilous Path* provides one of the most comprehensive analyses of UNHCR, looking at its evolution over time in light of the various High Commissioners in its history. A unique facet of UNHCR has been its dual role, being a "transmitter and monitor of refugee norms," but also an organization that "monitors compliance with international standards."[2] UNHCR grew out of refugee movements in Europe in the 1920s and expanded during and after World War II, particularly during the Cold War.[3] It is a normative organization and clings closely to its mandate and statute, enshrined in the 1951 Convention Relating to the Status of Refugees (CSR51).[4]

Today, however, it is also well known for being largely operational in the field, which is why it is such a good empirical focus for this study of IOs working on multiple levels and with a field presence in particular.[5] What began as a small office in the 1950s now has more than 7,600 staff in more than 125 countries. It has a budget of over US$3.5 billion and is largely based in the global South, with some 85 percent of the staff working in the field.[6] A large operational presence has not been without tensions, both within the organization (as some voice concern about the focus veering away from refugee protection to humanitarian assistance instead) and within the countries in which UNHCR operates. Loescher writes that staff must "negotiate access with national governments, implement programs with an array of partners, and endeavor to implement global policy in a local reality," and thus it is not surprising that UNHCR takes on many roles.[7]

Throughout its development, UNHCR has generally relied on a "toolbox" of several powers of persuasion and *modus operandi*. Understanding these methods of influence is crucial to examining UNHCR's changing roles with time—including its "domesticated" surrogate statehood—and to analyzing its increased, decreased or unchanged ability to influence state policy choices. The general "toolbox" of influence that emerges in the literature includes:

- Moral authority (e.g. "naming and shaming" countries[8]);
- Maintaining expertise (creating and holding technical expertise, knowledge, labels and categories relevant to refugees[9]);
- Issue-linkage (linking political, economic and humanitarian issues to influence state's behavior toward refugees; working with partners to achieve protection standards and/or durable solutions)[10];

- Material assistance, including C&M[11]; and
- Individual diplomacy[12] (e.g. individual High Commissioners using their political sway and personal relationships to foster specific outcomes).

First, UNHCR's moral authority in the eyes of states has generally been one of its most powerful methods of persuasion. It has always claimed "protection"[13] at the center of its mandate, focusing on the human rights of refugees and even thinking of itself as a lawyer representing refugees. Indeed, UNHCR's normative mandate makes it unique from other UN agencies and IOs. Gil Loescher, Alexander Betts and James Milner write, "UNHCR is the only global organization with a specific mandate to ensure the protection of refugees and to find solutions to their plight."[14] However, UNHCR's moral authority has also combined with the fact that it is an inherently political actor working with states to protect refugees.[15] It has thus had to operate with political wisdom as well. Loescher writes, "UNHCR has, to varying degrees of success, extended its moral authority to assert its agenda of refugee protection, while also linking refugee issues to states' material interests in order to gain greater leverage over state decisions."[16]

This combination of working from both moral and political perspectives has also meant that UNHCR works with a range of partners. Indeed, the foundation for its existence lies in principles and values, which inherently link it to other political actors: "UNHCR is . . . unable to pursue its mandate independently. Instead, UNHCR is structurally and operationally linked to a wide range of other actors in the international system, including donor and refugee-hosting states, other UN agencies, international, national and local NGOs," making it both an independent actor in the international system with a specific mandate and an organization "deeply enmeshed in a diverse and changing set of relationships with a growing number of other actors."[17] This is a double-edged sword, giving UNHCR the potential for more influence on state behavior toward refugees but also putting it in the difficult position of having to work with a large number of diverse actors with varied interests—everything from donor states to corrupt host governments to refugee groups to faith-based NGOs.

Having a High Commissioner also makes UNHCR unique to other UN agencies and presents an interesting case of the power of an individual within an IO to affect state decisions. The High Commissioner maintains significant moral authority and legitimacy, despite having little political authority.[18] In fact, High Commissioners have exercised considerable power over the trajectory and priorities of UNHCR and have "ushered in different phases of UNHCR's growth, its relations with states, and its relationship with the refugees it sought to protect."[19] High Commissioners have thus had to strike a balance between the moral and political methods of persuasion.

Loescher, for example, writes, "Most High Commissioners have realized that in order to have had any impact on the world political arena they had to use the power of their expertise, ideas, strategies, and legitimacy to alter the information and value contexts in which states made policy."[20] High Commissioners can also hold symbolic value as the lead figure of UNHCR and may even draw on personal relationships to achieve their ends.

Finally, UNHCR maintains technical expertise and knowledge over refugee matters, due to its specialization.[21] The sheer act of classification, fixing meanings, articulating and diffusing norms and being the holder of "knowledge, training, and experience that is not immediately available to other actors" is a powerful tool to UNHCR.[22] This also gives UNHCR legitimacy in the world and the ability to use these specialized skills and knowledge to benefit a refugee-hosting state. Loescher writes:

> Many new states were willing to adapt their behavior to UNHCR pressures for purely instrumental reasons. International humanitarian assistance has provided resource-strapped governments with the means to cope with influxes of refugees. Thus, through a mixture of persuasion and socialization, the UNHCR has communicated the importance of refugee norms and convinced many new states that the benefits of signing the refugee legal instruments and joining the UNHCR Executive Committee—either as a member or an observer—outweighed the costs of remaining outside the international refugee regime.[23]

Michael Barnett and Martha Finnemore also outline how the bureaucratic nature of UNHCR gives it autonomy: "Bureaucracies embody a form of authority, rational-legal authority, that modernity views as particularly legitimate and good. . . . The very fact that they embody rationality is what makes bureaucracies powerful and makes people willing to submit to this kind of authority."[24] In a similar vein, UNHCR is able to use framing and rhetoric as a tool of influence and a way to carry out its mandate.

Reflecting on its reach over history

UNHCR's reach has grown since its inception, and its historical trajectory also explains its evolution to surrogate statehood. As noted on p. 43, a signature development in UNHCR's history, and more importantly regarding its global influence, was its expansion from being a European-focused IO (emerging in response to refugees from World War II) to a global actor, beginning to work operationally on material assistance, rather than simply teaching norms of protection from a distance.[25] According to Loescher, this not only demonstrated greater autonomy on the part of UNHCR but was a turning point in which UNHCR began to have "an independent influence on events at the center of world politics."[26] By the 1980s, Cold War conflict and decolonization meant that nearly all of UNHCR's work was in the developing world. Care and maintenance programs (in contrast to a sole focus on protection) in Africa and Asia "exploded its budgets" with "the annual budget doubl[ing] each year from 1970 to 1980."[27] Large camps became more common, and UNHCR had a role in both establishing and maintaining camps, at times on behalf of host governments. UNHCR became entrenched in the habits of encampment, finding it difficult to change course.[28]

It is not surprising that the expansion of UNHCR has faced political challenges, with UNHCR's goals sometimes in tension with state priorities. During the Cold War, UNHCR was often caught in the middle of tense ideological opposites, receiving most of its funding from Western governments with geopolitical interests against communist regimes (or countries aligned with communist regimes and hence supporting intervention if it meant weakening a communist foothold) but continuing to expand into Africa and Asia, focusing on populations associated with those very regimes.[29]

In the 1990s, the securitization of refugees became a new norm as powers like the United States were less inclined to intervene in humanitarian situations and accept refugees or asylum seekers.[30] This caused UNHCR to further involve itself in situations of internal armed conflict as it sought temporary protection measures to contain refugees regionally, as opposed to allowing them to locally integrate or resettle elsewhere.[31] Consequently, repatriation became a popular focus, and UNHCR became less concerned with state sovereignty considerations and began to try to "tackle refugee-producing situations at or near their source."[32] UNHCR also became more entangled in comprehensive and integrated UN peacekeeping operations involving political and military actors of the UN, working with other displaced populations besides only refugees. This boosted the number of people of concern to UNHCR, "from 15 million in 1990 to a peak of 26 million in 1996," of which refugees only constituted 50 percent.[33] Consequently, this meant that UNHCR now looked like a broader-based operational agency driven by emergencies and part of "highly militarized and politicized situations."[34] Subsequently, UNHCR became "synonymous with large-scale international relief programs to victims of armed conflict and ethnic cleansing."[35] This also meant that technical standards of aid delivery and fulfilling material needs of refugees became the yardstick for measuring UNHCR's work, arguably taking the focus away from the original notion of legal protection and human rights.[36]

UNHCR faces a number of challenges in light of its own characteristics and the global climate in which it operates. As a highly networked, transnational actor, working with an array of partners ranging from governments to

NGOs, it can be subject to competition from other humanitarian players and is also party to the well-known "relief-development gap," where tensions between development actors and UNHCR are common and the struggle to identify when humanitarian assistance should shift into development is ever present.[37] In addition, given its constant need for donor support, it is hardly surprising that UNHCR and other agencies must compete for territory, visibility and funds like its other peers and may also be subject to pressure and political agendas from powerful donor states. An important issue that follows, therefore, is that UNHCR must not only navigate a relationship with the governments with which it is working (donor, host and sending governments) but also must maintain leverage and working relationships with other NGOs and IOs, given increasing partnerships.[38]

Similarly, in spite of the "toolbox" methods of influence outlined on p. 43, Loescher, Betts and Milner note that UNHCR is limited in how much it can assert its own autonomous agency.[39] It has successfully used moral authority and normative persuasion, as well as appealing to state interests; however, these have also been in tension with one another, "on the one hand appealing to the short-term realpolitik, and on the other hand to states' normative commitments to refugee protection."[40]

UNHCR has also struggled in balancing its responsibility to uphold the refugee regime versus its own organizational interests, which have not always been in sync with the interests of refugees.[41] This has affected its historical trajectory, as it has had to maintain a normative agenda while at times having to adapt or compromise its own mandate to remain relevant to states' concerns.[42] Overall, then, UNHCR is in a somewhat difficult, contradictory position, and thus questions remain regarding its role and influence:

> Its precarious place in world politics has made it an international organization that has had to respond to structural opportunities and constraints in order to survive and fulfill its mandate. Yet it has continued to maintain a significant degree of autonomy and the ability to influence states, in spite of its limited power.[43]

Domestication: UNHCR's varied domestic roles

Before homing in on UNHCR's surrogate statehood and what the framework can reveal about it, it is helpful to trace the other domestic-level roles UNHCR has taken. Indeed, some literature paints UNHCR as an instrument of states;[44] others as an autonomous political actor (Barnett and Finnemore 1999); and still others as a transnational/transterritorial actor (Loescher et al. 2008; Barnett 2001). These roles are not exclusive to one another; an IO like UNHCR may take on each of these roles at different times, or even in tandem, phasing from one to another with the passing of time. As with most IO literature, IR studies on UNHCR tend to focus on its global role, rather than the roles it takes at the domestic level. Certainly, other disciplines like anthropology or sociology have undertaken some domestic-level UNHCR studies (and policy-oriented studies on UNHCR as a surrogate state, though few in number, are examined in the next section), but these generally do not relate UNHCR's domestic role with its ability to influence the state.

First, a good portion of UNHCR-focused literature describes it as an instrument of states, or an actor dependent on state interests, whether looking at the global or domestic level. Scholars like Barbara Harrell-Bond (1989) and Barbara Harrell-Bond and Guglielmo Verdirame (2005), for example, have often criticized UNHCR for not putting the interests of refugees ahead of state priorities and its own internal priorities, being too ready to turn a blind eye to states' mistreatment of refugees or UNHCR itself mistreating refugees. Loescher, Betts and Milner (2008) do not find UNHCR as sinister but do discuss constraints on UNHCR's behavior in light of state and donor pressures. At the very least, UNHCR must maintain somewhat cordial relations with the host government in order to maintain access:

> In many instances, UNHCR has to engage with governments that are uncooperative, troublesome and even hostile to UNHCR. Given that the Office can only work in a country if it is invited to do so by the government, it ignores the importance of local politics at its peril. Governments have a range of mechanism[s] for frustrating the work of UNHCR, including preventing access to regions of the country, isolating UNHCR Representatives and denying entry for visiting missions from headquarters. An extreme consequence of ignoring these dynamics is the real danger of UNHCR being expelled from a country.[45]

The Uganda case study is one example of this tension, as a senior UNHCR official was expelled from the country for speaking out against the government's refugee policy.[46]

However, while there may be times when UNHCR acts as an instrument of state interests or at least prioritizing state interests above others, this book embraces the notion that it can be an autonomous actor in its own right at the domestic level. As Loescher writes, "The UNHCR has not just been an agent in world politics but a principal actor."[47] Constructivist perspectives perhaps offer the most analytic leverage in this respect because they not only leave room for the possibility that it can act autonomously but also focus on constitutive properties changing over time. Barnett and Finnemore, for example, emphasize how UNHCR's autonomy can grow over time, in large part due to its "expert status" in refugee matters and its ability to act independently in a given locale, often garnering greater trust from donors than the host government.[48] Loescher, Betts and Milner have also emphasized the ways in which UNHCR has grown in autonomy over the years, noting that it is not a passive actor with no agenda of its own.[49] Still recognizing the constraints from states and donors, the need to respect principles of state sovereignty and the mandate to focus on refugee rights, they write that it can also act independently, charting its own path:

> Although UNHCR has limited material capabilities, it has at times influenced the international political agenda and international responses to humanitarian crises through other sorts of power, such as authority and expertise. It has played a role both in framing the importance of refugee issues for states and in initiating discussions about policy proposals in response to humanitarian crises. In this sense, UNHCR has at times been a locus of power within the international political system.[50]

This autonomy therefore translates into some form of authority (or "locus of power"), particularly in cases where UNHCR is the most visible actor, such as in remote refugee-hosting areas. UNHCR's perceived expertise has allowed it to make decisions on the part of refugees, including how they are labeled and defined (often as powerless victims) and where and how camps would be constructed.[51]

Harrell-Bond's (1986) work offers perhaps one of the strongest critiques of UNHCR's authority and autonomy at the domestic level.[52] She looks critically at UNHCR's presence in Africa, noting that many governments have simply handed over "responsibility for policy and implementation to UNHCR and/or to an international voluntary agency."[53] In this respect, UNHCR's presence on the ground also merits authority. As Barnett writes, "Being 'an authority' and 'in authority' gives IOs and other actors the opportunity and the legitimacy to intervene in local affairs to help regulate what already exists and to help constitute something new."[54] They are also, therefore, able to frame their assistance vis-à-vis the state as they choose, all the while maintaining their own interests as well.[55] Thus, UNHCR represents an IO that can be somewhat authoritative and autonomous alongside states, at both global and local levels.

Merging the domestic and international at once, other literature illustrates how UNHCR acts as a transnational/transterritorial, multileveled actor. Views of this nature stray from the umbrella concept of domestication, embracing both domestic and international-level roles for UNHCR. However, they are still important for this research, as they provide a partially domesticated view of UNHCR. For example, Thomas Callaghy, Ronald

Kassimir and Robert Latham's *Intervention and Transnationalism in Africa: Global and Local Networks of Power* (2001), focuses on the structures and relations "in between" the "global" and "local"[56] and seeks to show how cross-boundary forces become directly involved in the constitution of forms of order and authority in social and political contexts ranging from the local, translocal and national to the regional and transregional.[57] Among one of the most important claims appearing alongside discussions on transnationalism—and a claim that is very relevant to this research—is that one actor's transnational nature and subsequent authority need not necessarily mean that another actor (i.e. a government) has less authority; it should not be assumed to be zero-sum. In other words, the involvement and power of an IO like UNHCR need not necessarily mean that local or national authorities are undermined or somehow have less authority (though sometimes this is the case).[58] In some cases, transnational phenomena may become "part and parcel of the political logics of the state itself, contributing to its ability to fulfill essential political imperatives such as extraction and redistribution," a point that will be demonstrated later in the case studies.[59] Similarly, Kassimir writes, "Much contemporary analysis emphasizes processes of the privatization, localization, and globalization of authority at the expense of the state. We need not assume that such processes are necessarily in a zero-sum relationship with sovereign states."[60] The case studies grapple with this further, considering different types of power platforms (e.g. power over laws, borders, people—citizens only or others, too—rhetoric, institutions or political and socioeconomic processes) where the state may lose, gain or share power or be unaffected.

Transnational, transboundary and transterritorial deployments all relate to different ways of understanding actors or networks working on multiple levels at once, including the domestic. Certainly, the categories cannot be divided up neatly, and thus, any analysis must take into account the ways in which they overlap. Broadly speaking, this view embraces a combination of global and local actors as part of the complex picture of authority. Rather than focusing solely on the state level, Barnett argues that politics can go beyond borders and strict understandings of the state and affirms scholars who consider different forms of networks of actors, many of which overlap on different levels of politics and thus avoid the oversimplified categories of "global" and "local."[61] He calls for the abandonment of the "territorial trap" of IR's tendency to follow a statist ontology, which understands authority only in terms of a sovereign state's territorial borders, noting that authority between the global and local can emerge from a bureaucratic entity such as UNHCR.[62] This perspective allows for a broader understanding of authority in light of IO involvement, particularly in states that may not be ideal Westphalian state types, with varied levels of political centralization and control over its territory. While this perspective looks beyond the "domestication" spectrum here, it does offer a view of how UNHCR can maintain its global identity and work domestically at the same time, a point relevant to this debate.

Recalling that transnational actors can be sources of norms[63] and can affect state policies,[64] domestic views of UNHCR can thus also consider its role as a transnational actor, working across boundaries and on multiple, overlapping levels from domestic and local, to international. The historical discussion of UNHCR's expansion on p. 45ff demonstrates how UNHCR works on multiple levels—from international offices in Geneva to national country offices to field and subfield offices.[65] Moreover, its transnational, multilayered nature collapses the space between the global and local in the context of IOs, demonstrating that the effects of authority are not just regulative, but constitutive, and that the constitutive effects are bound up with power to intervene in domestic spaces to alter the political and economic landscape.[66] Thus, UNHCR's domestic roles are inherently tied to its international ones.

An IO like UNHCR can therefore assert this authority domestically or internationally by holding "specialized knowledge" (also mentioned in the "toolbox"), creating rules and embodying rationality and technical knowledge, as well as maintaining the appearance of being apolitical, presenting itself as impersonal, technocratic and neutral, and the appearance of not exercising power but serving others instead.[67] An IO like UNHCR can thus be viewed as a self-deprecating actor, denying and asserting its authority at the same time.[68] In this respect, it is "delegated, layered, and textured, generated from organizational capacities and discursive linkages to the community, and effectively asserted and denied at the same time."[69] Thus, its transnational nature allows it to "intervene in local affairs to help regulate what already exists and to help constitute something new."[70] Finally, UNHCR's transnational nature points to another important theme in the theoretical and empirical research, which is that "domestication" of an IO like UNHCR does not mean that it ceases to be international but rather that it is acting in roles and on issues that are both foreign and domestic in nature. UNHCR's work with refugees is, after all, domestic in the sense that it takes place within the borders of the state; and foreign in that working with refugees is an act toward people of another state—an inherently international act.[71]

UNHCR's surrogacy and its ability to influence

> Several million Africans in refugee camps were effectively governed by the UNHCR, rather than by any state administration.[72]

Recalling that the framework first considers the domestic roles IOs can take and then zeros in on IO surrogate statehood, this section begins by describing how UNHCR takes on surrogate state properties more generally, drawing on the indicators discussed in the previous chapter and engaging with forced migration literature to demonstrate when and how this occurs. The second part of the framework—measuring how IO surrogacy affects its ability to influence the state in which it is working—is applied in each of the case studies. It is not possible to generalize all UNHCR influence in one fell swoop, but rather it varies according to each case. The section does, however, operationalize the measurements of influence, taking the wider theoretical indicators of perception of power, rhetoric, direct policy influence and affecting other actors' behavior and relating them to the empirics of UNHCR in PRS. This section, therefore, paves the way for the case studies by proving that UNHCR does indeed take on surrogate statehood and by considering when and how this occurs.

When and how UNHCR's surrogacy occurs

Forced migration literature is one of the only literatures with some scholarship on UNHCR's surrogate statehood (and even this literature does not relate it to IR theory more broadly, nor does it look beyond UNHCR). Variations on the idea have been written on from anthropological perspectives (e.g. Harrell-Bond 1986) but not in relation to IR theory or in relation to how IOs acting like surrogate states can affect state behavior. This section considers how UNHCR domesticates into a surrogate state through the empirical analysis of UNHCR's physical presence on the ground, taking it beyond a discussion of norms and ideas descending from an international actor to domestic actors. After all, UNHCR and other actors with similar structures do not just influence domestic structures from Geneva, Washington or New York but become "domesticated," hiring local staff, lobbying local and national authorities and even acting as a surrogate state by providing goods and services on the ground (in this example, managing camps or contracting others to help manage camps, but also administering nonrefugee sectors, e.g. paying local police salaries or paving roads). Indeed, in many of the remote areas in which it works, UNHCR is the most visible authority, not the state. UNHCR maintains its "international" standing while accumulating a "local" presence as well.

Drawing on Chapter 1's framework of "domestication," UNHCR can take on various roles along the spectrum, the most extreme of which is surrogate statehood. Recalling the indicators of surrogacy (service provision, forms of governance, perception of authority and physical presence), UNHCR has approached surrogate statehood in different cases. Indeed, recent studies have examined how UNHCR can take on the properties of states, in a sense governing and carrying out duties (e.g. service provision) that a state would normally be expected to provide in a given locale.[73] Michael Kagan, for example, cites refugees stating, "We live in a country of UNHCR."[74] Other studies show how common it is for UNHCR to take on state functions, doing everything from settling land disputes to paving roads or paying local police salaries—all in the name of refugee protection and indirectly connected to refugees, but certainly beyond the original purview of its work. Sometimes its surrogacy can even expand beyond refugee areas into local areas. As noted earlier, Crisp and Slaughter discuss UNHCR's surrogacy in terms of "territory (refugee camps), citizens (refugees), public services (education, health care, water, or sanitation) and even ideology (community participation, gender equality)."[75] Its ability to control resources (i.e. being the funder of many projects) also contributes to its surrogacy. (This idea resonates with broader IO scholarship, such as Latham 2001, 80–83; Obi 2001, 176.)

As noted earlier, UNHCR does not take on surrogate state properties immediately but rather in phases over time—an important variable discussed in each case study. Crisp and Slaughter write:

> UNHCR and other humanitarian organizations have assumed a primary role in the delivery and coordination of support to refugees, initially by means of emergency relief operations and subsequently through long-term "care and maintenance" programmes. Host country involvement has generally been quite limited.[76]

They also note that, in these cases, over time, the "notion of 'state responsibility' . . . has become weak in its application, while UNHCR and its humanitarian partners have assumed a progressively wider range of long-term refugee responsibilities."[77] Thus, they depict UNHCR as transitioning from a humanitarian actor to one that "shares certain features of a state" with the passing of time.[78] As noted earlier, PRS with UNHCR involvement are the most useful for examining instances where UNHCR takes on surrogate state properties.

This evolution to C&M and eventually surrogate statehood can be demonstrated by looking at changes in UNHCR's history. As highlighted earlier, UNHCR expanded from an organization originally focused only on refugees in Europe, to one that worked all over the world. With seemingly larger influxes, refugees began to be perceived as a source of political instability and social tension rather than victims of external aggression.[79] Developing countries were also being asked to bear a larger part of the refugee "burden," as European and other Western countries became increasingly closed to "burden sharing," instead favoring "regional solutions" that contained refugees. Developing countries followed suit, placing more restrictions on refugee admissions, ultimately bringing about more restrictions on refugee rights, closed or semiclosed encampments (rather than open rural settlements), fewer prospects for LI and self-reliance and the threatening of *refoulement* unless the international community met all refugee needs.[80] Coupled with ongoing conflicts and few possibilities for a durable solution, UNHCR was thus left to "run a network of huge camps" by the mid-1990s.[81] By this time, new humanitarian intervention norms were also in full swing, applying a rights- and protection-based doctrine that superseded state sovereignty, thus enabling UNHCR to maintain an identity and role that approached surrogate statehood. Thus, there are links between long-term encampment and UNHCR's surrogacy. States also had some incentive to keep refugees in camps, wanting them to remain visible as a way to discourage permanent settlement and to maintain development aid separately from refugee aid.

UNHCR's role in C&M programs of the 1990s is thus a clear example of its path to surrogate statehood and illustrates increased responsibility. Crisp and Slaughter write:

> A defining characteristic of the "care and maintenance" model was the extent to which it endowed UNHCR with responsibility for the establishment of systems and services for refugees that were parallel to, separate from, and in many cases better resourced than those available to the local population. In doing so, this model created a widespread perception that the organization was a surrogate state, complete with its own territory (refugee camps), citizens (refugees), public services (education, health care, water, sanitation, etc.) and even ideology (community participation, gender equality). Not surprisingly in these circumstances, the notion of state responsibility was weakened further, while UNHCR assumed (and was perceived to assume) an increasingly important and even preeminent role.[82]

They point to Tanzania in particular, saying that people were living "like babies in UNHCR's arms" or referred to UNHCR as their "father and mother."[83]

Hand-in-hand with C&M programs, UNHCR's extensive operational presence in the field also demonstrates how it can act as a surrogate state or even a territory of its own. Again, Crisp and Slaughter write:

> The ubiquity of UNHCR's personnel, offices, vehicles and logo in many long-term refugee camps often leads to confusion on this matter, a situation exacerbated by the fact that many government assets also

> carry the prominent inscription, "donated by UNHCR". When coupled with the physical separation of refugee camps, it is hardly surprising that refugees, local people and government officials should perceive such locations as extra-territorial entities, administered by an international organization with greater visibility and resources—and even legitimacy—than the state.[84]

Their study considers refugee camps to be the embodiment of UNHCR surrogate statehood, but as some of the case studies show, UNHCR's surrogacy can and has gone beyond refugee camp borders, extending its authority to local populations as well.

Why UNHCR becomes a surrogate state (motives, conditions): filling a void, passing of time, moral concerns

This research argues that UNHCR generally does not intentionally seek to take on surrogate statehood but rather finds itself filling a void with the passing of time and in the absence of the state. Of course some argue that UNHCR cannot help but take on more and more projects as it seeks more territory as a bureaucratic IO, sending it on a road to surrogacy, but as the case studies will show, rarely is UNHCR so intentional in its expansion—unaware of its presence, perhaps, but not necessarily intentional in its surrogacy. Scholars like Kagan (2011), for example, see UNHCR's surrogacy as a reluctant filling of a void—not a power grab. He even outlines cases where a state prefers UNHCR to take over some aspects of governance. He writes, "when state-to-UN responsibility shift happens, we should not hastily assume that it is the UN that wanted the shift to occur. There are powerful political forces that lead states in the south to want to transfer their responsibilities to the United Nations for their own benefit."[85] In other cases, the state may want to fulfill its obligations toward refugees, but it may be unable to do so, leaving UNHCR to "fill gaps in the international refugee regime that were not envisaged at the time of its establishment."[86] This picture of UNHCR as a "reluctant filler of a void" was echoed in many interviews for the case studies.

Pertinent to the African cases studied here, literature on African statehood also helps reveal why some states may be ripe for an IO like UNHCR to take on surrogacy (though, as the introductory and concluding chapters argue, this case is generalizable beyond Africa, as various authors and interviewees demonstrate, e.g. Kagan 2011, 4; UNHCR Official C 2013). Indeed, many African states struggle to govern remote areas, leaving power voids open for IOs like UNHCR. Scholars like Jeffrey Herbst (2000), for example, consider how geography and population distribution are directly linked to how well central authorities can consolidate power, noting that smaller states tend to have an easier time consolidating power.[87] This relates in part to ethnic makeup; minorities concentrated in single geographic areas can be difficult to govern.[88] Similarly, Christopher Clapham (1996) understands governance in Africa in part as a function of population density. He asserts that Africa is a sparsely populated, resource-rich continent that is difficult to govern because maintaining authority over population clusters and expansive unpopulated lands is challenging.[89] This, too, helps explains some conditions favoring IO involvement and potentially leaving an open door for UNHCR surrogacy in particular.

Population distribution and geography also have a direct bearing on how centralized a regime is, relations between the central and local authorities and the extent to which remote areas "feel" a state presence. These factors also provide conditions that might favor an IO like UNHCR to expand its work in a state, be welcomed by the state or act as a surrogate state. For example, Herbst writes that many African states struggle to project power over long distances.[90] He also considers how far centralized states in Africa have been able to broadcast power into rural areas by examining ongoing disputes over land tenure and notes that the role of local elites in the distribution of land is critical to their autonomy from the central state.[91] As the case studies will show, how well a central state apparatus can broadcast power to a remote, refugee-hosting area has direct bearing on the role taken by an IO like UNHCR and the policies adopted. Namely, if there is a void, an IO like UNHCR may see little choice but to fill it (possibly as a surrogate state) in order to continue its work.

Likewise, Ogaba Agbese and George Clay Kieh, Jr. (2007) write that a large proportion of Africans experience political life with little state presence, a key factor when examining the role of an IO like UNHCR taking on surrogacy and its subsequent influence on the state. This is due in large part to what they call state decay or "inversion," a state where the "bureaucratic infrastructure is unable to perform even the most fundamental policymaking and policy-implementing functions outside a severely restricted national urban core—often the capital city and its environs, plus one or two rural zones."[92] They argue that state inversion results in a radical decentralization of authority because the state cannot carry out its functions.[93] In turn, this leaves room for other actors—local social and cultural structures or other actors like UNHCR—to assume some of these functions.[94]

This void leaves many postcolonial African states ripe for foreign intervention, external governance, and/or a proliferation of NGOs and IOs like UNHCR. As Agbese and Kieh (2007) argue, many African states are shells of authority, not able to fully deliver goods or services without a combination of other actors' involvement. Drawing on their "inverted state" concept, there are some cases where state power is a mirage.[95] They write:

> Inverted states provide international actors with a relatively familiar pretend-administrative structure and a pretend-set of bureaucratic rules and offices. This familiarity encourages foreign powers and external actors to treat these political entities as states, but they fail to fulfill the 'positive sovereignty' function of states' ability 'to declare, implement and enforce public policy' (Jackson 1990, 29). In such cases, the bare remnants of a public sector remain, as communication and coordination of activities between state institutions largely ceases. The signpost 'Ministry of X,' the edifice of a government office building, and a weighty stack of (often dusty) official policy papers represent mere physical mirages of stateness. In inverted states, the state—as a collective set of national authoritative institutions monopolizing authority and military power and exercising policy on a national basis (Weber 1947; Dyson 1980)—is no longer recognizable as such.[96]

Furthermore, they highlight an increase in privatization of both domestic and international state functions as a result of this, in particular in relation to service provision. This has, in some ways, transferred decision-making power to other actors and ultimately resulted in "state contraction" (or the absence of central authority in a given locale) across the board.[97] These conditions help set the stage for an IO like UNHCR to assume surrogacy when there is a void left by the state.

Other scholarship points to this void by looking to postindependence conditions as factors that weakened African states, leaving them ripe for IO involvement as mediators from western governments. Clapham, for example, describes IOs' filling of a void where the state was unable to broadcast power as a "destating of external relations with Africa," noting that Africa's relations with the outside world were privatized by politicians and the displacement of traditional state-to-state relations as a result of the processes of globalization.[98] In addition, he notes that Western states often prefer to work through IOs rather than directly with states, implying that IOs can be proxies by which Western states interact with African states. He finds the proliferation of NGOs as a symbol of privatization between North/South relations.[99] Clapham also argues that globalization helped bring about the arrival of numerous NGOs, noting that this was yet another way in which Western states reduced their direct interactions with African states.[100]

Taken in the refugee context, some scholars (e.g. Harrell-Bond 1986, 13) argue that this lack of donor state engagement with the host state may be due to the assumption that host government institutions are too weak to respond to refugees or that they are too corrupt, oppressive or exploitative to engage with (in Milner 2009, 5). Thus, North/South political relationships can also create openings for IOs like UNHCR to take on larger functions, including substitution for the state, partially conferred upon it by donor states that prefer to work with it instead of the state. This is particularly likely when Western states may prefer to work through an IO like UNHCR instead of working directly with the state.

Other literature on institutions in Africa and power also reveals how an IO like UNHCR can assume surrogacy based on a void left by the state. Lund (2007), for example, reexamines how to understand power and the state in Africa, looking at institutions vis-à-vis state power. He finds power and authority to be fluid and elusive, in many cases in the hands of international institutions more than the state. He writes, "It seems that the closer one gets to a particular political landscape, the more apparent it becomes that many institutions have twilight character; they are not the state but they exercise public authority."[101] The notion that the state has absconded itself (by choice or otherwise) from some forms of governing, providing services and even protection in certain parts of its territory is perhaps the most relevant point to this research. Indeed, it directly relates to the ways in which the framework understands surrogacy to develop.

Changes in conceptions of sovereignty also help explain the evolution of UNHCR (and by extension IOs in Africa more broadly) to surrogate statehood. Indeed, some scholars argue that international actors no longer view the sovereign state in the same way, justifying intervention and a large IO presence in a way that ignores the desires of the state, in some cases dwarfing the state and its capacity. For example, Jackson (1990) argues that "internal sovereignty in parts of Africa is increasingly either very weak or non-existent" in the sense of a capacity even to preside over regime associates, much less control a specific territory.[102] Clapham has also written that some states "have been so thoroughly privatized as to differ little from territories controlled by warlords."[103] Moreover, it only further alters the perception of sovereignty when the international community steps in to serve the population at the exact moment a state appears in decline (e.g. "extraversion" in Callaghy et al. 2001, 13).[104] Debates about the sovereign state in the African context, therefore, form an important backdrop for this research on how IOs like UNHCR can evolve into surrogate states. In addition to outlining issues relating to power, responsibility, governance and influence, conceptions of sovereignty in African states help inform the roles of other actors, such as UNHCR. The extent to which sovereignty is exercised by the state or respected by the IO forms an important basis for analyzing how an IO like UNHCR can assume surrogate statehood and what the subsequent implications would be (see Chapter 6 for more).

Dolan and Hovil (2006) also point to another reason why UNHCR can take on surrogacy, which points to tensions about its own motives and identity. They argue that because it has moved away from a human rights focus (concerned with "holding duty-bearers to account" and not wanting to "let the real duty-bearers off the hook") to a humanitarian actor (more concerned with meeting human need), it is more prone to take on state responsibilities like service provision.[105] Consequently, the idea of "protection" takes on an expanded use. They write that this expanded view of protection

> involves humanitarian organizations in protecting the rights of beneficiaries by filling some of the gaps in state provision—such as the right to clean water in an IDP [internally displaced person] camp. In cases where these rights are not protected, non-state actors can substitute for the state. Responsibility extends upwards to the "international community," and downwards to include the non-governmental organizations that compromise the majority of humanitarian actors.[106]

These conditions and motives for surrogacy point to a tension about UNHCR's identity—put simply, whether it is more of a "lawyer for refugees" focused on traditional understandings of protection and advocacy or whether it continues down a path of C&M, meeting the physical needs of refugees as a humanitarian worker and feeling pulled to meet more and more of the physical day-to-day needs, potentially substituting for the state. Shifts in this direction help illustrate why and how it takes on surrogacy.

Sheer money can also be a condition or motivator for UNHCR to assume surrogacy. As a senior UNHCR official argued in 2013, there is a profit to be made in substituting for the government. Another senior NGO interviewee noted in 2013 that donors are far more willing to give in camp situations that are run by UNHCR than in situations of settlements or LI where UNHCR is likely to have a less prominent role. Consequently, UNHCR may feel pressure to show donors that it is taking on more and more responsibility and that refugees are in dire need for its assistance in every way, particularly in the absence of any other help from the host state. It is not surprising that donors tend to give to the most desperate of situations, and thus, it is also not surprising that UNHCR might feel pressure to portray a situation as desperate and their work as essential to refugee survival in order to obtain those funds. Surrogate statehood may inadvertently be a way of showing that refugees are in great need and hence that more funds should be given.

Finally, UNHCR may be motivated to assume surrogacy because of moral reasons. Staff may feel as though they have little choice but to craft programs so that they substitute for the state. Even if this means going beyond their mandate, they may feel that refugees would otherwise be left with no protection or assistance. For example, they may need to pave roads in order to get their trucks and supplies through to refugees; they may need to pay police that the state cannot afford to in order to ensure camp or settlement security; or they may need to provide locals with health, water, education and sanitation funds in order to alleviate tensions between the refugee and local populations. As Kagan writes, "Even if fully committed in principle to state responsibility, UNHCR is often trapped into accepting quasi-government functions indefinitely, fearful that if it pulls back refugees would simply be abandoned because host governments would turn out to be unwilling to step in," or that donor governments will not step up.[107] He writes that while this is far from ideal, a UN surrogate state may offer better protection for refugees.[108]

These moral reasons for assuming surrogacy may also "just happen" by default, rather than extensive planning. Indeed, UNHCR may have state-like responsibilities thrust upon it simply because the state is nowhere to be found. For example, when a critical juncture happens (e.g. a mass influx) and the state cannot respond, as has occurred in Kenya, UNHCR may have no choice but to follow the moral imperative to respond in ways that go beyond its original plans for refugee assistance. While surrogacy is more likely to happen over time, these emergency examples can also highlight conditions and motives for surrogacy.

Why UNHCR remains a surrogate state (what sustains its surrogacy)

UNHCR's surrogacy is sustained by a number of factors, some of which build on the conditions and motives for surrogacy noted in the previous section. For one, the organizational structure and traditions of UNHCR make it so that once it takes on surrogacy, it is difficult to change course (NGO Official A 2013). Indeed, if UNHCR expands its operations, raises funds from donors and builds its reputation around its role in a refugee situation, it is difficult to scale back operations once it has expanded. Staff do not want their jobs to be eliminated, and programs are often expected to expand in services and reach more people in need, rather than downsize (UNHCR Official N 2012). If donors continue to fund a surrogate state situation, it is difficult to change priorities. In other words, the pattern becomes difficult to break. As UNHCR takes on surrogate state roles with the passing of time, it easily falls into the pattern of running camps, falling back on what has worked with C&M in the past. One former senior UNHCR official stated in 2012:

> UNHCR is also an administration . . . like any administration has fantastic pools of operational comfort . . . you run camps, you have camp

> refugees depend on you so you're the good guy . . . basically you have a captive population . . . we have a whole structure . . . it's a system that works . . . in general there is a system that is reasonably tested and bureaucrats of the administration and after a while you know how you run it so why push things with governments?[109]

In some ways, then, inherent to surrogacy is the possibility that UNHCR stops trying to influence the government as it becomes entrenched in its own patterns. The case studies are thus cautious to account for this to avoid endogeneity between influence and surrogacy; for example, interviewees were pressed to describe the ways in which UNHCR continued to try to influence so as to tease out the nuances of the relationship.[110]

Also noted in the previous section, another reason for sustaining surrogacy includes an ongoing sense of moral obligation, which may continue to make UNHCR feel an obligation to maintain surrogacy. Finally, the government may feel even further removed from the situation and, rather than growing in expertise and staff that are knowledgeable about refugees, may find it easier to continue to abdicate responsibilities to UNHCR, only further sustaining its surrogacy.

Alternatives to why UNHCR takes on surrogacy

Thus far, this book has argued that IO surrogate states emerge when filling a void. However, there are those who argue that it is grabbing power more aggressively, not reluctantly filling a void left by the state. Among those critical of UNHCR, seeing it as an aggressive power-grabber that does not care for refugee needs but is only concerned with its own growth, are authors like Harrell-Bond (1986) and Jacob Stevens (1991; 2006). Stevens writes:

> As a brutal testament to . . . [UNHCR's] . . . contemporary failure, at least 3.5 million . . . refugees currently struggle for survival in sprawling camps in Africa and Asia . . . If it was originally a guarantor of refugee rights, UNHCR has since mutated into a patron of these prisons of the stateless: a network of huge camps that can never meet any plausible 'humanitarian' standard, and yet somehow justify international funding for the agency.[111]

Even worse, he argues that UNHCR is complicit in keeping camps going over long periods of time, perhaps to maintain control over the situation. As noted earlier, Barnett and Finnemore's (1999) study also outlines the "pathologies" of IOs and UNHCR in particular, noting that its bureaucratic drive to dominate knowledge and expertise on refugee matters has enabled them to make life-and-death decisions on the part of refugees, defining them as powerless victims.[112] Harrell-Bond (1986) has also offered critiques of UNHCR's role in caring for refugees in camps, particularly arguing that it has led to overdependency, lack of agency and a lack of self-reliance on the part of refugees. Each of these perspectives paints a portrait of UNHCR as an IO that is more concerned with its own power and growth (and thus grabbing at power wherever it can) than its core mandate.

It is also possible that UNHCR's path to surrogacy is the result of a combination of the two (filling a void and aggressively grabbing power), with UNHCR taking on different roles and characteristics at different times. Likewise, UNHCR may feel pressure from donors to solve problems and continually address need, causing them to take on more and more until surrogate statehood unintentionally occurs. Or UNHCR may be concerned about its reputation—it may need to look like it is achieving certain priorities, which may lead it to expand its work beyond its mandate, thus approaching surrogacy. As the case studies demonstrate, many of these work in tandem with the broader concept that UNHCR domesticates into a surrogate state in order to fill a void, and thus not all (with the exception of the view that UNHCR is power-hungry and aggressively taking power from the state) are opposing alternative explanations but are rather complementary.

Influence

Describing how and when UNHCR takes on surrogate state properties is one aspect of this research, but understanding what this means for its influence on the state—not as an international actor headquartered in Geneva, but working domestically from within—is the second part of the inquiry. While there is extensive forced migration literature on UNHCR's surrogacy, it offers little on what this means in terms of UNHCR's ability to influence the state. Only the case studies will carry out measurements of UNHCR's influence over the state, because it varies from case to case—indeed, that is the variation under scrutiny in this research. However, as summarized in Table 2.1, this section operationalizes the theoretical indicators from Chapter 1 to the UNHCR context in order to assess the case study outcomes.

Beyond more empirical specificity, there are few changes to the indicators from their theoretical versions. However, the indicator, "material shifts in refugee policy" does require some additional explanation for the UNHCR context considered in the case studies. While various policies are examined in the case studies, one of the clearest set of policies examined relates to both *de facto* and *de jure* forms of LI, as understood via freedom

Table 2.1 Indicators of IO influence operationalized to the UNHCR context

Indicator of influence	*Way to measure*
Change in perception of UNHCR as an authority	Perception (by local population, refugees and other groups) of who is in authority. The state may be seen as an authority but may have little presence, thus making UNHCR "feel" like the authority.
Shifts in responsibility, blame and expectations of who is responsible for services	UNHCR may take on responsibilities—e.g. service provision of water, sanitation, infrastructure, health etc.—that would otherwise normally be expected of the state. Also a mechanism, this may shift how refugees and local populations attribute blame for shortcomings in services (they may blame UNHCR more than the state—e.g. Landau 2008).
Material shift in refugee policy	Complete change in policy as a result of UNHCR's role. (This is difficult to attribute to UNHCR alone because so many factors go into policymaking. This can be measured in the refugee rights that UNHCR promotes, including those related to freedom of movement and right to work; often discussed through the lens of LI.)
Change in individual leaders' demeanor toward refugees	Influencing individual policymakers via one-on-one relationships, who in turn may influence policy choices.
Change in rhetoric	Rhetorical influence (UNHCR changes the terms or language of the debate, possibly symbolically).[113]
Change in other actors' behavior	Influencing other actors (e.g. local NGOs, IPs, donor governments or civil society) to apply pressure in a certain policy direction promoted by UNHCR and thus having an indirect means of influence.
Carrying out governance functions	Administration and adjudication of specific territories or locales (also an indicator of surrogate statehood), such as a refugee camp or settlement.
Directly writing policy	Helping to negotiate and write refugee-relevant policy by being "in the room" (writing it up, meeting with leaders, lobbying).

of movement and the right to work. The focus on LI within the case studies is certainly not the only way to test the empirical aspects of this theory (for example, one might examine other state policies toward refugees, including forced returns, freedom of movement or work permits), and it is for this reason that a wide range of LI-related policies are examined.

However, broadly speaking, studying LI policies is a good material fit for approaching this question for several reasons. First, LI tends to be advocated for by UNHCR (in various forms) but also tends to be the least favored durable solution by states. UNHCR's roles in promoting policies of return or resettlement, for example, are less likely to demonstrate an example where UNHCR influenced a state to do something it otherwise did not want to do because states generally prefer return or resettlement to LI—they were likely to choose those options anyway, and thus those policies are less likely to reveal UNHCR influence.[114] Focusing on LI thus narrows the scope of inquiry to a refugee-related policy that UNHCR advocates for and states almost always dislike. This provides an observable shift that is useful for comparison: a shift in LI policies within individual cases (e.g. Tanzania's shifts to LI) and across cases (why one state is more willing to consider LI than another). While a state's choice to enact a policy of LI might not be entirely contingent upon UNHCR's lobbying, it is more likely to show a case where UNHCR's input was heard (given that UNHCR promotes greater rights access through LI and states tend to avoid such policies). Thus, with careful process tracing and in tandem with other variables and indicators, studying policies of LI is a useful way to view UNHCR's influence on state decision-making vis-à-vis its surrogacy.

In addition, LI represents a policy that is inherently both domestic and foreign in nature, thus lending analytic leverage to this study's focus on multilayered (and specifically the domestic) interactions between IOs and states. Policies of LI also bring up a host of other aspects about state refugee policy, including the right to work and freedom of movement. Thus, LI covers other policy issue areas like human rights and protection, on which UNHCR tries to persuade states. Alone it cannot explain UNHCR's level of influence on a state all together, but it is one of several indicators that can point in that direction and reveal areas where a state considered UNHCR's input where it otherwise might have chosen otherwise.

As noted on p. 62, LI in the refugee context is generally defined in two different ways: 1) legally (*de jure*) in terms of refugees being granted citizenship in a legal capacity and 2) *de facto*, in terms of the reality of access to human rights, namely, the right to work and freedom of movement. While both are relevant to this study, the latter definition will be most commonly referenced. However, the legal aspects of LI in the former will not be ignored entirely, particularly because this book considers *policies* of LI, and policies are most easily seen via the law. This also relates to another important differentiation that must be made in relation to LI: for the purposes of this research, the study does not focus on how *successful* LI has been (i.e. the psychosocial aspects of integration, the extent to which refugees "feel" locally integrated or the complex shifts in identity among individuals or the collective group). While such aspects are certainly important to understanding the process of LI and the extent to which it is "successful," they are outside the scope of this research (as they would require sociological, psychological and anthropological inquiry).

Policies of LI are a major part of "material policy changes" examined in the case studies (e.g. the Self-Reliance Strategy (SRS/DAR) in Uganda or Tanzania's decision to naturalize refugees from Burundi that fled in 1972), but they are certainly not the only indicator of UNHCR's influence as a surrogate state. And while LI does help frame the case study chapters' discussion on refugee rights more broadly, and how states treat refugees in light of UNHCR's role and leverage, it is examined carefully with process tracing, and only in combination with other indicators before conclusions about influence are drawn. Moreover, there are times when UNHCR does not even advocate for LI, or where it does so halfheartedly or indirectly.[115] Similarly, LI is the result of a number of variables and is not necessarily indicative of influence: UNHCR may have more or less leverage, even if a decision on LI was unaffected. It is for this reason that the framework takes into account the other nonmaterial factors as well.

There are a number of additional explanations that indicate why a state may behave a certain way toward refugees, many of which are far more influential on the state's decisions than the role taken by UNHCR. Some include: international donor attention (the host state might be more willing to consider a more open policy if it is given adequate assistance to do so); the size of the refugee population (if there is a perception that the state is inundated with refugees, leaders might be more inclined to confine them to camps and minimize freedom of movement); the location of the refugee settlements (whether refugees are in a remote, border area or in urban slums might affect the state's policy considerations or other behavior toward refugees); or how culturally similar the refugee population is to the host population (refugees that share language, religion and ethnic ties with their hosts might be more welcome). Still other factors include timing (how long the country has hosted the refugee population), regional politics, economics, security, regime type, the amount and type of aid given, media representation/rhetoric associated with refugee population and the linking of development to policies of LI.[116]

More UNHCR surrogacy means less influence

The case studies will flesh out why UNHCR's surrogacy translates into less influence on the state, leaning on process tracing, literature and interviews. The framework's mechanisms (responsibility shifting and marginalization of the state) in particular help demonstrate why this is the case. In terms of responsibility shifting, for example, Kagan writes that UNHCR assumes "unnatural" roles "in order to fill gaps in the international refugee regime" as it takes on responsibility for delivering direct assistance to refugees.[117] In turn, the state may have little incentive to change course or listen to

UNHCR about its behavior toward refugees. Its decision-makers are likely to be content to let UNHCR pay for and carry out all responsibilities pertaining to refugees (and refugees and locals alike may not even expect anything from the state as UNHCR assumes surrogacy).[118]

For its part, UNHCR may be trapped, unable to leverage or pressure the government because it needs the government to continue to grant it access to do its work—work that it must continue to show its donors to maintain funding. Put simply, in these cases, UNHCR loses its ability to "responsibilize" the government because they are "in the same boat" and "do not want to rock that boat."[119] Chris Dolan and Lucy Hovil (2006), for example, illustrate this struggle in their research. As noted earlier, they assert that UNHCR has moved away from a human rights focus on calling a government out for not meeting its responsibilities, to a humanitarian focus, which instead concentrates on meeting human need.[120] This results in an expanded use of what "protection" entails and brings them further away from their original mandate.[121] In trying to play both roles, they argue that UNHCR is caught between "soft" and "hard" protection (challenging the state on its duties and obligations) and ultimately weakens its ability to argue for refugee rights.[122] They write, "the fundamental tension between relief and protection remains: humanitarians can only pursue these forms of protection activity to a certain (relatively limited) point, before their capacity to deliver services on the ground is jeopardized."[123]

Marginalization of the state also illustrates the relationship between UNHCR's surrogacy and influence. In cases where the state is marginalized, the sovereign state may exist only in the background, as it cannot reach the "front lines" in interacting in the daily lives of refugees. Kagan writes, "When host governments deflect the burden for caring for refugee populations onto international actors, they weaken the normal connection between territorial sovereignty and state responsibility for people who are present on their territory."[124] UNHCR may even appear colonialist, mirroring some of Monica Kathina Juma and Astri Suhrke's (2002) claims: "In large refugee settlements in Africa, Asia and the Middle East one can find a humanitarian infrastructure dwarfing local government and dominated by international agencies based in the West, funded by Western states and led by international staff."[125]

These local and national authorities may also be sidestepped because, as noted earlier, IOs like UNHCR hold the technical expertise and knowledge.[126] Juma writes, "The marginalization of state structures, and relations between humanitarian agencies and donors are mediated by a humanitarian techno-speak that justifies the patronage of international actors over local actors and capacities."[127] While UNHCR may appear to have authority and greater responsibility, the marginalized state is less likely to cede decision-making power, instead seeking to hold its power even more tightly to show that it is still relevant. A surrogate state UNHCR may simply "leave a bad taste in the government's mouth," making them less cooperative and less likely to be influenced. As Juma writes, "when humanitarian actors usurp government obligations, the latter's reaction turns negative."[128]

Certainly, these mechanisms are not the only way to understand the relationship between UNHCR's surrogacy and influence, and this research has even remained open to the possibility that IO surrogacy has no relationship to its influence on state behavior. The case studies also demonstrate an array of other factors (some of which echo the additional explanations for state refugee policy decisions mentioned in the previous section) that contribute to how well UNHCR can influence the state from the domestic level, including individual personalities/leadership, the ability of individual groups to lobby politicians, the ways in which politicians calculate audience costs and domestic politics in general. These can overlap or juxtapose scholarship on the ways in which IOs can influence a state more broadly (not as domestic actors, but at the international level) and also are in addition to the broader refugee context (how long refugees have been there, how the population perceives them, etc.). Resources are another important aspect that comes out in the case studies, as states are more likely to listen to UNHCR when there is a financial incentive to do so. For example, one senior UNHCR official stated in 2012 that he recognizes that the humanitarian sector is no different than the commercial sector—"if you have a big wallet or come in with resources, that will determine the pitch of your voice and leverage you have anywhere in the world."[129] Other factors might include: how well UNHCR seizes upon critical junctures or crucial moments, the effects of budget cycles on UNHCR's planning and execution,[130] patterns engrained in response practices (i.e. UNHCR's "habit" of encampment), UNHCR's ability to assuage state concerns about securitization and the sense of government ownership over refugee issues.

Introducing the case studies

The previous section operationalized the framework to the context of UNHCR, examining how it can take on surrogate statehood and broadly speaking, what this means for its ability to influence the state. The case studies illustrate this empirically, using the framework to understand UNHCR's surrogate state relationships (or lack thereof) with Kenya, Tanzania and Uganda. As Chapter 1 indicated, these three cases are comparable (they hold a number of variables constant, including all hosting large numbers of refugees for long periods of time, all experiencing long-term UNHCR involvement, all being in the same region, all being developing countries and all being former colonies). They are also generalizable to other UNHCR missions in other regions and some other IOs.[131]

Figure 2.1 Subview of the "surrogate state" end of the spectrum paired with state disposition

The cases show variation on several levels: the variables of surrogacy and influence vary (in terms of nonmaterial and material indicators, such as policy decisions toward refugees). The cases vary in state responses as well: ranging from partnership (Uganda) to abdication (Kenya). Recall from Chapter 1, the subview illustrated by Figure 2.1.

Which causes which (i.e. does abdication cause surrogacy or vice versa) is less important for this research. What is more important for this study is the variation on the DV: IO influence, empirically taken as UNHCR's ability to influence the state.

Conclusion

This chapter applied the theoretic framework to UNHCR. It described UNHCR's roles at the domestic level and its "toolbox" of influencing states. It explored different ways UNHCR has domesticated as outlined in the literature, focusing most heavily on the ways in which UNHCR takes on surrogate statehood and the ways in which this affects its ability to influence state policy decisions on refugees. It operationalized some of the framework's indicators, looking specifically at refugee policy formation in terms of LI. Finally, it introduced the case studies of Kenya, Tanzania and Uganda.

The issues up for debate in this research are complex and relate not only to major questions within IR, but also to the work of UNHCR. This chapter's discussion of surrogate statehood also relates to larger questions about state sovereignty and forms of UNHCR's power vis-à-vis the centralization of state authorities in Africa and global governance. The initial assumption that UNHCR's increased role, power and responsibility at the local level as a surrogate state would translate into greater policy influence implied that surrogate statehood might be another avenue of influence for UNHCR's "toolbox." Realizing that the inverse is true—that an IO like UNHCR can have greater local power and responsibility and yet not have that increase its ability to sway state decisions—has interesting implications for both IR theory and UNHCR's work. The next three chapters present case studies that grapple with these themes and bring the framework's claims to the "real world," before the final concluding chapter ties it all together.

Notes

1 Michael Kagan, "We Live in a Country of UNHCR: The UN Surrogate State and Refugee Policy in the Middle East," *New Issues in Refugee Research*, Paper No. 201, UNHCR Policy Development and Evaluation Service, 2011; Jeff Crisp and Amy Slaughter, "A Surrogate State? The Role of UNHCR in Protracted Refugee Situations," in *Protracted Refugee Situations: Political, Human Rights and Security Implications*, ed. Gil Loescher, James Milner, Edward Newman and Gary Troeller (New York: United Nations University Press, 2008), 123–140.

2 Loescher, *The UNHCR and World Politics: A Perilous Path* (Oxford: Oxford University Press, 2001), 5.

3 Loescher, *The UNHCR and World Politics: A Perilous Path*, 22ff.

4 Gilbert Loescher, Alexander Betts and James Milner, *The United Nations High Commissioner for Refugees (UNHCR): The Politics and Practice of Refugee Protection in the Twenty-First Century* (Routledge: New York, 2008).

5 However, many scholars would argue that it is still largely a top-down organization, a point that will be discussed throughout the case studies. As noted in the introductory chapter, other IOs such as the ICRC, UNDP or WFP might have similar roles. While the framework has not been constructed with NGOs in mind, it might also relate to large NGOs with a similar presence, such as the IRC.

6 UNHCR, "Displacement: The New 21st Century Challenge," *UNHCR Global Trends 2012*. Available from www.unhcr.org/51bacb0f9.html.

7 Loescher, *The UNHCR and World Politics: A Perilous Path*, 82.

8 See Loescher, *The UNHCR and World Politics: A Perilous Path*.

9 Michael Barnett and Martha Finnemore, "The Politics, Power, and Pathologies of International Organisations," *International Organisation* 53, no. 4 (1999): 699–732.

10 Alexander Betts, "Historical Lessons for Overcoming Protracted Refugee Situations," in *Protracted Refugee Situations: Political, Human Rights and Security Implications*, ed. Gil Loescher, James Milner, Edward Newman and Gary Troeller, 162–186 (New York: United Nations University Press, 2008).

Alexander Betts, "The Refugee Regime Complex," *Refugee Survey Quarterly* 29, no. 2 (2010): 12–37.

e.g. Indo-Chinese CPA, CIREFCA (International Conference on Central American Refugees).

11 See Loescher et al., *The United Nations High Commissioner for Refugees (UNHCR): The Politics and Practice of Refugee Protection in the Twenty-First Century*, 128.

12 See Loescher, *The UNHCR and World Politics: A Perilous Path*.

13 With a broad understanding of "protection" and, in some cases, an expanded interpretation of what "protection" encompasses.

14 Loescher et al., *The United Nations High Commissioner for Refugees (UNHCR): The Politics and Practice of Refugee Protection in the Twenty-First Century*, 73.

15 Loescher, *The UNHCR and World Politics: A Perilous Path*, 6.

16 Loescher, *The UNHCR and World Politics: A Perilous Path*, 6.

17 Loescher et al., *The United Nations High Commissioner for Refugees (UNHCR): The Politics and Practice of Refugee Protection in the Twenty-First Century*, 73.

18 Loescher et al., *The United Nations High Commissioner for Refugees (UNHCR): The Politics and Practice of Refugee Protection in the Twenty-First Century*, 73.
19 Loescher, *The UNHCR and World Politics: A Perilous Path*, 5.
20 Loescher, *The UNHCR and World Politics: A Perilous Path*, 5.
21 Barnett and Finnemore, "The Politics, Power, and Pathologies of International Organisations." However, Loescher is quick to note, "In recent decades, as a result of restrictionism on the parts of states, the UNHCR has lost its monopoly on information and expertise" (Loescher, *The UNHCR and World Politics: A Perilous Path*, 5).
22 Barnett and Finnemore, "The Politics, Power, and Pathologies of International Organisations," 708, 710. They go on to discuss how IO behavior is prone to "pathologies" (see 1999, 715ff for more).
23 Loescher, *The UNHCR and World Politics: A Perilous Path*, 6.
24 Barnett and Finnemore, "The Politics, Power, and Pathologies of International Organisations," 707.
25 Loescher, *The UNHCR and World Politics: A Perilous Path*, 8. See Loescher (2001, 105ff) for more on the "good offices" expansion.
26 Loescher, *The UNHCR and World Politics: A Perilous Path*, 8.
27 Loescher, *The UNHCR and World Politics: A Perilous Path*, 12.
28 One NGO interviewee in Uganda, who had worked in partnership with UNHCR for decades, described UNHCR as a massive ship that takes a very long time to make even small changes in its direction. This speaks to UNHCR's "character" more broadly. He also noted frustration in how long it could take the massive bureaucracy to act, noting an example of when Burundian refugees wanted to return to Tanzania and needed assistance, it took weeks before UNHCR could address the issue. While refugees were ready to go, they had to wait while UNHCR signed a formal tripartite agreement. He said, in the meantime, refugees were "walking and leaving."
29 Loescher, *The UNHCR and World Politics: A Perilous Path*, 10–13.
30 Note that forced migration literature uses the term "securitization" in a slightly different way than other IR literature. See, for example, Van Selm (2003) or Hammerstad (2011).
31 Loescher, *The UNHCR and World Politics: A Perilous Path*, 14–15.
32 Loescher, *The UNHCR and World Politics: A Perilous Path*, 14.
33 Loescher, *The UNHCR and World Politics: A Perilous Path*, 15.
34 Loescher, *The UNHCR and World Politics: A Perilous Path*, 15.
35 Loescher, *The UNHCR and World Politics: A Perilous Path*, 15.
36 Loescher, *The UNHCR and World Politics: A Perilous Path*, 15.
37 Loescher et al., *The United Nations High Commissioner for Refugees (UNHCR): The Politics and Practice of Refugee Protection in the Twenty-First Century*, 87; Richard Black and Khalid Koser, ed., *The End of the Refugee Cycle? Refugee Repatriation and Reconstruction* (Oxford: Berghahn Books, 1999); Sarah Deardorff Miller, "How Long Is Too Long? Questioning the Legality of Long-Term Encampment through a Human Rights Lens," Working Paper Series No. 54, 2009 Refugee Studies Centre, Oxford University.
38 Loescher et al., *The United Nations High Commissioner for Refugees (UNHCR): The Politics and Practice of Refugee Protection in the Twenty-First Century*, 91.
39 Loescher et al., *The United Nations High Commissioner for Refugees (UNHCR): The Politics and Practice of Refugee Protection in the Twenty-First Century*, 128–129.

40 Loescher et al., *The United Nations High Commissioner for Refugees (UNHCR): The Politics and Practice of Refugee Protection in the Twenty-First Century*, 129.
41 Barnett and Finnemore, "The Politics, Power, and Pathologies of International Organisations"; Barbara Harrell-Bond and Guglielmo Verdirame, *Rights in Exile: Janus-Faced Humanitarianism* (New York: Berghahn Books, 2005); Simon Turner, *Politics of Innocence: Hutu Identity, Conflict and Camp Life* (New York: Berghahn Books, 2010).
42 Loescher et al., *The United Nations High Commissioner for Refugees (UNHCR): The Politics and Practice of Refugee Protection in the Twenty-First Century*, 129.
43 Loescher et al., *The United Nations High Commissioner for Refugees (UNHCR): The Politics and Practice of Refugee Protection in the Twenty-First Century*, 129.
44 Barbara Harrell-Bond, "Repatriation: Under What Conditions Is It the Most Desirable Solution for Refugees? An Agenda for Research," *African Studies Review* 32, no. 1 (1989): 41–69; Harrell-Bond and Verdirame, *Rights in Exile: Janus-Faced Humanitarianism*.
45 Loescher et al., *The United Nations High Commissioner for Refugees (UNHCR): The Politics and Practice of Refugee Protection in the Twenty-First Century*, 82.
46 Refugee Law Project 2003.
47 Loescher, *The UNHCR and World Politics: A Perilous Path*, 6.
48 Barnett and Finnemore, "The Politics, Power, and Pathologies of International Organisations," 705, 710.
49 Loescher et al., *The United Nations High Commissioner for Refugees (UNHCR): The Politics and Practice of Refugee Protection in the Twenty-First Century*, 122.
50 Loescher et al., *The United Nations High Commissioner for Refugees (UNHCR): The Politics and Practice of Refugee Protection in the Twenty-First Century*, 122.
51 Barnett and Finnemore, "The Politics, Power, and Pathologies of International Organisations," 710.
52 Interestingly, she sees it both as giving in to state desires and pressures and also acting as its own autonomous actor.
53 Barbara Harrell-Bond, *Imposing Aid: Emergency Assistance to Refugees* (Oxford: Oxford University Press, 1986), 64.
54 Michael Barnett, "Authority, Intervention, and the Outer Limits on International Relations Theory," in *Intervention and Transnationalism in Africa: Global-Local Networks of Power*, ed. Thomas Callaghy, Ronald Kassimir and Robert Latham, 47–68 (Cambridge: Cambridge University Press, 2001), 62.

Of course, IO power is distinctly tied to authority both moral and expert authority, delegated or legal-rational authority, setting and voicing norms and rules, having regulative and constitutive power, classifying, labeling, investing in meaning and information and turning it into knowledge, monopolizing knowledge, acquiring expert status, building coalitions with domestic and transnational actors to influence states etc. (Michael Barnett and Martha Finnemore, *Rules for the World: International Organisations in Global Politics* (Ithaca, NY: Cornell University Press, 2004); Bob Reinalda and Bertjan Verbeek, *Autonomous Policy Making by International Organisations* (London: Routledge, 1998); Biermann and Siebenhüner 2009 in Nina Hall, "Moving Beyond Their Mandates? How International Organisations Are Responding to Climate Change," D.Phil thesis, University of Oxford, Oxford, United Kingdom, 2013, 29.
55 Barnett, "Authority, Intervention, and the Outer Limits on International Relations Theory," 61–62.

56 They define "global" as a term that refers to some kind of claim about the range of forces operating across space and "local" as being either a discrete element within that global range or simply a site or phenomenon subject to global forces that are external to it (Thomas Callaghy, Ronald Kassimir and Robert Latham, "Introduction: Transboundary Formations, Intervention, Order, and Authority," in *Intervention and Transnationalism in Africa: Global-Local Networks of Power*, ed. Thomas Callaghy, Ronald Kassimir and Robert Latham, 1–22 (Cambridge: Cambridge University Press, 2001), 6. They look at how "external" and "internal" forces intersect to alter political outcomes and are quick to problematize notions of "internal" and "external" commonly made by IR and comparative scholars, choosing instead to merge them into "transboundary formations" that link global, regional, national and local forces through structures, networks and discourse (Callaghy et al., "Introduction: Transboundary Formations, Intervention, Order, and Authority," 3–4).

57 Callaghy et al., "Introduction: Transboundary Formations, Intervention, Order, and Authority," 6–7. They avoid privileging the state, considering NGOs and IOs as equally important actors in politics. Their discussion on transnationalism is also linked to theories of globalization, interdependence and broader claims about authority and sovereignty. With regards to authority, for example, they write that groups and institutions establish boundaries: "When the UN High Commission for Refugees establishes a refugee camp in some locale it must establish who is a refugee and who is not, what it will do for them and what it will not, and how it will do it or what the effects will be if it does not" ("Introduction: Transboundary Formations, Intervention, Order, and Authority," 9).

58 Barnett, "Authority, Intervention, and the Outer Limits on International Relations Theory," 63. There is no finite amount of power, and one's increase need not mean another's decrease (James N. Rosenau, *Turbulence in World Politics: A Theory of Change and Continuity* (Princeton, NJ: Princeton University Press, 1990)). Roitman also affirms that transnational networks or power are not necessarily undermining a regime's power and in some cases may even create new ways of generating wealth or be complementary or reciprocal (Janet Roitman, "New Sovereigns? Regulatory Authority in the Chad Basin," in *Intervention and Transnationalism in Africa: Global-Local Networks of Power*, ed. Thomas Callaghy, Ronald Kassimir and Robert Latham (Cambridge: Cambridge University Press, 2001), 241–243).

59 Roitman, "New Sovereigns? Regulatory Authority in the Chad Basin," 253.

60 Ronald Kassimir, "Producing Local Politics: Governance, Representation, and Non-State Organisations in Africa," in *Intervention and Transnationalism in Africa: Global-Local Networks of Power*, ed. Thomas Callaghy, Ronald Kassimir and Robert Latham (Cambridge: Cambridge University Press, 2001), 95; Cyril I. Obi, "Global, State, and Local Intersections: Power, Authority and Conflict in the Niger Delta Oil Communities," in *Intervention and Transnationalism in Africa: Global-Local Networks of Power*, ed. Thomas Callaghy, Ronald Kassimir and Robert Latham (Cambridge: Cambridge University Press, 2001), 192.

61 Barnett, "Authority, Intervention, and the Outer Limits on International Relations Theory," 55.

62 Barnett, "Authority, Intervention, and the Outer Limits on International Relations Theory," 47. He problematizes rigid understandings of "global" and "local," arguing that it generates simplistic "domestic/foreign" distinctions or "inside/outside" views of global politics (citing R.B.J. Walker, *Inside/Outside: International Relations as Political Theory* (Cambridge: Cambridge University Press, 1993)).

63 Grace Skogstad, ed., *Policy Paradigms, Transnationalism, and Domestic Politics* (Toronto: University of Toronto Press, 2011), 17.
64 Thomas Risse-Kappen, ed., *Bringing Transnational Relations Back In: Non-State Actors, Domestic Structures and International Institutions* (Cambridge: Cambridge University Press, 1995).
65 Gilbert Loescher, James Milner, Edward Newman and Gary Troeller, ed., *Protracted Refugee Situations: Political, Human Rights and Security Implications* (New York: United Nations University Press, 2008), 74.
66 Barnett, "Authority, Intervention, and the Outer Limits on International Relations Theory."
67 Barnett, "Authority, Intervention, and the Outer Limits on International Relations Theory," 60.
68 Barnett, "Authority, Intervention, and the Outer Limits on International Relations Theory," 60; Barnett and Finnemore 1999, 708.
69 Barnett, "Authority, Intervention, and the Outer Limits on International Relations Theory," 60.
70 Barnett, "Authority, Intervention, and the Outer Limits on International Relations Theory," 62.
71 Milner, for example, writes that refugee movements are by nature both domestic and international events James Milner, *Refugees, the State and the Politics of Asylum in Africa* (Basingstoke, UK: Palgrave Macmillan, 2009), 9.
72 Christopher Clapham, *Africa in the International System: The Politics of State Survival* (Cambridge: Cambridge University Press, 1996), 257.
73 Jeff Crisp and Amy Slaughter, "A Surrogate State? The Role of UNHCR in Protracted Refugee Situations," in *Protracted Refugee Situations: Political, Human Rights and Security Implications*, ed. Gil Loescher, James Milner, Edward Newman and Gary Troeller (New York: United Nations University Press, 2008), 123–140; Turner, *Politics of Innocence: Hutu Identity, Conflict and Camp Life*.
74 Michael Kagan, "We Live in a Country of UNHCR: The UN Surrogate State and Refugee Policy in the Middle East," *New Issues in Refugee Research*, Paper No. 201, UNHCR Policy Development and Evaluation Service, 2011, 4 (Citing Grabska's (2008) research with refugees in Egypt).
75 Crisp and Slaughter, "A Surrogate State? The Role of UNHCR in Protracted Refugee Situations," 131–132.
76 Crisp and Slaughter, "A Surrogate State? The Role of UNHCR in Protracted Refugee Situations," 124.
77 Crisp and Slaughter, "A Surrogate State? The Role of UNHCR in Protracted Refugee Situations," 124.
78 Crisp and Slaughter, "A Surrogate State? The Role of UNHCR in Protracted Refugee Situations," 124–125.
79 Crisp and Slaughter, "A Surrogate State? The Role of UNHCR in Protracted Refugee Situations," 126.
80 Crisp and Slaughter, "A Surrogate State? The Role of UNHCR in Protracted Refugee Situations," 128.
81 Crisp and Slaughter, "A Surrogate State? The Role of UNHCR in Protracted Refugee Situations," 128, referencing Stevens 2006.
82 Crisp and Slaughter, "A Surrogate State? The Role of UNHCR in Protracted Refugee Situations," 131–132.
83 Crisp and Slaughter, "A Surrogate State? The Role of UNHCR in Protracted Refugee Situations," 132; Harrell-Bond 1986, 91.

84 Crisp and Slaughter, "A Surrogate State? The Role of UNHCR in Protracted Refugee Situations," 137.
85 Kagan, "We Live in a Country of UNHCR: The UN Surrogate State and Refugee Policy in the Middle East," 6.
86 Crisp and Slaughter, "A Surrogate State? The Role of UNHCR in Protracted Refugee Situations," 123.
87 Jeffrey Herbst, *States and Power in Africa: Comparative Lessons in Authority and Control* (Princeton, NJ: Princeton University Press, 2000), 146. He develops a typology of African states based on population-distribution maps. In his first group, he finds that countries with certain political geographies (e.g. large countries with a high population density that is not contiguous) find it difficult to consolidate power. His second group includes "hinterland" countries: those that are large but do not have dispersed areas of high population density. This group may have its highest population density in small areas of the country, making it hard to govern. His third group, that which has a geography most favorable for the consolidation of power, has most of the power in the capital. These countries tend to be small, though not always peaceful. The final group in Herbst's typology includes countries with neutral political geographies (e.g. Kenya, Uganda and Zambia) (*States and Power in Africa: Comparative Lessons in Authority and Control*, 161).
88 Herbst, *States and Power in Africa: Comparative Lessons in Authority and Control*, 146.
89 Clapham, *Africa in the International System: The Politics of State Survival*, 28–9.
90 Herbst, *States and Power in Africa: Comparative Lessons in Authority and Control*, 173.
91 Herbst, *States and Power in Africa: Comparative Lessons in Authority and Control*, 174.
92 Ogaba Agbese and George Klay Kieh, Jr., ed., *Reconstituting the State in Africa* (Basingstoke, UK: Palgrave Macmillan, 2007), 46. Lund, for example, mentions taxation as one indicator of state formation (Achille Mbembe, *On the Postcolony* (Berkeley, CA: University of California Press, 2001); Charles Tilly, *Coercion, Capital, and European States, AD 990-1990* (Cambridge: Blackwell, 1990) but adds that "in places where central government institutions do not reach at all, alternative forms of tax may emerge," including services provided by organizations (Christian Lund, ed., *Twilight Institutions: Public Authority and Local Politics in Africa* (London: Wiley-Blackwell Publishing, 2007), 695).
93 Agbese and Kieh, *Reconstituting the State in Africa*, 54.
94 See Clapham (1996, 44–55) for more on postindependence governance in Africa and the ways in which states began to rule as top-down, one-party, monopoly states. This arguably further sets the scene for forms of governance that are ripe for IO surrogate states.
95 Agbese and Kieh write, "Scholars have recently depicted African states in decline as 'soft,' 'weak,' 'collapsed,' 'failed,' 'shadow,' or 'quasi' states (Rothchild 1987; Forrest 1994; Zartman 1995a; Helman and Ratner 1992–3; Reno 1995b; Jackson 1990)" (*Reconstituting the State in Africa*, 45). They prefer the concept of "state inversion," which depicts state decay in stages over time and is marked by a withdrawal from state institutions (*Reconstituting the State in Africa*, 45–6; Azarya and Chazan 1987).
96 Agbese and Kieh, *Reconstituting the State in Africa*, 47.
97 Joseph Semboja and Ole Therkildsen, eds. *Service Provision Under Stress in East Africa: The State, NGOs and People's Organisations in Kenya, Tanzania and Uganda* (Copenhagen: Centre for Development Research, 1995).

98 Clapham, *Africa in the International System: The Politics of State Survival*, 256.

99 Clapham, *Africa in the International System: The Politics of State Survival*, 258. He attributes the expansion of NGOs in Africa to post-Cold War changes in international politics, as well as a decline in respect for national sovereignty and a merging of humanitarian assistance with military protection from the international community (259). He goes on to discuss how NGOs affected Western civil society's ways of shaping the management of African external relations, which ultimately affected the distribution of power. Even NGOs that appear to be nonpolitical can easily shape the political landscape, particularly on multiple levels (at the local and national levels):

> [T]he 'de-stating' of Western relations with Africa led to the establishment of institutions through which to reduce the role of the state both in the internal management of African societies and in their relations with the outside world. To the extent to which they became effective and autonomous organizations, these 'southern NGOs' in turn became intermediaries which took African international relations beyond the sphere of the state. (Clapham, *Africa in the International System: The Politics of State Survival*, 264)

100 Clapham, *Africa in the International System: The Politics of State Survival*, 258.

101 Lund, *Twilight Institutions: Public Authority and Local Politics in Africa*, 1. "The blurred boundary between state and non-state is often more conspicuous in Africa than in other places because of the many challenges to a grand state formation project" (Lund 2007, 679). He continues,

> [I]t is not only institutions of public authority that provide representations of the state. . . . [O]ne is struck by the irony of a systematic myth of the unity and coherence of the state. An idea of a powerful state with intention, a higher rationality and a project is manifested in receptions, seminars and inaugurations, draped in the ineluctable banners with slogans of determination, designed to instill trust in its capacity to do what states are supposed to do. This is contrasted with the incoherence and incapacity of the state, the multiple parallel structures and alternative sites of authority (chiefs, vigilantes, political factions, hometown associations, neighborhood groups) that deny any notion of unity or rationality in the singular. (Twilight Institutions: Public Authority and Local Politics in Africa, 689)

102 In Thomas Callaghy, Ronald Kassimir and Robert Latham, ed., *Intervention and Transnationalism in Africa: Global-Local Networks of Power* (Cambridge: Cambridge University Press, 2001), 197.

103 Clapham, *Africa in the International System: The Politics of State Survival*, 273.

104 This may or may not change the balance of power, as Barnett reminds us that power ought not necessarily be viewed as zero-sum—an IO assuming some power does not necessarily mean that state has less power. And yet it seems that some power reconfiguration is inevitable in these cases, and when the state appears weak and IOs strong at a domestic level, the state can also begin to look irrelevant. Case studies consider some of these power-related issues.

105 Chris Dolan and Lucy Hovil, "Humanitarian Protection in Uganda? A Trojan Horse?" Humanitarian Policy Group Background Paper, Overseas Development Institute, 2006, 3. Available from www.odi.org.uk/sites/odi.org.uk/files/odi-assets/publications-opinion-files/381.pdf.

106 Dolan and Hovil, "Humanitarian Protection in Uganda? A Trojan Horse?" 3.

107 Kagan, "We Live in a Country of UNHCR: The UN Surrogate State and Refugee Policy in the Middle East," 7.

108 Kagan, "We Live in a Country of UNHCR: The UN Surrogate State and Refugee Policy in the Middle East," 1–2. More broadly, Kagan points to a responsibility shift emerging from basic North/South global inequalities, all of which relate to burden sharing (notably that governments in the global south have tended to bear a greater load) (Kagan, "We Live in a Country of UNHCR: The UN Surrogate State and Refugee Policy in the Middle East," 2). He proffers that minimal attempts at resettlement are not enough and instead that UNHCR's role in host countries can be another form of burden sharing. He writes, "UNHCR's ability to deliver aid to desperate refugees in the south offers northern states a channel by which to funnel assistance monetarily while simultaneously helping host governments in the south to keep refugees from imposing a burden on their own societies" (Kagan, "We Live in a Country of UNHCR: The UN Surrogate State and Refugee Policy in the Middle East," 3). Juma touches on similar points, writing that when some governments claim to be overwhelmed and cry out for greater burden sharing, the response tends to be one of government abdication of refugee responsibilities, "thus making them UNHCR's responsibility" (Monica Kathina Juma, "The Political Economy of Building Local Capacity," in *Eroding Local Capacity: International Humanitarian Action in Africa*, ed. Monica Kathina Juma and Astri Suhrke (Uppsala: Nordiska AfrikaInstitutet, 2002), 171).

109 UNHCR Official J 2012.

110 Moreover, at the very least it is still helpful to know that surrogacy and influence are paired in this way.

111 In Crisp and Slaughter, "A Surrogate State? The Role of UNHCR in Protracted Refugee Situations," 123.

112 Barnett and Finnemore, "The Politics, Power, and Pathologies of International Organisations," 710; Liisa H. Malkki, *Purity and Exile: Violence, Memory and National Cosmology among Hutu Refugees in Tanzania* (Chicago: University of Chicago Press, 1995); Kevin Hartigan, "Matching Humanitarian Norms with Cold, Hard Interests: The Making of Refugee Policies in Mexico and Honduras, 1980–89," *International Organisation* 46, no. 3 (1992): 709–730; Barbara Harrell-Bond, Karim Hussein and Patrick Matlou, "Contemporary Refugees in Africa: A Problem of the State," in *Africa: A Handbook*, edited by Sean Moroney (London: Facts on File Publications, 1989).

113 For example, a Tanzanian NGO official stated that UNHCR works in a perpetual emergency: "even when it is not an emergency, it treats it like an emergency" (NGO Official F 2013). Another called UNHCR a "frenzy that feeds on itself" and recalled the perpetual emergency lens through which UNHCR works, at times to maintain donor attention and funds, other times to stay in charge and at other times because it is the model it has always used (NGO Official D 2013; UNHCR Official O 2013).

114 As will be discussed later, UNHCR almost always says that it promotes LI, but there are times when it tries harder than others, and there are even those who accuse it of getting in the way of LI at times. There is even the possibility that the more it assumes surrogacy, the less likely it is to advocate for a shift in policy among the government, thus making it seem as though influence and surrogacy may have an endogenous relationship. This challenge is also refuted in the cases and concluding chapter.

115 See, for example, Harrell-Bond and Verdirame, *Rights in Exile: Janus-Faced Humanitarianism*, or Turner, *Politics of Innocence: Hutu Identity, Conflict and Camp Life*. This is discussed further in later chapters.

116 See Milner 2009 for more.

117 Kagan, "We Live in a Country of UNHCR: The UN Surrogate State and Refugee Policy in the Middle East," 3. Kagan draws on Isaiah Berlin's classic distinction between positive and negative liberties:

> Host governments' role is limited to protection of negative liberties. . . . As a result, host governments can substantially live up to their end of the bargain by literally doing nothing. They can 'protect' refugees simply by restraining themselves from deporting them, through a policy of benign neglect. UNHCR and its partners bear the heavier load by taking responsibility for refugees' registration and status determination, healthcare, education, nutrition and livelihood assistance. (3)

Kagan's conclusion is ultimately pragmatic. He writes,

> The assignment of responsibility for protecting rights should be to the institution best positioned to carry out the duty. As a default rule, the state should usually be responsible because in the international arena states are presumed to have the clearest ability and authority to act. But there are situations where either state capacity is lacking or political constraints lead governments to be unwilling to use it. In these situations, the United Nations may be best able to promote the protection of refugees by taking on some of the responsibility for refugee protection. (164)

118 E.g. Kagan, "We Live in a Country of UNHCR: The UN Surrogate State and Refugee Policy in the Middle East," 3; Landau 2008.

119 UNHCR Official N 2012.

120 Dolan and Hovil, "Humanitarian Protection in Uganda? A Trojan Horse?," 3.

121 Dolan and Hovil, "Humanitarian Protection in Uganda? A Trojan Horse?," 3.

122 Dolan and Hovil, "Humanitarian Protection in Uganda? A Trojan Horse?," 4.

123 Dolan and Hovil, "Humanitarian Protection in Uganda? A Trojan Horse?," 4. They continue, "The Country Director of a large INGO summed up the dilemma . . .: 'We are prepared [to raise difficult issues], but I am not authorized to have [my organization] closed down. . . . It is rarely better for us to leave'. A field-worker reiterated this point, saying: 'On the ground we want to do a good job, but there is an element of real compromise. We are always thinking, what will the state do?' . . . In Uganda, the government told NGOs to remain silent on issues of government responsibility' (Dolan and Hovil, "Humanitarian Protection in Uganda? A Trojan Horse?," 12).

124 Kagan, "We Live in a Country of UNHCR: The UN Surrogate State and Refugee Policy in the Middle East," 3.

125 Kagan, "We Live in a Country of UNHCR: The UN Surrogate State and Refugee Policy in the Middle East," 5.

126 Barnett and Finnemore, "The Politics, Power, and Pathologies of International Organisations."

127 Juma, "The Political Economy of Building Local Capacity," 181–182.

128 Juma, "The Political Economy of Building Local Capacity," 175.

129 UNHCR Official N 2012.

130 UNHCR Official A 2013.

131 E.g. Kagan, "We Live in a Country of UNHCR: The UN Surrogate State and Refugee Policy in the Middle East," 5.

3 Kenya

- **Refugee-hosting policies and history in Kenya**
- **UNHCR's domestication and surrogacy in Kenya**
- **UNHCR's influence on Kenya**
- **Conclusion**

UNHCR's domestication in Kenya provides a clear example of an IO's surrogate state role coupled with state abdication. UNHCR has had a presence in Kenya for decades and expanded its responsibilities and activities in the 1990s, when a large influx of Somali refugees arrived in the Northeastern Province (NEP). It assumed surrogacy over time, to the point where refugees and locals alike viewed it—not the government—as the authority in charge of many aspects of life. However, while one might assume that greater autonomy, authority and power in the NEP would translate into influence over the Kenyan government's decisions on refugee issues, this does not appear to be the case. Despite its role as a surrogate state—carrying out activities and funding projects—UNHCR has not gained greater influence in terms of material (e.g. policies advocating for greater protection and refugee rights) or nonmaterial measures. This chapter presents the case of Somali refugees in Kenya via a brief introduction to the relevant history, politics and refugee policy. It then applies the framework, outlining the ways in which UNHCR domesticates into a surrogate state—the conditions and motives, examples of surrogacy and why its surrogacy has been sustained. The chapter then examines UNHCR's ability to influence the state, explaining why it is less influential as a surrogate state.

Refugee-hosting policies and history in Kenya

Brief general history

Kenya was a British colony until 1963, when Jomo Kenyatta became the first president after more than a decade of rebellion. Amidst political instability, Kenya became and remained a single-party government under President Daniel arap Moi from 1969 until 1992, when multiparty elections were held and President Mwai Kibaki was elected. The government has been plagued by corruption and fraud, as well as tensions with neighboring Somalia over land disputes. It has also had its share of recent ethnic and political clashes. Kenya's postcolonial history is also marked by *harambee*, a self-help concept (meaning "all pull together" in Swahili) embraced under Kenyatta as a means of local community development and unity and which has informed some refugee policy.[1]

Kenya has hosted some of the highest numbers of refugees in recent decades from more than 10 countries, a large number of which are from Somalia. There are an estimated 450,000 Somali refugees in Kenya, consisting of both recent and more historic waves of migration in response to civil war in the 1980s and subsequent instability since. Most are in Dadaab, in the NEP, as well as in the slums of Nairobi. Kakuma Camp in the northwestern part of Kenya also hosts a majority of Sudanese refugees, as well as Somalis, Ethiopians and Congolese refugees, with more than 80,000 residing there. In total, UNHCR estimates that there are 559,000 "persons of concern" in Kenya. While nearly all refugees in Kenya have significant needs, drought, famine and protracted instability in Somalia prove the Somali refugee situation as one of today's most difficult PRS.[2] This chapter will focus on Somali refugees in Dadaab's camps.

In the past, Kenya had a strong local nonstate relief capacity, consisting of mostly indigenous resources: churches and other civil society organizations.[3] Kagwanja writes, "Kenya's refugee policy right from the colonial era oscillated . . . between 'hospitality' and 'hostility' to refugees and asylum-seekers."[4] He notes that Kenya saw itself as a transit state for refugees: "whenever refugees did not threaten its interests, it closed its eyes to them and gave a free sway to NGOs to manage refugee affairs."[5] Harrell-Bond and Verdirame (2005) describe a similar story, arguing that, before 1990, the government controlled refugee policy with an approach of "benign neglect, allowing refugees to settle freely in towns and cities to secure their own means of livelihood as best they could."[6] They write that it was, for the most part, an open door, laissez-faire policy until the 1990s when refugee numbers spiked.[7] As discussed in later sections, Kenya's more recent refugee policy has been marked by abdication and a strict focus on security. In response, UNHCR and its partners have assumed blanket responsibility for refugees, operating "care and maintenance" camps since the early 1990s.

According to Anna Lindley and Anita Haslie (2011), there are generally two refugee populations in Kenya: protracted refugees who fled in the 1990s and more recent refugees who have fled violence in the 2000s. Dadaab's refugee camps were established in 1991 to host approximately 90,000 refugees.[8] In light of famine and drought, the population is now more than five times that, and Dadaab is essentially Kenya's third largest city. What was meant to be a "temporary situation" is now protracted, with some refugees having been there for over 20 years.[9] Conditions in Dadaab have always been difficult and have only worsened with the scale of new arrivals. As Lindley and Haslie summarize, recent years have demonstrated increased government involvement, heightened security concerns and crises within the camps to accommodate new arrivals.[10]

Relations with NEP, securitization

Historically, central authorities in Nairobi have always had a tense relationship with the NEP since its colonial days.[11] Under British rule, it was seen as a constant threat of rebellion. Even today Somalia sees this portion of Kenya as rightfully Somalia, and thus today's government of Kenya (GoK) (currently led by President Uhuru Kenyatta as of April 2013 and formerly under President Mwai Kibaki) tends to distrust people in the region. One senior UNHCR official stated that some Kenyans in NEP do not even view themselves as Kenyan, but rather in occupied Somalia.[12] Another asserted that the people are nearly one and the same and that it is difficult to tell the difference between Somali Kenyans and Somalis.[13] And yet another noted that issues between the central government and NEP existed long before there were refugee issues there.[14] It comes as no surprise, then, that this area was kept isolated and devoid of development or investment.[15] Milner writes:

> It has been argued that "the North of Kenya is a peripheral region . . . where, since colonial times, opponents have been sent" (Pérouse de Montclos 1998, 168 . . .). It is an arid and sparse region, a space of relegation where the government has invested little since independence and which, in turn, has contributed little or nothing to the national economy. . . . it has been "placed on the periphery of a very centralized state" . . . (Pérouse de Montclos 2001, 297). It is . . . geographically, economically and politically far from the core of power in Nairobi, and therefore a suitable place to contain a perceived threat.[16]

According to Milner, the underdevelopment and repression of Somali Kenyans in NEP is rooted in colonialism and has precluded the integration of Somali refugees in Kenya, keeping them viewed as a threat.[17] There were a number of attempts at secession into a unified Somali state, which resulted in the British implementing a state of emergency in the 1960s. The state of emergency was not lifted until 1991 when Moi allowed UNHCR and other organizations to respond to the mass arrival of Somalis.[18] Subsequent *shifta* wars, or guerrilla campaigns of secession from Kenya, prompted Kenyatta to respond with intense military spending and fighting.[19] A coup attempt against Moi in 1982 only further securitized domestic politics in Kenya, resulting in policies meant to ensure that members of his ethnic group would rise to power, as well as mass human rights violations to protect his regime. All of this only contributed further to portray Somalis as a threat and the justification of their repression on the grounds of national security.[20] One senior UNHCR official who had worked in Dadaab for several years stated, "Not surprisingly, Kenyans see Somalis as a threat . . . military or police have seen it as a foreign country they've been sent to and it's a 'why me?' scenario."[21]

Scapegoating refugees as economic and security threats are also convenient tactics for some politicians: as one UNHCR interviewee stated, "soapbox politics take over, particularly if you want to divert attention from a corruption scandal, of which there were quite a few, then you immediately start a 'Somali scare.'"[22] Milner roots some of this in the process of democratization, noting that the arrival of multiparty elections meant that politicians found it useful to stigmatize or employ anti-Somali rhetoric and antirefugee sentiments to gain political traction.[23] Likewise, it is not uncommon for local Somali Kenyans to blame economic or environmental problems on the refugee population.[24] Finally, the current "war on terror" since the terrorist attacks of September 11, 2001, on the US, coupled with international donor pressure and concerns of al-Shabaab's[25] presence in Kenya have also contributed to Kenya's strict, security-focused policies toward refugees and the shift from laissez-faire policies of the past.

Confinement and encampment

Kenyan refugee policy has been defined by encampment for decades, demonstrating a significant shift from the earlier postindependence days. A spike in refugee numbers between 1991 and 1992—an increase from 16,000 to 427,278—was one major reason that Kenya adopted policies of confinement and encampment.[26] The government saw refugees as a threat and sought to keep them isolated from urban areas.[27] With the influx, Kenya asked UNHCR for assistance prompting seven new camps to be opened in 1992. Milner writes that these camps "cover[ed] a large portion of land; refugees were transferred to camps, and the government transferred responsibility for camp management to UNHCR."[28] Refugees were continually required to reside in the camps and were not allowed to move freely or gain employment.

More recently, refugees have been increasingly identified with al-Shabaab, generating Kenyan fears about Muslim extremism and terrorism and resulting in Kenyan police operating with "clumsy, heavy-handed and militarized action against a wide section of the Somali population."[29] And yet encampment has hardly solved Kenya's problems: Dadaab's camps are known for their insecurity and are often subject to banditry, kidnappings and robberies.[30] As will be discussed in the next section, the refugee policy of encampment in Kenya centered on abdicating responsibility to UNHCR and pushing refugees to the margins, politically and geographically.[31] It has only been security concerns that have lured it to have more involvement. Recent history has maintained much of this tradition, favoring encampment pending return (not LI and limited resettlement).[32]

While encampment still dominates, there have been some important changes since 2006. First, the government passed legislation putting itself in charge of refugee registration and reception and setting out a legal framework that governs refugees and establishes some procedures.[33] It took on camp management as well, and a Department of Refugee Affairs (DAR) was established (though it has now been disbanded).[34] This would seem a positive step for refugees, but it has unfortunately taken place in conjunction with a large influx of refugees in 2011 and 2012, exacerbating tensions in Dadaab's camps, and the subsequent increased securitization of the Somali presence in Kenya.[35] In October 2011, the GoK even suspended the registration of new refugee arrivals, claiming that Dadaab's camps were too full and that accommodating more refugees would be a threat to national security.[36] Kenya now hopes to return refugees to a safe zone within Somalia, though it is dubious whether conditions for return will really emerge. Nevertheless, the 2006 legislation is a significant step, given GoK's previous abdication.[37] It is discussed further at the end of this chapter.

UNHCR's domestication and surrogacy in Kenya

The previous section provided background and context for understanding the role of UNHCR in Kenya vis-à-vis the government's behavior toward refugees. This section examines one of the ways UNHCR domesticates in Kenya: as a surrogate state.

Surrogacy and abdication (conditions and process)

> In Kenya, the government has institutionalized a laissez faire attitude towards refugees and views them as the responsibility of UNHCR. This indifference has left UNHCR with no alternative but to take over what is in effect *a state responsibility*.[38]

UNHCR domesticated in Kenya, moving beyond an advisor from Geneva, a resource or funder or projects, or a transnational actor working through a network of local actors, to an actor working on the domestic level, which, over time took on surrogate state properties. Before the 1990s, local Kenyan organizations had dealt with refugees, in many cases integrating or resettling them locally, in spite of Kenya's hostility toward refugees.[39] For the three decades following independence, international actors like UNHCR kept a distance from "on the ground operations," working instead through local actors.[40] The 1990s, however, represent a turning point in Kenya's refugee history and one where international involvement skyrocketed. From 1991 onward, international actors "sidelined and eventually eclipsed" these local NGOs.[41] With large numbers of refugees arriving at the border, some local actors were overwhelmed, and thus in the 1990s, Kenya relied on UNHCR to take on more responsibility. Kagwanja writes:

> This period saw a meteoric growth of the UNHCR Branch Office in Kenya, from a staff of eight to more than 50 officers. The period was also characterized by a reinforcement of the link between UNHCR and international NGOs such as Care International, the Lutheran World Federation (LWF) and the International Rescue Committee (IRC). This relationship manifested in expanding programs at the NGO level.[42]

Harrell-Bond and Verdirame note this period as a major shift in the balance of power, one where UNHCR assumed expansive power over refugee policy and the government began to perceive refugees as "UNHCR's problem."[43] This resulted in tensions between the GoK and UNHCR and the perception that UNHCR held its own "territories" of power outside the state. Recall the relationship between surrogacy and the state from Chapter 2, as illustrated in Figure 3.1.

The influx alone did not drive UNHCR to surrogacy in the NEP but rather the gap in refugee assistance left by the absence of the Kenyan central government. Some literature describes UNHCR's ascension to surrogacy as a power grab that pushed local and state actors aside, while other studies describe it as stepping in when Kenya asked for assistance. Kagwanja, for example, writes that once on the scene in the 1990s, "international organizations progressively excluded local actors, entrenched themselves and

Figure 3.1 Subview of the "surrogate state" end of the spectrum paired with state disposition

expanded their institutional power and influence, in effect, making their own exit or 'devolution' of responsibility to local actors difficult."[44] He also talks about competition and duplicating efforts by IOs, rather than encouraging and strengthening local capacity. Kagwanja would argue that Kenya's request of assistance from UNHCR paved the way for the hegemony of UNHCR and its international NGO partners and for the marginalization of local capacity in the refugee arena. (However, it is important to note that his focus is on local actors more than central authorities.)[45] Similarly, Harrell-Bond and Verdirame would also argue that UNHCR marginalized the national government during the 1990s, pushing it out of refugee assistance rather than supporting it.[46]

However, while both arguments have their merits, this study takes an historical view, which demonstrates that Kenya was not likely to want extensive involvement in the NEP, nor did it have the capacity in staff or funds to carry out large-scale refugee assistance. Thus, rather than "grabbing for power," it was more likely "filling a gap" as the years passed. This does not mean that UNHCR did not sideline local actors, as Kagwanja argues, or that it accidentally took on this role but rather that it did not have the discipline to resist the "mission creep" that led it to expand into a surrogate state.[47]

Indeed, as outlined on p. 83, there is also evidence that Kenya willfully yielded power over refugee affairs to UNHCR. Rather than abiding by international standards of refugee protection, or at the very least actively governing the areas in which refugees resided, the GoK found it more strategic to put all refugee responsibility on UNHCR and its partners.[48] Milner writes, "Notwithstanding the principle that the primary responsibility for refugees lies with the host state, 'a deliberate choice was made by Kenyan government officials in the 1990s to largely cede refugee affairs to UNHCR.'"[49] He cites one senior Kenyan official, stating that refugees were "the UNHCR's responsibility, not ours."[50] Part of this was due to the sheer number of refugees arriving and Kenya's inability to cope. The magnitude of the refugee influx from Somalia also paved the way for UNHCR to morph into a surrogate state. As noted on p. 81, in 1991 refugee numbers rose steeply from 16,000 to 427,278 by the end of 1992, thus overwhelming the *ad hoc* system and prompting Kenya to ask for international help from UNHCR.[51]

Donor states have also played an important role in the trajectory of Kenya's refugee policy and UNHCR's path to surrogacy. Lindley and Haslie (2011) write that, while donor states may not have much moral authority to influence Kenya's policy, the fact that they trust IOs like UNHCR more than the government is yet another reason why Kenya has not had a direct role in refugee assistance; it is simply more strategic to let international actors that can obtain the funds do the work. Subsequently, it is not surprising that there have been tensions regarding UNHCR's handing over of responsibilities to government actors, which GoK sees as "rooted in the organization's own institutional self-interest."[52] One interviewee emphasized the role of donors in indirectly encouraging encampment and not LI, partially to be pragmatic, but also because:

> [T]hey do not push Kenya because they do not want to accept liability, and do not want Somali refugees [for resettlement]. The US and UK are very interested in stabilizing Somalia and thus will avoid criticizing the GoK because they know that it is key . . . they won't withdraw support. Kenya knows that they use it for surveillance [of terrorist threats], and they know how to use this to their advantage . . . [especially because they need the aid].[53]

These conditions parallel many of those listed in the framework as conditions for IO surrogate statehood, including a void for the IO to fill.

Examples of UNHCR's surrogacy

As a result of these conditions making Kenya ripe for IO surrogacy, UNHCR's role as a surrogate state can be seen via the indicators from Chapter 1 (physical presence, service provision, governance and perception of authority). In response to whether UNHCR was a surrogate state in Kenya, one UNHCR official immediately smiled and shook his head, stating, "It's true, you know."[54] First, it can be seen via service provision to refugees. One example of this is the C&M model that has been in place in Dadaab for the last two decades. By itself, C&M does not necessarily signify surrogacy, but in conjunction with the other indicators, a clearer picture of surrogacy emerges. UNHCR's surrogate statehood even extends beyond refugees, to service provision and involvement in funding and governing the local community. Milner writes that in addition to caring for refugees:

> UNHCR . . . runs a number of programs designed to support the local community and authorities in Dadaab. In addition to providing monthly monetary incentives, equipment and transportation to the local police, UNHCR has constructed 14-room barracks in each of the camps and in Dadaab town, an 80-room administrative block for the District Office—complete with water and electricity, canteen and compound fencing. UNHCR has invested more than US$440,000 since 1995 to rehabilitate and improve roads and airstrips in the Dadaab region. Since 1992, it has constructed and maintained almost 30 water boreholes for the local population, installed water and electricity to the Dadaab

> Primary School, rehabilitated livestock boreholes, and provided water tanks for the local population. UNHCR has also provided free medical care to the local population since 1992. Finally, UNHCR has been involved in a range of environmental projects, contributing over US$4 million to environmental rehabilitation projects.[55]

In addition, UNHCR as a surrogate state has also taken over some governance functions, resembling administration in the form of refugee status determination (RSD) and camp management. Until recently, UNHCR has had complete control over RSD procedures with its partner implementing organizations, despite trying to persuade the government to have a more active role.[56]

The perception of UNHCR as an authority—both in the eyes of refugees and locals—also demonstrates its surrogate statehood, even showing examples of locals looking to UNHCR on governance issues rather than the central authorities. The state was more or less a distant echo to local politicians, and the authority to go to was often UNHCR, not the central government.[57] Even a senior GoK official and former Minister of Refugees agreed, discussing how those both refugees and those in the local government did not feel like the central government was in charge: "the people feel abandoned . . . not so closely attached to the national government."[58] A senior UNHCR official that had worked in Dadaab, for example, stated that local officials knew to seek resources from him, trying to extort money from him before even considering petitioning the government. He stated, "as far as they're concerned, I'm being given a large bag of gold coins which it was up to me to spend however I wanted, and if they threatened and abused me enough, then I would be forced into giving them what they wanted and letting the refugees starve."[59] Thus, he was seen as an authority, and locals sought assistance from him rather than their regional and national counterparts.

Even security provided by the state was often funded by UNHCR. Kagwanja writes:

> District officers in refugee-hosting divisions interpreted their duties in a strict sense as ensuring the security of the Kenyan citizens while refugees were the responsibilities of UNHCR and partner NGOs . . . the DO considered refugees as outside his brief and never entered the camp unless he was invited by the UNHCR when there is a security problem, especially involving refugees and the locals. The feeble presence of the state in camps was accentuated by the inability of the national refugee administration to make its influence felt beyond Nairobi. The refugee Directorate in the Ministry of Home Affairs, for instance, had no representatives in the camps. *UNHCR became so powerful that it*

> *was brokering land deals with the local population without consulting either the central government or the local administration.* For instance, in 1999 the resident officer in Kakuma camp negotiated a deal with Turkana elders to acquire more land to set up a new camp.[60]

UNHCR's surrogate statehood can also be seen through individual refugee's perceptions of its role. Whereas national authorities were seldom present in the lives of refugees (and many locals for that matter), UNHCR's presence evoked the perception that it could take care of individuals beyond legal protection. Horst, for example, talks about this responsibility shift over time, with refugees wanting UNHCR to do everything for them.[61] She cites Collins (1999), noting, "When the husband goes to town in order to earn an income, this is much easier when he can leave his family in the care of UNHCR."[62]

The perception of UNHCR as the authority in charge is also reinforced by what some may call "mission creep." As noted in the previous chapter, in many cases, UNHCR has little choice but to carry out tasks far beyond its mandate because they will otherwise be unable to carry out refugee protection. For example, Kagwanja writes that, because the state was also unable to offer adequate security around the camps, UNHCR was forced to subsidize local security personnel and to establish local police stations—activities far outside its original refugee protection mandate.[63] One interviewee stated, "The government provides security, paid by UNHCR. UNHCR pays the per diem (vehicles, police stations, $11M USD of UNHCR security budget goes to this . . .)."[64] Thus, even if the government has some role in this, UNHCR is seen as the authority behind it.

Why it stays a surrogate state

> You don't make a lot of money off . . . 'responsibilizing' the government . . . where you make a lot of money is substitution [for the government].[65]

A number of factors offered by the framework help explain why UNHCR's surrogacy in Kenya perseveres. At the very least, UNHCR and the GoK maintain surrogacy as long as it is in their interest. As noted on p. 84, Kenya continues with the status quo because it is happy to have UNHCR both carry out the work and pay for it as well. Also, after years of UNHCR carrying out refugee protection, the GoK may have little knowledge and expertise on the subject and may not have staff well trained to take over. Thus, UNHCR has created a niche for itself that the government has lost the opportunity in which to grow.

For its part, UNHCR, though outwardly reluctant to take on surrogacy, has an interest in pleasing its donors and thus does not want to appear to be scaling back from any projects. On the contrary, expansion is what brings in new funds, which makes going beyond the refugee protection mandate tempting. One UNHCR official stated that UNHCR's current role in Kenya and in other PRS puts UNHCR in a difficult place, as it becomes the key resource mobilizer, continually failing to "responsibilize" the government. He claims that within the organization, "it is not really rewarded" to truly seek solutions that empower the government to make sure that "I will not be necessary." In other words, technically speaking, humanitarians should seek to "put themselves out of a job," but the organization does not always carry on this way, instead taking on more and more. He continues, "That's why in Kenya, which is quite stable [and thus capable of responding to refugees], you will have 'capacity-building' for 20 years" as opposed to turning over responsibilities to the GoK.[66] In other words, to "stay in business," UNHCR may not always seek solutions that would put an end to their operations in Kenya.

This relates directly to arguments that UNHCR's structure makes it difficult to downsize once it has expanded. As noted earlier, scholars like Barnett and Finnemore (1999) argue that this is true in bureaucratic organizations like UNHCR, which are often wired to continually seek expansion. One NGO official interviewed even talked about UNHCR being like a big oil tanker that is very difficult to turn around once it is moving in one direction: "the captain can try to turn the wheel, but it is going to be a long, gradual turn, and one will not see results for a long time."[67] Thus, part of the reason UNHCR maintains its surrogate state role in Kenya relates to both what is in its interest and in its nature.

He also notes that protracted cases generate money for UNHCR and donors sitting on funds that need to be used and that "responsibilizing" governments instead does not bring in as much money. As noted earlier, he states, "You don't make a lot of money off that . . . where you make a lot of money is substitution [for the government]."[68] Furthermore, he states, "There is little incentive for UNHCR to leave. . . . Contrary to the commercial sector, we are not cost-conscious and there is a mismatch between donors . . . we don't have the incentive to really look for a sustainable solution." He argues that UNHCR is (intentionally or unintentionally) out to keep its staff in the field. Likewise, he and another interviewee noted that one-year budget planning cycles and staff rotations only further promote short-term objectives and employees that are trying to climb the ranks, rather than focusing on finding long-term solutions.[69] These budget cycles also deter thinking on long, strategic views that incorporate development and private sector actors, which most agree are much needed in PRS.[70] This breeds inconsistency: "we go left for two years, then we go right for two years . . . we don't have long times . . . it's a cultural thing . . . and is linked to how the organization would like to see itself: responding to emergencies." He continues, "There is no go in and go out, it's go in . . . and stay."[71] Another senior UNHCR official stated, "We are stuck in emergency response attitude,"[72] which means more encampment and confinement, and continued surrogacy.

Though cynical, this UNHCR official concluded by saying that UNHCR's substitutionary, surrogate state role can perpetuate PRS. He stated,

> We become fat and happy and occupy space . . . that space is very difficult for any government, even if they would wish—and sometimes they don't wish—there is no incentive to take that on . . . there is no real authority . . . refugees are the business of UNHCR . . . UNHCR deal with this.[73]

Indeed, governments remain happy to save money and accept what he calls the "economic colonialism" placed on them. He also admitted that the "analytical process" by which UNHCR would leave would require knowledge of where they (UNHCR) "would like the government to be in five or ten years."[74]

Another related reason for the maintaining of surrogacy relates to donor preferences to channel funds through IOs more than directly to governments. This encourages UNHCR's continued role as surrogate state. Indeed, scholars (Milner 2009; Harrell-Bond 1986; Kagwanja 2002; Rutinwa 2002) indicate that many Western donor states do not trust governments directly and thus prefer to give aid through UNHCR. These states may have some humanitarian motives but are also concerned with doing so out of self-interest: for example, Somalia is a security issue for the West in a post-9/11, terrorism-focused world, and thus Kenya is a strategic partner. Western states therefore have interest in continuing to fund UNHCR's surrogate state presence, further lessening any incentive to pull back from its surrogate statehood.

However, this is not to say there are not well-intentioned reasons for surrogacy as well. Indeed, the previous section noted UNHCR's reluctance at filling the void (rather than a power grab), and many UNHCR staff interviewed also expressed a genuine sense of moral obligation to do some of the activities that make it appear to be a surrogate state. They argue that it is difficult to protect refugees when a situation is not secure, roads are not paved or water not potable. Thus, if the government is not willing or able, they are driven to take on other projects such as these in order to continue their work. They also argue that local development projects are essential to their work because they keep tensions between refugees and locals low, as locals may otherwise resent refugees receiving more international assistance. A different senior UNHCR official emphasized the need for UNHCR to take on the role of peacemaker amidst its mandate to refugees, maintaining peace with host communities and government authorities. He stated, "if we don't fulfill some of their demands we are also endangering refugees' lives" and paying police, providing vehicles and other things is a "way of making sure our work can continue. We do not feel hostage. In a way, yes, but somehow we manage to find our way . . . it all depends on personalities on the ground."[75] In light of these comments, it is not hard to see the ways in which UNHCR slides into surrogate statehood, sometimes unintentionally.

UNHCR's influence on Kenya

More surrogacy leads to less influence

What does UNHCR role as a surrogate state with Kenya's Somali refugees mean for its ability to influence the state? At first glance, it would seem that its increased responsibility and authority at the local level would mean greater power and influence over state decisions on refugee issues. Instead, this research finds that Kenya's surrogacy actually lessens its ability to influence the state. As shown in Figure 3.2, an array of additional explanations for UNHCR's level of influence helps to demonstrate why surrogacy has these effects (or lack thereof) on Kenya's behavior toward refugees.

Recalling the indicators outlined in the framework in Chapter 1, UNHCR in Kenya has less influence. First, while it is perceived as an authority in Dadaab among locals and refugees, both responsible for many services and governance functions, and blamed when services do not come through, it has had little effect on Kenya's policies. Top Kenyan leaders remained largely unconvinced on refugee protection issues important to UNHCR, continuing to see refugees solely as a security threat.[76] Concerns about spillover violence and terrorism have made the state less open to hear any other refugee-related ideas or policies, particularly UNHCR's concerns with protection and human rights.[77] One interviewee commented that Kenyans are growing tired of their troop involvement in Somalia and that security wings

Figure 3.2 Influence, surrogacy, and state reaction combined

of the government would happily kick out all refugees immediately if they could, even if their Department of Refugee Affairs (DRA) is more tame and tempered.[78] Likewise, the need to confine refugees to camps until they can return has remained unchanged, despite UNHCR's advocacy otherwise. UNHCR has had little participation in advising or formulating state refugee policies, and even though the government sets refugee policy, it feels little ownership over the refugee issues, given its abdicationist stance.

In addition, regional and international pressures on Kenya greatly affect Kenya's policy decisions and how willing the state is to listen to UNHCR. Milner writes that, when the Somali refugee crisis occurred in 1991, Moi was also feeling pressure from the international donor community, which had suspended aid to Kenya, citing the need for it to democratize and prioritize human rights.[79] The Moi regime had to comply and allow refugees to enter, given its heavy reliance on aid, and Kenya subsequently won praise and more international assistance.[80] Kenya now uses diminishing donor support as a reason for restrictive policies that ignore UNHCR calls for greater refugee freedoms. More recently, the US war on terror since 9/11 has greatly affected the Somali economy and its politics, including stronger anti-American sentiments among some, and greater US pressure on Kenya to be a counterterrorism partner—all of which domino into Kenya's refugee policy considerations and how willing it is to change the status quo or consider input from UNHCR. In addition, African Union and the East African Community (EAC) pressures also factor into Kenya's refugee policy choices, as have their commitments to international conventions and treaties like CSR51.[81]

How refugees are perceived also affects how willing Kenya is to listen to UNHCR. For example, Kenya has often framed refugees as terrorists or economic refugees, rather than "true" refugees. This in turn has meant more restrictive policies and less concern for UNHCR's attempts to lobby for greater refugee rights. Also individual leadership and the relationships between government officials and UNHCR (and its partner NGOs) also affect the relationships of influence—perhaps even more so than roles of surrogacy or otherwise. And, as noted earlier, government structure (centralization, leadership styles and whether Kenya is "out to prove" its authority) also factor in to how much it can be influenced by UNHCR.

Thus far, UNHCR's role as a surrogate state has been unable to overcome these factors that make it difficult for UNHCR to influence GoK's behavior, summarized in Table 3.1.

One example of this lesser influence can be found in UNHCR's inability to successfully lobby for greater refugee rights, particularly in terms of freedom of movement and the right to work (most commonly exhibited in *de facto* LI). UNHCR explicitly states that it advocates for refugees to

Table 3.1 Summary of UNHCR in Kenya: IO surrogacy, state abdication, low influence

UNHCR in Kenya (Somalis): IO surrogate state/state abdication			
Indicator of influence			
Is UNHCR perceived (by locals, refugees or other actors) as a power or authority in the locale in which it is working?	Yes	Are state policies toward refugees in line with UNHCR's priorities?	No
Does UNHCR receive blame when services are not provided? Is it seen (by locals, refugees or other actors) as responsible for things generally attributed to the state?	Yes	Does the GoK feel a sense of "ownership" over the refugee 'issue'?	No
Has UNHCR been able to change leader's minds on decisions?	No		
Has UNHCR changed the rhetoric of the issue?	No		
Has UNHCR affected other actors' behavior (local authorities, refugees, locals, other NGOs?)	Yes	= Low influence	
Does UNHCR participate in forms of local governance?	Yes		
Has UNHCR participated in directly writing and/or shaping policy?	No		

have greater access to their human rights. Of course how it does this varies from case to case. In Kenya, UNHCR officials acknowledged that they had few ways to encourage policy shifts. One senior official stated that LI was more likely to happen "by stealth" (e.g. via intermarriage, but not an official policy), and another stated, "they don't even want to hear about it . . . once you start talking about it, the government will start keeping their distance."[82] Similarly, an NGO official stated, "You can't even say 'local integration' among government officials of Department of Refugee Affairs. You can't say the word before they have said 'no.'"[83] Likewise, another UNHCR official commented on the label of LI, noting that calling a policy "local integration" has a negative connotation.[84] In other examples, Lindley and Haslie note that UNHCR gave in to pressure from Kenya to try to stem the flow of incoming Somali refugees and to encourage repatriation through a "preventative zone" in Somalia near the Kenyan border.[85] This is arguably the opposite of greater protection through LI.

Certainly, there are a number of reasons that Kenya does not consider LI in particular or more open policies more broadly (and it is possible that material policies in Kenya would never be swayed by UNHCR, which is why this study looks at nonmaterial indicators of influence as well). What is evident in these material policies, however, is that UNHCR has not been able to alter or affect change in such policies or bring its protection and rights-oriented agenda to the forefront of Kenya's decisions on how to treat refugees. Its surrogacy not only positions it to maintain the camps that continue such restrictive policies but also locks it into a position where it has little leverage to negotiate for change. UNHCR must maintain access, leverage and good relations with the GoK but also feels "trapped" to fund "everything" endlessly, even if it is unable to advocate for change and greater access to refugee rights.[86]

UNHCR's surrogacy has also led to less influence because it "disincentivized" the Kenyan government from wanting to change the status quo, which included UNHCR paying for refugee programs. Even where the surrogate state UNHCR in Kenya has tried to lobby the state to take on more responsibility, such as with the 2006 Refugee Act—even funding the government's refugee department to encourage more government "ownership" of refugee issues—it has backfired and left the government less inclined to be influenced by UNHCR.[87] One senior UNHCR official stated quite bluntly (in reference to Kenya) that UNHCR should not fund government refugee departments. He stated, "You know the worst thing we have ever done was create the government counterpart in areas where we are the government counterpart fully funded by UNHCR. . . . I think there are many situations where we have a refugee ministry or commission totally dependent on funding by UNHCR."[88] He indicated that this produces a department that is self-interested and difficult and that tends "to manipulate the situation to their own needs, and to make sure the refugee situation continues so that they can get funds . . . they have no interest in a solution, or they sabotage solutions."[89] Numerous other UNHCR colleagues agreed with this,[90] and yet it surprised some donor government officials.[91] Ultimately, then, UNHCR's surrogacy in this case made it less able to lobby for solutions or changes in the refugee status quo.

The government's perception of UNHCR's surrogacy also means that UNHCR has less influence on the state. For example, interviewees seemed generally resigned to the fact that UNHCR would remain in Kenya for some time, that the situation was unlikely to change and that it would therefore maintain surrogacy for some time. Interestingly, most NGO, UNHCR and government interviewees discussed future plans for refugee affairs as if UNHCR were a permanent fixture in Kenya. Even as the new constitution of 2010 brings greater centralization of refugee affairs under the government and the government is taking on new responsibilities for refugees, no interviewees entertained the notion that UNHCR would not be part of the picture in a big way. In fact, expectations of UNHCR's continued surrogacy were so engrained in people's minds that several interviewees even mentioned the government considering charging rent to UNHCR for continuing to serve refugees on government land.[92] This demonstrates both a lack of ownership "felt" by the government on refugee matters and also demonstrates that UNHCR as a surrogate state is perceived as a permanent fixture in Kenya. Both leave the GoK with little incentive to change the status quo on refugee responsibility or authority and thus little interest to be influenced by UNHCR to change course, improve refugee conditions or provide refugees with greater access to their rights.

Applying the mechanisms to understand why UNHCR as a surrogate state has less influence

The previous section demonstrates some of the ways UNHCR's ability to influence Kenya is affected by its surrogacy. Applying the mechanisms, however, helps uncover some of the deeper reasons behind its lessened ability to influence the state. The mechanisms (marginalization of the state and shifts in responsibility/blame) work hand-in-hand to help clarify why there appears to be an inverse relationship between UNHCR's surrogacy in Kenya and its ability to influence the state. Put simply, when UNHCR took on responsibility for responsibilities toward refugees (and to some extent locals in NEP), it marginalized the state and left it off the hook from having to carry out or pay for any of the refugee-related assistance and protection. Kagwanja states it clearly: "Here, the government is spoken of in the past tense, mocking its claim to be in-charge."[93]

Likewise, the remote, impoverished region's local economy has been centered on aid, something that has also empowered UNHCR and its partners as the givers of such aid, while at the same time further marginalizing the Kenyan state. Kagwanja writes that, while the state hoped that hardships in the district would force refugees back to Somalia and that local communities would benefit from the aid that comes from swarms of international actors, "refugee aid became an integral part of the politics of local development in refugee-settled areas."[94] Thus, what may have seemed like a strategic plan in the beginning (abdicating refugee responsibilities to UNHCR to obtain more aid and to avoid caring for refugees) backfired into a power vacuum that UNHCR filled, rendering the state isolated in an area it was most concerned about controlling.[95]

This translates into less influence for several reasons, clarified by tracing Kenya's decision-making logic. First, as a rational, self-interested actor, Kenya thus saw no incentive to change the status quo of UNHCR paying for everything and doing all the work and subsequently had no incentive to listen to UNHCR when it came to refugee rights such as the right to work and freedom of movement. As UNHCR Official N (2012) noted earlier, the opportunity to "responsibilize" the government is lost; he fears that UNHCR has fostered a climate where UNHCR and other IOs provide free support, often completely substituting for the government in its responsibilities to address humanitarian needs.[96] Several others agreed, noting that UNHCR loses leverage when it pays for "everything."[97] UNHCR Official N stated, "Too frequently I had a feeling that senior UN officials are allowing themselves . . . to be kept hostage by host governments. . . . This is linked to personal ambition . . . private interest . . . and it becomes . . . the UN like Santa Claus . . . you are there to channel funds and resources in an uncontrolled manner without asking for anything in return."[98] Kenya thus has no incentive to listen to UNHCR on refugee policy because the status quo allows it the flexibility to continue to see refugees as a security threat without addressing any assistance or rights-related issues. In turn, UNHCR upholds this view as a surrogate state meeting refugee needs and footing the bill but forfeits its ability to have input in the process.

A marginalized state also means that the government is "let off the hook" (UNHCR Official N 2012) on refugee issues (also blame shifting) because it is not on the front lines of refugee assistance. It also does not develop staff and expertise that respond to refugees (e.g. Barnett and Finnemore's (1999) discussion of IO specialization and knowledge). In turn, a stalemate emerges where UNHCR does the work and has the expertise, assuming forms of authority and responsibility, but the government still makes the policies—even if it is uninformed and lacks the expertise to do so. This relationship leaves UNHCR with less influence, again held hostage to carry out the work but with little say over policies. (Some even argued that GoK even "dug in" further, ignoring UNHCR and showing that it was in charge, even as it knew UNHCR carried out all the programs.) Juma and Kagwanja summarize it well:

> The government . . . allowed the agency to take on a wide spectrum of responsibilities which are normally the preserve of the host state, giving it untrammelled powers in refugee administration. . . . [B]y marginalizing itself from the refugee arena, the state contributed to the loss of the experience and capacities accumulated over the years, and stifled the emergence of new capacity for humanitarian intervention. . . . On their part, the agencies seized the chance to step into the breach created by the withdrawal of the state from refugee governance. Paradoxically, this turned the refugee arena into a sphere where UNHCR and its partners assumed untrammelled control over refugee affairs, without the corresponding power to protect refugees. This became the bane of asylum in Kenya and the pitfall of refugee protection.[99]

Thus, the stalemate of a more powerful UNHCR in refugee affairs, but with little influence on the state, begins to resemble an odd marriage where both parties lose. Though it may have clout when it comes to regional and local decision-making, UNHCR is still bound by the state, particularly when security rhetoric is invoked. After all, Kenya is still able to set a tone of security threats—again seeing refugees almost entirely through the security lens and using security-related concerns as a "trump" card.

Also, responsibility/blame shifting means that UNHCR bears the brunt of public opinion and expectation as a service provider and in turn rests its reputation on its ability to keep providing such services. This means that it is less likely to "rock the boat" or "push the envelope," as some interviewees put it, because it needs to maintain access, both to carry out its work and thus please donors and for moral, humanitarian obligations. (Many staff felt a genuine moral, humanitarian duty to care for refugees and recognized that some trade-offs were worth it in order to maintain access, including lobbying the government to change its behavior.) For example, one senior NGO official explained that UNHCR has given up on promoting LI, knowing well that the government has no interest in it and not wanting to upset authorities that grant them field access to refugees.[100]

Similarly, Lindley and Haslie write that UNHCR has received extensive criticism for its "'soft diplomacy' in the face of 'hard' human rights concerns regarding border closure, *refoulement*, and the massive congestion of Dadaab, for fear of jeopardizing relationships with the government."[101] One interviewee stated that UNHCR's budget helps give it some leverage, but in the end, it struggles to assert its priorities ("a rights-based approach," as he calls it) because "governments have learned how to deal with troublemakers . . . if you want to come in here you need approval . . . governments are very conscious to select the representatives to make sure no well-known troublemakers and that the government has leverage on that person."[102] Another senior NGO interviewee stated that UNHCR does not lobby for LI because they feel that it is not their place to lobby for policy. He stated that their approach is: "We are here invited by the Kenyan government not to make trouble . . . so if anyone pushes it should be donor states or IOM or someone else."[103] This means that UNHCR is not in a position to lobby the GoK on policy or to influence changes in its behavior or attitudes toward refugees. As argued here, this is partially rooted in UNHCR's substitution for the state.

Similarly, as UNHCR took on the major operational responsibilities of running the camps (responsibility shifting) its ability to hold the Kenyan and donor governments to account on protection issues was widely perceived as having diminished, as it depended on these governments for access and funding for the camp operations.[104] One official stated that the more UNHCR did, the less power it had.[105] This is also reflected in the sentiments cited on pp. 87–88, whereby UNHCR officials felt that funding the Department for Refugee Affairs, for example, left their hands tied to advocate more freely. Another UNHCR lawyer also pointed out that providing some services only gets UNHCR so far:

> You do whatever you have to [in the face of little government involvement] . . . and . . . initially it looks really appealing, but you notice very quickly that . . . there are very few things that UNHCR can do . . . if the government is not involved . . . it's a fake impression, a freedom you don't really have. . . . I can't issue a birth certificate to a newborn"[106]

And yet the interviewee also acknowledged that people in NEP consider UNHCR as responsible for many of these state functions and that "It is difficult to change the mindset of people that this is actually government responsibility."[107]

Responsibility shifting also led to less influence because UNHCR became bound up in meeting expectations, rather than lobbying for change. Regarding paving roads, providing vehicles and topping up government salaries, one senior UNHCR official stated, "The government takes it as one of the things that we should do—they wouldn't look at it as a favor."[108] Another senior regional UNHCR official even described UNHCR as the "donor government arm," meaning that it is an agent more than its own autonomous actor.[109] He recognized that on one hand, UNHCR was the "ultimate middleman" between donors and beneficiaries and that it did not want to be the "conductor" because the government should be responsible. At the same time, he stated that governments that advocated for sovereignty on the one hand, also sometimes said, "Oh, UNHCR they are your refugees" and thus the confusing paradox of power and responsibility that complements UNHCR's surrogacy.[110]

Conclusion

This chapter has examined UNHCR's surrogacy with Somali refugees in Kenya. It first outlined the history and context of Kenya's refugee policies since independence and looked closely at the ways in which UNHCR's role has evolved into surrogate statehood, including the conditions under which it assumes surrogacy, why surrogacy is sustained and indicators of surrogacy. It outlined the ways in which Kenya is an abdicationist state, putting security above all else and practicing abdication with its refugee responsibilities. Ultimately, the case shows that UNHCR's surrogacy, though laden with greater authority and responsibility at the local level, does not render

UNHCR greater influence with the state on refugee matters, nor does it overcome forces that minimize its influence (e.g. Kenya's continued view of refugees as a security issue, regional/international pressures and various forms of rhetoric). Refugees are viewed almost entirely through a security lens, and the NEP continues to be a dangerous, undesirable part of Kenya in the eyes of central authorities. Consequently, GoK's abdication of responsibilities to UNHCR has only further isolated the GoK from a region they are most concerned about. Refugees are still confined to camps, reliant on aid and are unable to return. Thus far, UNHCR has had very little ability to change any of these policies or rhetoric and continues trapped in its surrogate state role.

Theoretically, Kenya proves the counterintuitive finding of this study's framework: an IO can take on greater authority, autonomy and responsibility—becoming a surrogate state that provides services, performs governance functions and as perceived as a local power—but not have greater influence over the state's behavior or decisions. In fact, in this case, the IO actually had less power because its surrogacy took away opportunities to hold the state accountable in a policy capacity. For its part, the state's abdication left a void for the IO to take on more surrogacy and left the state marginalized from the relevant issue area (refugees) and free from responsibility or blame. For all the negative ways this may have affected the state (e.g. isolating it from a region it was concerned about), it gave the state less of a reason to alter the status quo and thus little reason to listen to UNHCR.

Kenya will continue to be interesting to follow in the future, both for the empirical implications for UNHCR's role in PRS and for the continued study of domesticated IOs (and surrogate state IOs in particular). Recently the government has begun to take on greater responsibility for refugees, slowly absorbing some duties from UNHCR (though the 2006 Refugee Act, which finally entered into effect in 2009, continues to need better enforcement and implementation). Refugee populations are changing (they are younger and more technologically connected to the rest of the world), and the new Kenyan Constitution of 2010 calls for a decentralization of power, granting more decision-making capabilities to county-level politicians (although refugee matters are still expected to be controlled from the center). And despite a recent court ruling in favor or refugees (ruling against the government's push to force urban refugees into camps), the GoK still largely views refugees as a security threat and prefers to maintain the status quo until they return home.

In other words, some advances are being made, but it remains to be seen whether UNHCR's surrogacy and its low level of influence will change in Kenya. This speaks to broader questions about domesticated IOs as surrogate states, including how well they can disengage from their roles or change their level of influence. It also relates to broader IR issues of sovereignty and power balances between states and IOs working domestically. While there appear to be no limits as to how much responsibility an IO can take on, there are limits on its influence and power. These issues are discussed further in Chapter 6.

Notes

1 General information is taken from the University of Iowa (Kenya Information Page. Available from www.uiowa.edu/~africart/toc/countries/Kenya.html, 2012). For more general Kenyan history, see Charles Hornsby, *Kenya: A History Since Independence* (New York: Palgrave Macmillan, 2012).

2 Melanie Teff and Mark Yarnell, "Somali Refugees: Ongoing Crisis, New Realities," Refugees International Field Report, 19 March 2012. Available from www.refugeesinternational.org/policy/field-report/somali-refugees-ongoing-crisis-new-realities.

Also see James Milner, *Refugees, the State and the Politics of Asylum in Africa* (Basingstoke, UK: Palgrave Macmillan, 2009), 85.

3 Peter Mwangi Kagwanja, "Strengthening Local Relief Capacity in Kenya: Challenges and Prospects," in *Eroding Local Capacity: International Humanitarian Action in Africa*, ed. Monica Kathina Juma and Astri Suhrke, 94–115 (Uppsala: Nordiska AfrikaInstitutet, 2002), 99.

4 Kagwanja 2002, 100.

5 Kagwanja 2002, 100.

6 Barbara Harrell-Bond and Guglielmo Verdirame, *Rights in Exile: Janus-Faced Humanitarianism* (New York: Berghahn Books, 2005), 31.

Until 1987, Kenya had very few refugees. Those that arrived in the late 1980s were skilled Ugandans, viewed as contributing to Kenya's development and prosperity and thus being welcomed with "tempered hostility" (Kagwanja 2002, 98, in Milner, *Refugees, the State and the Politics of Asylum in Africa*, 86). In light of this, Kenya's earlier policies were more open and less restrictive, granting individual status by the government, freedom of movement, access to employment and various social rights.

7 Harrell-Bond and Verdirame, *Rights in Exile: Janus-Faced Humanitarianism*, 31.

8 Dadaab is made up of several camps: Ifo, Hagadera and Dagahaley.

9 Anna Lindley and Anita Haslie, "Unlocking Protracted Displacement: Somali Case Study," Working Paper 79, Refugee Studies Centre, Oxford University, Oxford, United Kingdom, 2011, 27.

10 Lindley and Haslie, "Unlocking Protracted Displacement: Somali Case Study," 28.

11 Milner, *Refugees, the State and the Politics of Asylum in Africa*, 101.

12 UNHCR Official B 2012.

13 UNHCR Official C 2012.

14 UNHCR Official D 2012.

15 Milner, *Refugees, the State and the Politics of Asylum in Africa*, 101.

16 Milner, *Refugees, the State and the Politics of Asylum in Africa*, 105.

17 Milner, *Refugees, the State and the Politics of Asylum in Africa*, 101.

18 Milner, *Refugees, the State and the Politics of Asylum in Africa*, 101–102.

19 Parlevliet 2012.

20 Milner, *Refugees, the State and the Politics of Asylum in Africa*, 104.
21 UNHCR Official B 2012.
22 UNHCR Official B 2012.
23 Milner, *Refugees, the State and the Politics of Asylum in Africa*, 105. The Refugee Consortium of Kenya writes:

> Experience has shown that in the run-up to elections many politicians will not hesitate to manipulate the refugee situation as an electioneering gimmick. Members of Parliament have been known to distort facts and stereotypes and vilify refugees as the sole source of increased crime and insecurity, proliferation of illegal arms and scarcity of resources. They have even been known to point to humanitarian assistance to refugees in the camps as evidence that refugees allegedly enjoy a better lifestyle than the locals. (Milner, *Refugees, the State and the Politics of Asylum in Africa*, 105–106; see also Monica Kathina Juma, "The Political Economy of Building Local Capacity," in *Eroding Local Capacity: International Humanitarian Action in Africa*, ed. Monica Kathina Juma and Astri Suhrke, 159–196 (Uppsala: Nordiska AfrikaInstitutet, 2002), 6).

24 Milner also points out that there are varied viewpoints of security on the part of Kenyan officials, depending on whether they work in or near the camps or in Nairobi (see *Refugees, the State and the Politics of Asylum in Africa*, 100ff, for more).
25 Al-Shabaab (fully named Harakat al-Shabab al-Mujahideen), or "the Youth," is a Somali militant group tied to terrorist groups like al-Qaeda and fighting for a fundamentalist Islamic state in Somalia. The US and other Western states consider it a terrorist organization, and it has been linked or directly responsible for a number of terrorist attacks in Somalia and elsewhere in Africa. For more, see (Jonathan Masters, "Al-Shabab," *Council on Foreign Relations Background Page*, 2013. Available from www.cfr.org/somalia/al-shabab/p18650).
26 Milner, *Refugees, the State and the Politics of Asylum in Africa.*
27 Kagwanja, "Strengthening Local Relief Capacity in Kenya: Challenges and Prospects," 99.
28 Milner, *Refugees, the State and the Politics of Asylum in Africa*, 87.
29 Lindley and Haslie, "Unlocking Protracted Displacement: Somali Case Study," 27.
30 Milner, *Refugees, the State and the Politics of Asylum in Africa*, 85.
31 Monica Kathina Juma and Peter Mwangi Kagwanja, "Somali Refugees: Protracted Exile and Shifting Security Frontiers," in *Protracted Refugee Situations: Political, Human Rights and Security Implications*, ed. Gil Loescher, James Milner, Edward Newman and Gary Troeller (New York: United Nations University Press, 2008), 221.
32 One interviewee described three levels of Kenya's current refugee policy: the national level, which wants to look tough on terrorism and is only interested in return; the regional/district levels in Dadaab and Kakuma, who have small local populations in comparison to the refugee population and are interested in political and financial gain from the refugees (he states, "there is a lot of money to be made and a lot of votes to be counted"); and the tribal component, representing a diverse and complex political tug-of-war, with Somali Kenyans wanting LI (so as to boost their voting constituency) (UNHCR Official C 2012).
33 Sara Pavanello, Samir Elhawary and Sara Pantuliano, "Hidden and Exposed: Urban Refugees in Nairobi, Kenya," Humanitarian Policy Group Working Paper, Overseas Development Institute, 2010.

34 UNHCR Official C 2012.
35 Lindley and Haslie, "Unlocking Protracted Displacement: Somali Case Study," 4.
36 Teff and Yarnell, "Somali Refugees: Ongoing Crisis, New Realities," 2012.
37 Lindley and Haslie, "Unlocking Protracted Displacement: Somali Case Study," 22.
38 Juma, "The Political Economy of Building Local Capacity," 175, emphasis added.
39 Kagwanja, "Strengthening Local Relief Capacity in Kenya: Challenges and Prospects," 103, 170.
40 Kagwanja, "Strengthening Local Relief Capacity in Kenya: Challenges and Prospects," 103.
41 Kagwanja, "Strengthening Local Relief Capacity in Kenya: Challenges and Prospects," 102.

> [T]he events of the early 1990s marked a significant shift to a new refugee regime in Kenya. On the one hand, the involvement of foreign NGOs and UNHCR guaranteed external resources at a time when the numbers of refugees exceeded Kenya's capacity to absorb them through its generous, if somewhat laissez-faire, policy. On the other hand, the emergency nature of the response of the NGOs, and of UNHCR, did not include any effort on their part to preserve the positive aspects of the pre-1991 refugee regime. (Kagwanja, "Strengthening Local Relief Capacity in Kenya: Challenges and Prospects," 109, citing Verdirame 1999, 57)

42 Kagwanja, "Strengthening Local Relief Capacity in Kenya: Challenges and Prospects," 104.
43 Harrell-Bond and Verdirame, *Rights in Exile: Janus-Faced Humanitarianism*, 33–35. Both UNHCR and Kenyan government officials also noted this (UNHCR Official M 2012; GoK Official A 2012).
44 Kagwanja, "Strengthening Local Relief Capacity in Kenya: Challenges and Prospects," 13.
45 Kagwanja, "Strengthening Local Relief Capacity in Kenya: Challenges and Prospects," 104.
46 Harrell-Bond and Verdirame, *Rights in Exile: Janus-Faced Humanitarianism*, 33.
47 This need not necessarily be a negative: in some cases, UNHCR staff might argue that they had no choice but to take on this role in order to help alleviate the suffering of refugees. See Chapter 1 for more on motives for surrogacy.
48 Milner, *Refugees, the State and the Politics of Asylum in Africa*; Lindley and Haslie, "Unlocking Protracted Displacement: Somali Case Study," 23.
49 Helton 2002, 161 in Milner, *Refugees, the State and the Politics of Asylum in Africa*, 88.
50 Milner, *Refugees, the State and the Politics of Asylum in Africa*, 88. In another example, a Kenyan official in Dadaab responded to a question about state obligations to refugees at the height of the rapes scandal in 1993, saying, "it was not Kenya's responsibility to investigate what happened in the camps" (Kagwanja, "Strengthening Local Relief Capacity in Kenya: Challenges and Prospects," 106).
51 Milner, *Refugees, the State and the Politics of Asylum in Africa*, 87.
52 Lindley and Haslie, "Unlocking Protracted Displacement: Somali Case Study," 26.
53 NGO Official B 2012.
54 UNHCR Official N 2012.
55 Milner, *Refugees, the State and the Politics of Asylum in Africa*, 95.
56 Kagwanja, "Strengthening Local Relief Capacity in Kenya: Challenges and Prospects," 109; UNHCR Official C 2012. See Kagwanja ("Strengthening Local Relief Capacity in Kenya: Challenges and Prospects," 109) for more.

57 UNHCR Official K 2012.
58 GoK Official 2012.
59 UNHCR Official B 2012.
60 Kagwanja, "Strengthening Local Relief Capacity in Kenya: Challenges and Prospects," 105, emphasis added. To be fair, it is not necessarily the case that UNHCR sought out this powerful role. Indeed, UNHCR has engaged in numerous initiatives to empower refugees and locals to respond more directly to community needs (e.g. "Operations Continuity Plan") (Teff and Yarnell, "Somali Refugees: Ongoing Crisis, New Realities"). Moreover, Teff and Yarnell report that UNHCR only had some 13 protection staff for nearly half a million refugees in Dadaab, thus demonstrating that they were still short on staff.
61 Cindy Horst, "Vital Links to Social Security: Somali Refugees in the Dadaab Camps, Kenya," New Issues in Refugee Research, Working Paper No. 38, UNHCR, 2001, 7.
62 Horst, "Vital Links to Social Security: Somali Refugees in the Dadaab Camps, Kenya," 8.
63 Kagwanja, "Strengthening Local Relief Capacity in Kenya: Challenges and Prospects," 106.
64 NGO Official B 2012.
65 UNHCR Official N 2012, emphasis added.
66 UNHCR Official N 2012.
67 NGO Official 2013.
68 UNHCR Official N 2012, emphasis added.
69 UNHCR Official N 2012; UNHCR Official A 2012.
70 UNHCR Official A 2012.
71 UNHCR Official N 2012.
72 UNHCR Official A 2012.
73 UNHCR Official N 2012.
74 Implying that UNHCR would somehow have influence over the status of the government in 5 to 10 years. In spite of this, this particular official felt he had excellent standing in UNHCR, good relations with the government and that prospects for policies promoting refugee rights (like policies of LI) in Kenya would become possible. Ultimately, this interviewee felt strongly that UNHCR needed to stay rooted in its principled approach: "We handed over thirteen brand new Land Cruisers . . . but that in itself is not what refugee protection is about . . . our loyalty must be to the refugees . . . it's when you stop and go down the road where you try to accommodate other needs . . . when you try to please or to position yourself you become a political actor" (UNHCR Official C 2012).
75 UNHCR Official C 2012.
76 GoK Official 2012.
77 UNHCR Official K, 2012. Kagwanja ultimately finds that "assistance—whether local or international—can only be of limited effectiveness when the state views humanitarian crises through a prism of national security and is itself implicated in causing or accentuating the emergency" ("Strengthening Local Relief Capacity in Kenya: Challenges and Prospects," 13).
78 NGO Official B 2012.
79 Democratization also had mixed effects on responses to refugees at local and national levels, as politicians sometimes found it convenient to scapegoat refugees to attract votes.

80 Orwa 1989, 226 in Milner, *Refugees, the State and the Politics of Asylum in Africa*.
81 Kagwanja and Juma, "Somali Refugees: Protracted Exile and Shifting Security Frontiers," 230ff.
82 UNHCR Official C 2012.
83 NGO Official B 2012.
84 UNHCR Official C 2012.
85 Jennifer Hyndman, *Managing Displacement: Refugees and the Politics of Humanitarianism* (Minneapolis: Minnesota University Press, 2000); Lindley and Haslie, "Unlocking Protracted Displacement: Somali Case Study," 28–29.
86 UNHCR Official E 2013; UNHCR Official L 2013; UNHCR Official C 2013.
87 At first glance, the 2006 Refugee Act may be seen as a possible way that the state's behavior changed amidst UNHCR's surrogacy (perhaps because of its surrogacy or in addition to a number of factors). After all, UNHCR lobbied for the Act to be passed, which includes implementing the 1951 Convention, 1967 Protocol and 1969 Organisation of African Unity (OAU) Convention, all outlining a clearer legal framework for dealing with refugees. However, a closer look reveals that it has not relieved UNHCR of its duties in Dadaab, granted refugees more rights in terms of freedom of movement or the right to work, or amounted to greater will or capacity to carry out its implementation. For these reasons, interviewees expressed that it has not granted them more influence (and possibly less, as seen on p. 97) (Pavanello et al., "Hidden and Exposed: Urban Refugees in Nairobi, Kenya").
88 UNHCR Official C 2013.
89 UNHCR Official C 2013.
90 UNHCR Official L 2013; UNHCR Official E 2013.
91 USG Official G 2013.
92 NGO Official B 2012; UNHCR Official A 2012.
93 Kagwanja, "Strengthening Local Relief Capacity in Kenya: Challenges and Prospects," 105. In spite of reforms since 2006, a surrogate state UNHCR continues to marginalize local authorities from responding to refugees as well, encouraging continued abdication and thus the status quo of containment, encampment and few refugee rights or LI. One interviewee stated that local actors were completely "isolated" and "excluded . . . it has been the central government talking to UNHCR and the agencies" (NGO Official B 2012). Kagwanja argues, for example, that what was once a rigorous and comprehensive local humanitarian response mechanism has been overtaken by the influx of aid agencies and IOs, leaving local response capacity a "pale shadow of what it was" before the 1990s ("Strengthening Local Relief Capacity in Kenya: Challenges and Prospects," 97, 115). He holds that "whether intended or not, after intervening, international agencies bypassed, weakened and marginalized indigenous capacity" (98).
94 Kagwanja, "Strengthening Local Relief Capacity in Kenya: Challenges and Prospects," 105.
95 One senior UNHCR official outlined this blunder on the part of GoK, noting that the "Kenyan's could've played this one smarter" if they had been more involved and considered developing the region rather than allowing resentment toward GoK to build, getting refugees "on your side and not wanting to go along with al-Shabaab" (UNHCR Official B 2012). Similarly, a former refugee official in the Kenyan government stated that it was a mistake for Kenya

to be absent from refugee management, stating, "We lose the opportunity to have a hands on approach to the security issues that come with the hosting of refugees" (GoK Official A 2012). Another senior UNHCR official also stated bluntly that security and local demands give an impression of lawlessness and that national authorities are somewhat impotent (UNHCR Official G 2012). Of course the occasional heavy-handed military presence along the border reinforces some central authority presence, and since 2006, the GoK has been more involved in refugee matters, but it is still appears that abdication has generally translated into isolation on the part of Kenyan authorities (UNHCR Official B 2012; Milner, *Refugees, the State and the Politics of Asylum in Africa*; Kagwanja, "Strengthening Local Relief Capacity in Kenya: Challenges and Prospects," Lindley and Haslie, "Unlocking Protracted Displacement: Somali Case Study").

96 See also Chris Dolan and Lucy Hovil, "Humanitarian Protection in Uganda? A Trojan Horse?" Humanitarian Policy Group Background Paper, Overseas Development Institute, 2006. Available from www.odi.org.uk/sites/odi.org.uk/files/odi-assets/publications-opinion-files/381.pdf.

97 UNHCR Official E 2013; UNHCR Official L 2013.

98 UNHCR Official N 2012.

99 Juma and Kagwanja, "Somali Refugees: Protracted Exile and Shifting Security Frontiers," 220–221.

100 UNHCR Official B 2012.

101 Lindley and Haslie, "Unlocking Protracted Displacement: Somali Case Study," 26.

102 UNHCR Official N 2012.

103 NGO Official B 2012.

104 UNHCR Official B 2012; UNHCR Official D 2012; UNHCR Official H 2012; Lindley and Haslie 2011, 26.

105 UNHCR Official C 2013.

106 UNHCR Official D 2012.

107 UNHCR Official D 2012.

108 UNHCR Official C 2012.

109 UNHCR Official A 2012.

110 UNHCR Official A 2012.

4 Tanzania

- **Refugee-hosting policies and history in Tanzania**
- **UNHCR's domestication and surrogacy in Tanzania**
- **UNHCR's influence on Tanzania**
- **Conclusion**

Tanzania provides a look at two cases in one: UNHCR's role with Burundian refugees that fled in 1972 and with Burundian refugees that fled in the 1990s.[1] Certainly, there are many other groups of refugees that Tanzania has hosted, but these two groups provide an interesting and unique comparative view of UNHCR's varied roles and its subsequent ability to influence the state. Indeed, for the former, UNHCR had very little role. For the latter, it was a full-fledged surrogate state, thought of by some refugees as "father and mother" or to some women as a husband.[2] This chapter briefly outlines the relevant postindependence history that has informed UNHCR's evolution in Tanzania and the disposition of the state toward refugees. It then focuses on the different ways UNHCR domesticated in the two cases, as an advisor and partner to the government for the 1972 Burundian refugees and as a surrogate state for the 1990s Burundian refugees. It considers the conditions and motives for these different roles and then analyzes the levels of influence UNHCR had on Tanzanian behavior toward refugees. As predicted by the framework, the different roles produced very different levels of influence. In particular, UNHCR's surrogacy led to less influence.

Refugee-hosting policies and history in Tanzania

General background, ujamaa *and Nyerere*

Broadly speaking, Tanzania has been viewed as one of the more stable and peaceful countries in Africa in recent decades. Under German colonial rule in the late nineteenth century, and later under British control, it gained independence in 1961, remaining in the British Commonwealth. Both during and after colonial rule, it struggled with poverty, poor infrastructure and economic decline (particularly in the 1980s) and has subsequently hosted a number of international actors attempting to intervene in various issue areas. Tanzania's general characteristics are also important to its identity and policy formation and subsequently to the role IOs take within its territory. Drawing on the relationships between geography, population distribution and the exertion of power, Jeffrey Herbst (2000) describes Tanzania as a "compact country" in terms of population density, with a "rimland population," or one that sees most of the population concentrated along the borders of the country. According to Herbst, this type of geographical landscape presents significant challenges to state building and maintaining centralized rule.[3]

The political trajectory of Tanzania has also been affected by the movement away from traditional chief leadership, particularly in light of clashes between chiefs and state authorities seeking modernization.[4] Indeed, postcolonial Tanzania brought a different political context, where politicians needed to "establish themselves nationally, due to both the mandate given by the British and the fragmented basis of ethnic support," particularly in light of Tanzania's heterogeneous population spread across a diverse landscape.[5] These conditions form an important basis for the role taken by UNHCR, as discussed later in this chapter.

In this postindependence context, the movement of *ujamaa* emerged in the 1960s and 1970s under Tanzania's first prime minister, Julius Nyerere. *Ujamaa* was a form of socialism that tried to ideologically transform the peasantry through a "villagization" program, massive education campaign and system of state corporatism.[6] It was meant to be an "African" model of development and stressed that individual identity was obtained by one's place in the community. It created a one-party system and the institutionalization of social, economic and political equality through a central democracy and stressed Tanzanian self-reliance. It fostered a Tanzanian identity where everyone learned Swahili (instead of a tribal identity and language) and required all youth to learn the principles of *ujamaa*.[7] The ambitious attempt at social engineering came on the heels of independence and the desire to promote national unity above all else, requiring all people to live together in villages. Herbst sees the ideas behind *ujamaa* as hardly surprising, given the country's political geography of population centers largely along the rim of the country.

Although it ultimately did not succeed, *ujamaa* played an important role in shaping the political landscape in the decades that followed. Most notably, its belief in unity sustained the Tanzanian population through economic collapse and uncertainty in the 1980s.[8] It also produced a pattern of uncritical reverence for the national leadership and ruling party and a reverence for the national language of Swahili as a marker of Tanzanian political identity.[9] Landau even writes that it brought about an "obsession with centralized control, unity and unanimity."[10] Most importantly, he writes that this context set the scene for a Tanzanian population that does "not demand that government takes responsibility for the citizens' material welfare."[11] All of these factors form important context for the role of UNHCR in Tanzania and how the state responds to refugees.

Refugee-hosting policies in Tanzania: an overview

Tanzania has been widely studied in humanitarian and forced migration scholarship and has generally been viewed as one of the more generous models of refugee hosting and assistance. One senior UNHCR official even called it "a humanitarian superpower in 2012," reflecting on its openness, cooperation and generosity with refugees over the years.[12] He argued that its sense of hospitality stemmed from its leadership and that it explains why Tanzania has hosted so many refugees for so long and why it considered granting refugees more rights through LI policies when the "rest of the world was doing the opposite."[13] Juma and Suhrke write that Tanzania has been among the most elaborate, progressive and politically motivated states responding to refugees—providing an open door and even some opportunities for naturalization as a way to support wars of independence, liberation, pan-Africanism and African socialism.[14] Likewise, others like Loren Landau (2008) and James Milner (2009) write how Tanzania has developed a reputation as one of the most hospitable countries of asylum in the world.[15]

However, Tanzania's approach toward refugees has changed over the years and has not always been one of hospitality and generosity. As Bonaventure Rutinwa (2002) outlines, Tanzanian refugee policy is marked by several distinct phases, moving from open to restrictive. During the first phase (1960s), local groups responded to refugees with little involvement from the central government or other organizations. Refugees were generally welcomed under Nyerere, as a sign of solidarity with independence movements. Refugees were integrated under *ujamaa* and were granted freedom of movement and the right to work. During the 1960s and 1970s, Tanzania hosted tens of thousands of refugees, who were granted land and encouraged to be self-sufficient. At this point, UNHCR was only a funder of projects and did not have an operational presence on the ground.[16]

The second phase (late 1960s to early 1980s) was marked by the Tripartite Agreement,[17] which labeled a Tanzanian NGO (Tanganyika Christian Refugee Service (TCRS)) as the main actor, the government as a "junior participant" and UNHCR as the nonoperational funder.[18] This shared approach was largely successful in terms of financial burden sharing, as UNHCR paid for most of the settlements in conjunction with the World Food Programme (WFP) and TCRS, with the government of Tanzania (GoT) only bearing some 14 percent of the cost of settlements in 1972.[19] It also enabled Nyerere to continue to accept refugees and "freedom fighters" fleeing wars of national liberation, earning him both domestic and foreign political clout. UNHCR's involvement was still defined as a funder, and largely nonoperational, but this would soon change.[20]

In the late 1970s and early 1980s, Tanzania shifted to a system where UNHCR and other IOs began to oversee relief supplies to refugees. Local response mechanisms were generally replaced by international actors.[21] At the same time, *ujamaa* eroded, and Tanzania's economy crashed as cash crops prices declined.[22] Nyerere's predecessor, Ali Hassan Mwinyi, was forced to follow strict IMF measures, which also affected policies toward refugees.[23] Tanzania scaled back on social services across the board and became more restrictive toward refugees. This opened the door for greater international involvement to "fill in the gap" in responding to refugees, as Tanzanian authorities were increasingly less capable to provide basic services to its own citizens, let alone refugees.[24] At the same time, the early sentiments of hospitality, brotherhood and pan-Africanism that made Tanzanians welcoming to refugees were eroded with frustration and concern at the growing scale and scope of refugee influxes, their protracted nature and feelings of abandonment by the international community.[25]

Tanzania's most significant shift in terms of refugee policy and international involvement occurred in the 1990s (Rutinwa's third phase). In the wake of economic collapse, state officials began to call for more international burden sharing and refugees began to be seen as a "problem" or a threat.[26] The perfect storm arrived soon thereafter, when, as Milner puts it, "It was against this backdrop that Tanzania received hundreds of thousands of refugees from Burundi and Rwanda in the 1990s."[27] Between October and December of 1993 alone, more than 300,000 Burundians fled to Tanzania.[28] By 2001, Tanzania hosted over 500,000 refugees, at the time the highest refugee population in Africa.[29] By this point, UNHCR was fully operational, and responsibility for refugees was relegated to the international community.[30] In contrast to previous decades, all refugees were now required to stay in settlements or camps.[31] Landau writes,

> These settlements were significantly different from those of the past: instead of semi-permanent, self-sustaining communities mimicking prototypical Tanzanian villages, these camps were visibly temporary and required residents to be almost completely dependent on handouts for their daily rations. And as the influx continued, the Tanzanian government became increasingly restrictive of refugees' economic activities.[32]

These camps were also much closer to the border than previous settlements had been. The camps were internationally managed, overcrowded and marked by food shortages and increased crime in and around the camp areas.[33]

The 1998 Refugee Act also demonstrates Tanzania's increasingly restrictive policies.[34] The Act aimed to show that Tanzania was in control of the refugee situation and to "'signal disengagement from the Open Door policy of the Nyerere administration' and to 'assure the populace' that the government was 'determined to address the problem of seemingly endless refugee influxes.'"[35] Tanzania's policies were also driven by the sentiment that the international community was not doing its fair share in assisting refugees and that there were not enough resources for both refugees and Tanzanians—feelings that further drove policies of encampment and confinement. Ironically, at the same time Tanzania felt that it was not getting enough international support in the form of donor resource commitments, international actors like UNHCR were assuming unprecedented roles on the ground. Whereas earlier decades showed local actors taking the lead in responding to refugee inflows and subsequently implementing greater LI, the 1990s saw these actors increasingly marginalized, and decisions were instead made between UNHCR and the central government.[36] Rutinwa even goes so far as to write that the 1990s was a period of "total dominance by UNHCR and international NGOs of relief administration."[37]

Since 2000, Tanzania has continued to have restrictive policies on Burundian refugees from the 1990s, focusing on return as the favored solution (e.g. the 2003 National Refugee Policy). Harsh conditions in camps remained, and the international community struggled to maintain donor interest in the protracted situation. The GoT stated that it wanted to be "refugee free" by 2010, which was interpreted in a range of ways (from being committed to finding durable solutions, to simply wanting to be rid of the "problem of refugees").[38] By 2007, repatriation of the 1990s cases was in full swing, and a few years later in 2009, Tanzania took the surprising move to consider integrating the long-time 1972 Burundian refugee caseload.

The 1990s and 1972 Burundian refugee cases were viewed as completely separate from one another, with interviewees even calling the closure of camps for the 1990s refugees "coincidental" to the integration of the 1972 cases.[39] LI for the 1972 group was based on a 2006 study carried out by UNHCR, which found that most refugees in this group of 218,000 were already well integrated, self-reliant and wanted to stay in Tanzania. Despite numbers being much higher than anticipated, Tanzania had to follow through with the naturalization process, resulting in some 162,000 people being given Tanzanian citizenship.[40] By December 2009, 11 camps from both the 1972 and 1990s cases were closed, leaving only 2 camps.[41]

Tanzania's shifts from open hospitality and integration to encampment and restrictive policies that view refugees as a threat and a problem are the result of complex shifts in Tanzania's economic, political and cultural history. These shifts do not just form context and background to Tanzania's refugee situation and policy decisions but directly inform the timing and nature of UNHCR's role and subsequently its ability to influence the state as a surrogate state, as discussed in the following sections.

However, other factors besides UNHCR's surrogacy, of course, influenced Tanzania's decisions about refugees. As Milner argues, many explanations for refugee policy decisions have little to do with the actual presence of refugees, but rather broader political, economic and historical factors.[42] Among those already mentioned, interviewees emphasized timing and luck (the ability of leaders to seize upon historical moments or openings for policy changes, e.g. UNHCR Official T 2012); the personalities and personal relationships between leaders[43] (e.g. Nyerere's vision; NGO Official F 2013); policy precedent ("how the emergency starts determines how it ends"; e.g. UNHCR Official O 2013); and the effects of decentralization, multipartyism and democratic reforms.[44]

As this chapter demonstrates, these explanations do not refute or reinforce the relationship discussed here (between surrogacy and influence); the explanations are not mutually exclusive, and reality shows that a myriad of explanations account for UNHCR's ability to influence state behavior. The task at hand is demonstrating how surrogacy affects influence. As this chapter argues, even when it cannot be isolated completely, careful interviewing and background literature review demonstrate that greater IO surrogacy does not translate to greater influence.

UNHCR's domestication and surrogacy in Tanzania

1972 Burundian refugees: UNHCR the observer, advisor and partner

UNHCR has domesticated in very different ways in Tanzania, as demonstrated in the two different cases examined here. Among the 1972 Burundian refugees, it took a very minimal role. On the spectrum of domestication shown in Figure 4.1, it might be labeled a "distant observer" or, in light

Figure 4.1 Spectrum of UNHCR's domestication in Tanzania, comparing roles with 1972 and 1990s Burundian refugees

of its later role in carrying out a census and informing the government in 2006, as an "informant," "advisor" or "partner." Because this study is more focused on surrogacy than any other type of domestic-level role, this section will focus heavily on UNHCR's role with the 1990s Burundian refugees, where it was a surrogate state. However, the 1972 case forms a useful point of reference for comparison, especially when drawing conclusions about influence in later sections.

The 1990s Burundian refugees and UNHCR's surrogacy: "UNHCR Islands"

In contrast to its role in 1972, UNHCR's role in Tanzania with the 1990s caseload of Burundian refugees was that of a surrogate state. Indeed, it took on service provision, forms of governance including adjudication and administration, was perceived as being in authority and essentially managed its own "territory" (and, to some extent, local areas as well). As Landau writes, this role for UNHCR has brought about a "seemingly paradoxical set of logics and discourses insinuating international actors [i.e. UNHCR] into roles normally associated with the domestic state."[45] This section outlines the conditions and motives leading to UNHCR's surrogacy, examples of it and what sustained it.

Conditions and motives leading to surrogacy

First, the conditions that helped bring about surrogacy were similar to those that brought about surrogacy in Kenya. The scale and scope of the refugee influx in the 1990s made Tanzania feel overwhelmed, abandoned and frustrated. In contrast to early phases that embraced refugees under Nyerere, the Tanzanian government of the 1990s felt that it simply could not cope with large numbers (e.g. some 700,000 refugees arrived in less than a year, Milner 2009, 119).[46] Tanzania's restrictive policies thus reflected fear of instability and concerns that the refugee situation was part of a never-ending cycle.[47]

Funding was, of course, also at the heart of such policies, and Tanzanians felt strongly that the international community was not doing its share of responsibility sharing.[48] One NGO senior official stated, "Tanzania feels cheated by the international community."[49] Another UNHCR official stated that Tanzania felt like it had "paid more than its share to carry this load of people coming."[50] These conditions left Tanzania frustrated and turned off to refugee assistance and thus created an opening for UNHCR to assume an expanded role that eventually led to surrogacy.

A similar condition for UNHCR's surrogacy in the 1990s was abdication on the part of Tanzania and a lack of "ownership" of the refugee situation—thus creating a void in refugee programs that UNHCR could fill. Rutinwa, for example, describes how international actors took on much greater responsibility in the 1980s and 1990s onward. He argues that this shift occurred in part because the Tanzanian government was trying to accommodate international organizations and donors who did not trust the authorities and preferred to channel aid through IOs.[51] With the Tripartite Agreement, local actors were thus sidelined, and donors were able to provide aid through international partners.[52] Rutinwa argues that this encouraged the Tanzanian state to abdicate its responsibility to refugees by making asylum contingent upon the receipt of foreign humanitarian aid.[53] It also demonstrates that Tanzania had little choice in the matter. He writes, "by relinquishing control over relief operations to UNHCR and INGOs during the Rwanda emergency, Tanzania was being pragmatic. The government realized that this was the only way to ensure that enough resources would be raised to deal with the situation."[54] It knew that donors preferred to give money through UNHCR and large INGOs and thus:

> Contrary to established wisdom, Tanzania did not invite international agencies to administer refugee programmes because it had lost administrative capacity to do so. Rather, the Tanzanian government did so as a response to the approaches preferred by aid agencies and donor states and institutions on whom it depended for its resource capacity to deal with refugee situations.[55]

Moreover, as time went on, the government was not even privy to assistance delivery agreements between UNHCR and its IPs, and eventually, many donors lost interest all together.[56] Therefore, abdication was arguably a result of donor funding preferences. This, in turn, left a gaping hole for UNHCR to fill, and thus it took on a role of substitution for the state in Tanzania.

Recalling the framework's stated links between surrogacy and state level of involvement, abdication tends to be paired with greater levels of IO surrogacy, and partnership with lower levels of IO surrogacy, which is what is observed in Figure 4.2.

Again, it is possible that there is a circular causality in this relationship: abdication may open the door for surrogacy, but surrogacy may also

Figure 4.2 Subview of the "surrogate state" end of the spectrum paired with state disposition

cause greater abdication. This is not a problem for this argument, however, because simply recognizing that the two are paired is enough for analyzing the main relationship under analysis (surrogacy and influence) here. Either way, the state practiced abdication of responsibilities to refugees in the 1990s, its leaders content to let UNHCR (and its partners) fund and carry out all refugee projects. This is in contrast to the 1972 caseload, which had very little involvement from UNHCR.

UNHCR's surrogacy was also paired with the practice of encampment itself, which by definition forces long-term reliance on aid. While UNHCR's values and rhetoric stress freedom of movement and the avoidance of camps because they tend to obstruct refugees' access to their rights, UNHCR has unfortunately gotten used to assisting refugees in camp settings. It finds it easier to deliver aid and to offer security for refugees.[57] Camps are also easier logistically and administratively: refugees are in one place, so it seems easier to access, process and keep track of people and to distribute aid. Some even argue that donors prefer to give to camp situations more than to others.[58] This leads to C&M roles for UNHCR, and whether it was intentional or not (UNHCR would say that camps are not desirable and that they simply assist as best as possible given the policies in the host state) leads to long-term service provision, a key indicator of surrogacy. Sometimes this service provision even extends to local communities (UNHCR may assist locals as well to reduce tensions between locals and refugees), only further connoting UNHCR's surrogacy.[59]

A final condition that helped lead to UNHCR's surrogacy in Tanzania was the diminishing and sidelining of local actors. Certainly, some of this also happened as a result of UNHCR's surrogacy, but literature indicates that local actors were being silenced and deemed incapable by international donors and the government (who wanted to please the donors) long before UNHCR assumed surrogate statehood. Rutinwa (2002), for example, writes that local actors were weakened as early as during Nyerere's rule which focused on a strong central government ("Africanization") and the nationalization of nearly everything (schools, for example, or groups providing social services). This meant the subsequent removal of local response mechanisms that might have otherwise assisted refugees. In his view, then, "This might have made the intervention of external actors in a situation of a mass influx inevitable."[60]

Ujamaa also contributed to weakening local powers that otherwise might have played important roles in refugee responses. As Landau observes, national unity, self-reliance and peace trumped territorial, tribal, linguistic or cultural identities, which arguably further made Tanzania ripe for an organization like UNHCR to assume surrogacy.[61] Furthermore, he argues that despite its aims, *ujamaa* ironically produced a *de*participation in national politics and identity: "the simultaneous incorporation of the citizenry into a national system of values while excluding them from material, active participation in the objectives or design of these new arrangements" had the effect of diminishing citizens' expectations of their political leaders.[62] Local authorities also felt less ownership of refugee projects, which Rutinwa argues made such projects less sustainable and leads to xenophobia, donor fatigue and avoidance at the central level.[63] All of this set the stage for local response mechanisms to be discredited in the name of large, international-scale interventions and hence for UNHCR to fill the void as a surrogate state.[64]

Examples of surrogacy

UNHCR took a lead role in refugee assistance in the 1990s, and it did not take long for it to morph into a surrogate state. Rutinwa writes that this decade was marked by "the consolidation of control of relief work by UNHCR" and its many IPs.[65] As an operational partner, UNHCR's offices in Tanzania expanded rapidly:

> UNHCR established two additional and autonomous sub-offices in Ngara, and Kigoma; a logistics office at Mwanza airport on Lake Victoria; an office at the headquarters of every district in which there were refugees, and field offices in every camp in the country with the exception of Mwisa in Karagwe. Fleets of cars and other heavy equipment were brought in and staff, both expatriates and local, recruited to run various UNHCR programmes.[66]

In conjunction with domestic partners like TCRS and international partners like the IRC, UNHCR became part of a massive protracted C&M program for the 1990s caseload of Burundian refugees in Tanzania.

Expanded operations do not necessarily signify surrogacy but, in tandem with other indicators, do point to surrogacy. For example, UNHCR became a major service provider for refugees (and some locals) in the 1990s. Indeed, the shift from state-provided services to UNHCR-provided services is clear. UNHCR's service provision in Tanzania demonstrates surrogate statehood because UNHCR has, at times, provided services to refugees completely separate from the government—in other words not as a subcontracted actor or simply an actor carrying out an order in partnership or as an agent. In fact, Rutinwa writes that unlike the 1960s and 1970s, the Tanzanian government was "not privy" to assistance delivery arrangements made by UNHCR and its partners.[67]

Also noted as a condition on p. 108, another indicator of UNHCR's surrogacy in Tanzania in the 1990s relates to the decline of local responses to refugees. For example, Landau's research found that national donor governments tended to ignore local officials, preferring to liaise with aid agencies like UNHCR.[68] As a result, local actors ended up appealing to UNHCR for the funding of some local projects, not national authorities as one might expect. In other words, UNHCR was the perceived authority to "do business with." For example, UNHCR records show numerous funding proposals and projects that were presented to UNHCR by local officials. Landau writes of UNHCR's Kigoma office receiving proposals from locals requesting money for prisons, schools, roads and even a political party office. Local officials linked these projects to damage incurred by the refugee presence, which they viewed as UNHCR's responsibility, not national authorities.[69] These perspectives thus further demonstrate UNHCR's surrogacy with the 1990s Burundian refugees and can be both indicators of surrogacy or conditions for future surrogacy depending on when they occur. Ultimately, they demonstrate that UNHCR was perceived to be the main authority in the area.

Similarly, Turner writes:

> The perception of UNHCR as an omnipotent other that controls their lives from above remains pervasive in the camp setting. It is the ultimate locus of power, for better or for worse. While being perceived as the agent that emasculates them and reduces them to helpless receivers of alms, it is also seen as the ultimate source of recognition. The refugees do not "resist" it. Rather, they must relate to it and make the best of it.[70]

While this research does not view UNHCR as quite so malevolent, Turner's research does point to perceptions of its authority and "statehood." The camp setting, therefore, emulates the notion that UNHCR holds some form of state-like authority. Turner continues,

> The formal state is suspended, and a technical agency—UNHCR—operates as an apolitical surrogate authority. . . . [P]ublic authority is produced partly by the powers that UNHCR delegates to these actors and partly by the power bases that they manage to build up in the gaps in UNHCR's system.[71]

Likewise, a Tanzanian Foreign Minister quoted by Rutinwa stated that "refugee camps were 'UNHCR islands' in which the Tanzanian government had no role, apart from providing security around them (*The Guardian* (T) 17 February 1999)."[72] Another stated that local authorities had no role except for "gathering taxes once in a while . . . (Harrell-Bond 1986; Rutinwa 1996, 24)."[73]

Government officials in the local community have also perceived UNHCR as a surrogate state. Landau, for example, cites an American Foreign Service official responding to a question about Kigoma region's political and social conditions. He answered, "it depends a lot, to be honest, on what the UNHCR does. . . . They are basically administering the region."[74] Likewise, he cites a Kigoma regional planning officer who said that many international agencies "'think they [UNHCR] have replaced the role of the government.'"[75] These perceptions only increased as UNHCR became more operational, NGO involvement increased, and expatriate staff became more common.[76]

"Separateness" has also fostered the perception that UNHCR is running its own little island, isolated from the rest of Tanzanian society, in some ways outside the law. These perceptions are rooted both in the day-to-day governing carried out by UNHCR in the camps, and in the set-up of the camps, where they are seen as "a temporary, exceptional space. . . . Here, the Tanzanian state decides that the refugees are a threat to the nation state and puts them in this exceptional space, which is at once both inside and outside the law."[77] In some cases, this translated beyond the camps, giving locals a sense of "UNHCR governance" as well.

UNHCR's presence among 1990s Burundian refugees has made it a political actor to engage with. For example, it has affected political campaigns, including rhetoric, speeches and writing. Landau cites one politician who said, "if elected, he promised to collect the regional commissioner and go to Geneva, where he would insist that UNHCR dedicate a quarter of its Tanzania budget to help locals, a figure he claimed to be mandated in the UNHCR Charter (Nzanzungwanko 2000, interview)."[78] As absurd as this seems from an international perspective, it demonstrates the ways in which UNHCR's presence and role became embedded into Tanzanian politics on every level. In this example, rather than speaking about what he would do vis-à-vis the Tanzanian government, he focused on relations with UNHCR as the perceived provider of services and power to be brokered with.

UNHCR's surrogate state presence can also be seen via its economic and political effects on Tanzania. Landau, for example, opens his book with an example of a truck advertising for the country's ruling political party, noting that the truck would not have been possible were it not for the presence of humanitarian actors. He writes:

> The grader's presence and its symbolic manipulation represent far more than domestic political strategies and electioneering. Were it not for a set of events and processes extending into neighboring Rwanda, Burundi, and the DRC, as well as Geneva, Washington, London and Brussels, the massive machine would never have come up the barely

> passable road form the regional capital. Only the influx of tens of thousands of refugees from Tanzania's neighbors and millions of dollars of aid from Europe, Japan, and North America made the ruling party's grand entrance possible.[79]

Other literature points to UNHCR's effects on the local economy, which also demonstrates the size of its footprint in the region as a surrogate state.[80] Landau writes:

> One NGO worker remembered that when he arrived in Kibondo in 1997, only two buses a week passed through the town, there were very few consumer goods for sale in the local shops, and there was only one telephone line out of the town. By 2004, there were three or four bus services a day, each bringing a wide range of fresh consumer goods into town, and two companies providing coverage for mobile telephones (interview, Kibondo 2004; IRIN 2002b).[81]

These changes not only signify the results of UNHCR's large presence as a surrogate state, but also show how locals, to some extent, "felt" more contact with international actors than national authorities—also pointing to the perception that UNHCR was the authority in charge, not the state. This is partially rooted in the funding of projects, but also rhetoric, physical presence and visibility. UNHCR, for example, was highly visible in remote parts of Tanzania where national authorities are considerably less visible. In Landau's interviews, he found that "Kasulu residents could almost universally name more international than state actors."[82] One interviewee even listed the "Department of the Red Cross" when asked to identify five government ministries or agencies, indicating just how integrated the international organizations had become into local government practices.[83] He concludes that people saw UNHCR as the established regional development agency and that it—not the national authorities—was blamed for any problems residents experienced, especially in relation to refugees. Ultimately, then, the large presence of international aid actors in the 1990s Burundian refugee case, affected the political landscape in various ways, including linking local and international actors directly and shifting blame and responsibility away from national authorities and onto UNHCR, the substitute state.[84]

Why surrogacy was sustained

Many of the reasons why surrogacy was sustained in Tanzania (1990s) are similar to the conditions for its emergence and the indicators that it is happening. Put simply, UNHCR maintained surrogacy because few of the actors involved (with the exception of the refugees) had an incentive to change the status quo. Tanzania's leaders were content to let UNHCR do all the work and pay for it, too. As discussed in Landau's analysis, Tanzania even benefited politically from UNHCR's surrogacy, allowing UNHCR to take public blame for things the state would otherwise be blamed for. In turn, this role allowed Tanzanian citizens to look favorably on the state and remain more patriotic.[85]

Some interviewees also argued that UNHCR's surrogacy was sustained because the government wanted to benefit from its presence in terms of development. As noted on p. 116, UNHCR's presence brought significant development to a remote part of Tanzania. Thus, Tanzania may have continued to foster UNHCR's surrogacy because they sought the development for the region that comes with large-scale international refugee assistance.[86]

One senior NGO official who worked in northwestern Tanzania for more than 10 years stated that at one point Tanzania saw refugees as a way to develop the land: "it was like, 'let them have that [land] . . . please for God's sake, cultivate, produce food, take this . . . we can use it and tax it!'"[87] Another senior NGO official indicated that development was not something Tanzania should be grateful for but rather that it was viewed as an expected benefit: "Development was expected . . . we're not 'happy' with it . . . in Tanzania there is a belief . . . let the guest come, the guest usually comes with some blessings and we all share with some blessings."[88] In addition, Milner writes, "refugee settlements were organised not only to produce subsistence crops but also export-earning crops, such as coffee and tobacco, which were sold through parastatals, gaining valuable foreign currency for Tanzania."[89]

For its part, UNHCR did not fight its surrogacy or try to end it as quickly as possible. Instead, it took on more and more responsibility and authority, both in the name of assisting refugees more fully and to grow its own organizational operations. Indeed, UNHCR as an organization cannot help but seek to expand in its work, further pleasing donors and having the freedom to work on its own terms rather than being constrained by the state (recall Chapters 1 and 2's discussion of the literature on bureaucratic organization's tendencies, as well as Barnett and Finnemore 1999). As Rutinwa puts it, UNHCR worked its way to the top of hierarchical relationships between the state and local authorities, a position it would find hard to give up.[90] In addition, the state could not change the fact that donor governments often preferred to work through UNHCR, further sustaining its role as a surrogate state.[91]

UNHCR's surrogacy among the 1990s Burundians in Tanzania finally came to an end when the government and UNHCR facilitated large-scale repatriation to Burundi from 2005 onward. See Milner (2009) for more on Tanzania's refugee policy shifts, which also shed light on UNHCR's role.

UNHCR's influence on Tanzania

The previous section demonstrated that UNHCR's role with the 1972 Burundian refugees was minimal and certainly not a surrogate state. In contrast, its role with the 1990s Burundians was one of surrogacy. But in response to the "so what?" question, what does this mean for UNHCR's ability to influence the state? Does its role as a surrogate state affect state behavior toward, or decisions about, refugees? Drawing on the material and nonmaterial indicators of influence discussed in the theoretical framework, the two cases demonstrate the "less is more" relationships expected. Indeed, the case where it took on less surrogacy (1972) translated into greater influence than the case where it took on more surrogacy (1990s). This again speaks to the broader theory that, while an IO like UNHCR may amass greater responsibility and authority in a given locale, this does not necessarily mean greater influence on state behavior toward refugees.

UNHCR's role with the 1972 Burundian refugees was not one of surrogacy, which in the end enabled it to better influence state behavior toward refugees. It had very little involvement with this group for most of their time in Tanzania (at first glance, then, not showing more influence). Where UNHCR's level of influence is relevant and visible, however, is in recent years when Tanzania considered following through on a decades old promise by Nyerere that this group would be integrated and naturalized. While the government certainly receives credit for its openness to granting citizenship to this group, interviewees were also quick to say that this would not have happened had UNHCR not been present and had it not been seen as a trusted and reliable partner by Tanzanian stakeholders.[92] Most notably, UNHCR was a provider of information (it carried out the census, wrote the report and informed the Ministry of Home Affairs (MHA)) and a facilitator. (It organized interviews in the settlements with Burundian refugees and helped transport lawyers to carry out the 17-step process in the region, so as not to require all 162,000 refugees to travel to Dar es Salaam.) It also enabled the GoT to feel continued "ownership" of the process but also held it accountable when it tried to renege on the promise to offer citizenship (for example, UNHCR Official T 2012 noted that the GoT had not expected such a high percentage of the 1972 Burundians to want to stay, assuming more would want to return; when it heard that some 80 percent wanted to remain and gain citizenship, it considered going back on its offer, but UNHCR held it accountable and the GoT ended up following through after all). Thus, its relationship and role as more of a partner and facilitator, not a surrogate, enabled it to promote, encourage and successfully lobby for the state to treat the refugees differently than it was otherwise inclined to (certainly, leadership, history and other factors played significant roles in contextualizing Tanzania's decisions, but as demonstrated here, UNHCR's role was also an important factor—not mutually exclusive, but in addition to these explanations—helping to explain the outcome).

In contrast, UNHCR was a surrogate state to the 1990s Burundian refugees, operating a C&M model for decades. It had little influence over policy, rhetoric or leader's views on refugees. In part because it was so involved as a surrogate state, it had more difficulty speaking out or holding the MHA accountable. Refugees remained encamped with less access to their rights—something UNHCR protested but was trapped in being unable to respond to because it needed to maintain access and good relations with the GoT.[93] Indeed, UNHCR was less able to speak freely or hold the government accountable on refugee protection issues because it was so enmeshed in the refugee response and needed to be able to keep access and supplies coming to a region where it ran enormous projects. Unfortunately, this inadvertently only further entrenched the long-term encampment, endless C&M and lack of solutions that UNHCR sought to move beyond. As interviewees discussed, it did not have the freedom to "rock the boat" as a surrogate state.

Interviewees also gave the impression that GoT felt the need to prove that it was still in charge in response to UNHCR's surrogacy. The former Minister of Home Affairs was the most forceful in emphasizing that the power never left his office. For example, he stated that he would listen to other arguments from UNHCR and its partners, but "in the end I am the MHA and this is what I've decided . . . it is not up for discussion."[94] He argued that, while UNHCR and MHA did work together, he would "never allow" UNHCR to take on policy decision-making roles and does not believe any government should ever "abdicate its supremacy at any point in time" because the UN has different interests than the state. (He did not, however, refute the surrogate state characteristics discussed, including service provision and perception of authority; he simply chose to come to a different conclusion about the label that should be used for UNHCR's surrogacy.)[95]

Likewise, a senior UNHCR official said that, in spite of its responsibility and authority in some areas, UNHCR does "not have the privilege to say what we want . . . you can't push a certain thing . . . we can only react."[96] NGO Official F (2013) also stated that "the government was never weak. . . . The government was always in charge." And despite the high levels of funding coming from UNHCR, MHA officials said that they still felt free to "impose [their] own decisions . . . and to disagree even if UNHCR is paying top-up salaries."[97] A senior NGO official also stated that "UNHCR is sometimes bullied" by the government, particularly if the lead individuals do not have the right working relationships.[98]

Certainly, not all of these elements of influence (or the lack thereof) are rooted in UNHCR's surrogacy with the 1990s Burundians; some are more general, and all interviewees have their own subjective opinion. However, many of these comments demonstrate how surrogacy put UNHCR in a less-influential position with the 1990s caseload. In fact, they work in tandem with other explanations for UNHCR's lessened influence (such as economic downtown and/or frustration at the protracted nature of the situation).

In sum, unlike the 1972 example, UNHCR's surrogate state role with the 1990s Burundian refugee population granted it some forms of authority, legitimacy, governance and power at the local level but did not translate into influence over Tanzania's broader refugee decisions,[99] as summarized in Tables 4.1 and 4.2.

Mechanisms of marginalization of the state and responsibility shifting

Applying the mechanisms of state marginalization and responsibility shifting shed light on why these relationships of influence ("less is more") occurred. First, in reference to the 1990s surrogate state UNHCR, whether it chose it through abdication or had no choice as UNHCR assumed surrogacy, the Tanzanian state was marginalized and responsibility and blame

Table 4.1 Summary of UNHCR in Tanzania (1972 Burundians): no IO surrogacy, state partnership, high influence

UNHCR in Tanzania (1972 Burundians): no IO surrogacy/partnership state			
Indicator of influence			
Is UNHCR perceived (by locals, refugees or other actors) as a power or authority in the locale in which it is working?	No	Are state policies toward refugees in line with UNHCR's priorities?	Yes
Does UNHCR receive blame when services are not provided? Is it seen (by locals, refugees or other actors) as responsible for things generally attributed to the state?	No	Does the GoK feel a sense of "ownership" over the refugee "issue"?	Yes
Has UNHCR been able to change leader's minds on decisions?	Yes		
Has UNHCR changed the rhetoric of the issue?	Yes		
Has UNHCR affected other actors' behavior (local authorities, refugees, locals, other NGOs?)	Yes	= High influence	
Does UNHCR participate in forms of local governance?	No		
Has UNHCR participated in directly writing and/or shaping policy?	Yes		

Table 4.2 Summary of UNHCR in Tanzania (1990s Burundians): IO surrogacy, state abdication, low influence

UNHCR in Tanzania (1990s Burundians): IO surrogacy/abdicationist state			
Indicator of influence			
Is UNHCR perceived (by locals, refugees or other actors) as a power or authority in the locale in which it is working?	Yes	Are state policies toward refugees in line with UNHCR's priorities?	No
Does UNHCR receive blame when services are not provided? Is it seen (by locals, refugees or other actors) as responsible for things generally attributed to the state?	Yes	Does the GoK feel a sense of "ownership" over the refugee "issue"?	No
Has UNHCR been able to change leader's minds on decisions?	No		
Has UNHCR changed the rhetoric of the issue?	No, still securitized		
Has UNHCR affected other actors' behavior (local authorities, refugees, locals, other NGOs?)	Yes	= Low influence	
Does UNHCR participate in forms of local governance?	Yes		
Has UNHCR participated in directly writing and/or shaping policy?	No		

in northwestern Tanzania was placed on UNHCR. This translated into less influence (material and nonmaterial) because the GoT could give a façade of control, while not having to do any of the work (e.g. fund programs or carry them out). As Landau argues, this model allowed Tanzanian citizens to maintain a positive view of the government because they could shift expectations for service provision to UNHCR, thus blaming UNHCR rather than the government when services were not provided. He writes, "This process was remarkably effective in reforming the government's role as benefactor, without entering it into logics of blame and responsibility. In doing so, it shows its generosity and concern without taking direct responsibility for or accepting a recurrent duty to provide such services."[100]

In some cases, there was a blatant effort on the part of government officials to transfer responsibility for public service initiatives (and failings) to international actors.[101] Landau writes, "By blurring lines of responsibilities, officials and politicians were provided with additional mechanisms and incentives for 'shirking.' Both local and national officials rarely missed an opportunity to publicly blame international actors for the district's problems and the administration's own weaknesses."[102] For example, he cites an election observer saying that refugees were the reason for the region's difficulties and that because of this the international community has to take its share of the responsibility.[103] The unexpected result that Landau uncovers, then, is that Tanzanians have a "heightened loyalty to their nation, territory and political leadership, while expectations of and material interactions with the state have declined."[104]

This relationship ultimately put UNHCR in a weaker bargaining position (even if it was paying for everything, carrying out most of the projects and harnessing authority at the local level) to influence refugee policy decisions at the state level. Tanzania had no interest in changing the status quo and would thus not be interested in listening to UNHCR's suggestions for policy changes that encourage greater access to refugee rights or move away from encampment. As various interviewees stated, UNHCR loses its ability to speak out or protest the status quo when it substitutes for the state.[105]

Rutinwa's research on responsibility shifts yielded similar results: "What used to be acknowledged as state responsibility has enabled the state to shirk responsibility." Citing a Tanzanian foreign minister, he writes, "'Tanzania had no responsibility for whatever transpired in the camps' (*The Guardian* (T) 17 February 1999."[106] Because of this, it was not in Tanzania's interest to listen to UNHCR to the extent that it would change the status quo. Arguments about greater access to rights, including freedom of movement or the right to work, simply fell on deaf ears. Likewise, UNHCR had few ways of convincing Tanzania to reconsider encampment, confinement and long-term dependence on aid, because Tanzania had no incentive to pay for and carry out refugee programs itself.

UNHCR in the 1990s example also had less influence as a result of its surrogacy because it could not speak out as freely (recall Dolan and Hovil 2006). Assuming surrogacy placed UNHCR in a position where it had to maintain good relations rather than, say, protest long-term encampment more wholeheartedly. It was expected to carry out responsibilities that should have been borne by the state and could not assume the moral authority and protection-focused role it might otherwise have had in a less operationally-focused situation. At the same time, Tanzania was less engaged and had less expertise and thus also had less interest in hearing from other actors like UNHCR about refugee policies, instead preferring continued abdication.

Addressing the other side: arguments that UNHCR did not take on surrogacy and arguments that it took on surrogacy but that this gave it greater influence on the state

To address "the other side," it is worth noting that there are some who refute the idea that UNHCR took on surrogacy with the 1990s Burundian refugees example. Some described its role as more of a partner, catalyst, patron or even diplomat. One senior UNHCR official noted that UNHCR could "facilitate, arrange or create a forum" but was not a substitute for the government.[107] Others gave the impression that UNHCR acted as a patron more than anything else.[108] The former MHA even emphasized that Tanzania *expected* UNHCR to pay for things. In reference to granting citizenship to the 1972 Burundians, he stated, "UNHCR is supposed to pay for the citizenship of these people."[109] Still others, particularly in the GoT, argued that UNHCR's role was entirely dependent on individual relationships between leaders.[110] This theme was echoed in many interviews and does not refute the arguments made in this chapter, but rather adds to them. Indeed, friendships and personal relationships were an important facet mentioned by most interviewees in each of the case studies.

Returning to the notion that UNHCR took on surrogacy with the 1990s Burundian refugees example, there are a few arguments that imply that UNHCR's surrogacy increased its ability to influence the state. Scholars like Harrell-Bond (1986) note at various points that UNHCR did have strong influence over policy. At one point, Rutinwa even states that UNHCR implemented policies, with national authorities only "nominally involved."[111] And while he does not say that UNHCR *made* policies, Landau writes that policies made by the parliament were interpreted at the local level by UNHCR, as the government was largely absent from these areas and UNHCR had considerable "administrative oversight" and "latitude" in how the policies were implemented.[112]

In light of the previous arguments of this thesis gleaned from interviews and the literature, however, these "arguments from the other side" do not necessarily refute the notion that surrogacy and influence are inversely related. Rather, they point to additional variables that help complete the picture of complex power relations, which is discussed in the next section.

Reflections on UNHCR's surrogacy, influence and sovereignty

Surrogate statehood need not necessarily imply that a state is somehow less sovereign, just as earlier discussions indicated that IO surrogacy and state power are not necessarily zero-sum. However, the relationship between UNHCR's surrogacy and influence does generate some interesting themes pertaining to state sovereignty and power, particularly showing that while surrogacy may not increase influence on policies relating to refugees, it can affect how other ideas and concepts are thought about and, in some cases, can result in power transfers. As Landau writes, "If . . . sovereignty is the right to ration life, at the very least we have witnessed a shift of sovereignty away from state institutions and into the hands of private groups."[113]

In relation to this case study, UNHCR's presence as a surrogate state in Tanzania has also raised questions about the nature of its sovereignty.

Landau writes, "Even after the aid dollars dry up and the refugees return home, these dynamics will have changed how citizens relate to one another, the state, the territory they inhabit and a set of processes—displacement and humanitarianism—that are an under-explored form of globalization."[114]

UNHCR's large presence in refugee-hosting areas also bridged the "local" and "international," in different ways, in some cases bypassing national-level authorities and thus further bringing into question how the sovereign state controls parts of its territory that have direct links with international actors. In addition to bringing political attention to remote areas of Tanzania that were previously ignored, Landau writes, "through these events, remote rural governments and populations have become enmeshed in governmental practices extending regionally to Dar es Salaam, Kigali, Bujumbura and Kinshasa and to international organizations and donors in Europe and North America."[115] Thus, UNHCR's surrogate statehood in the case of the 1990s Burundians created a direct line of contact—international UNHCR staff directly in contact with local officials in remote regions, in some cases bypassing the traditional state apparatus at the national level.

In addition, UNHCR's authority over geographic space (e.g. camps and their surrounding areas) has affected Tanzania's sense of sovereignty and power processes. Indeed, everything from how refugees are quantified to where camps are placed is political, and international aid groups like UNHCR play central roles in these decisions.[116] In addition, Tanzania's association between its values and its geographic territory and the perception that an international organization is largely administering a portion of its territory has significant repercussions. Landau writes:

> A local and domestic focus is critical for understanding the causal mechanisms and importance of socio-economic and political transformations. . . . But while relations with those across political borders have always served as catalysts of political change (Spruyt 1994; Tilly 1990), transformations of the state and sovereignty are increasingly intractable when one only considers domestic actors and processes (see Das and Poole 2004; Powell 1991). The fact that the incorporation of international actors into logics of blame and responsibility helps account for Kasulu's transforming governmental practices challenges the territorial basis for domestic politics and the classical Weberian state.[117]

Landau is not arguing that UNHCR has "usurped government responsibilities or commandeered state sovereignty under the guise of good intentions" nor is he asserting that UNHCR entirely administers the refugee-hosting regions in which it works.[118] Certainly, UNHCR is bound by the national authorities in many ways and could be expelled from the country at any time. However, the nuances mentioned here mark important shifts that relate to sovereignty, Tanzanian identity and policy formation. Indeed, authority and sovereignty are complicated by UNHCR's domestic role, particularly a role that has fluctuated over time, moving from a distant advisor to a surrogate state.

Conclusion

This chapter has examined two examples in Tanzania: Burundian refugees that fled in 1972 and those that fled in the 1990s. It considered UNHCR's domestication via drastically different roles with each of the groups and subsequently the varied outcomes in terms of its ability to influence Tanzania's decisions and behavior toward refugees. UNHCR had a relatively hands-off approach with the 1972 cases, with little involvement until 2006 when it carried out a census to assist the government in integrating some 162,000 Burundians from this group. Although UNHCR had less responsibility and authority with this group, it was better able to advise and lobby the government to keep its promise of citizenship for this group. This group had been welcomed by Nyerere as fellow Africans struggling for freedom and were allowed to move freely and work, thus becoming *de facto* integrated in Tanzania.

In contrast, the 1990s cases arrived in a post-*ujamaa*, post-Nyerere climate and were confined to camps and forced to rely on aid, provided largely by a UNHCR surrogate state. UNHCR's surrogacy with this group was filling a void where the GoT was not responding. Both UNHCR and the GoT had little reason to alter the status quo: UNHCR maintained a large presence and significant power in the remote region, and the GoT benefited from UNHCR's presence because blame and responsibility was placed on UNHCR, not the government, when services were not provided or conditions deteriorated. According to Landau (2008), this enabled the state to look stronger and to be more popular among citizens.

In line with the framework, the greater the surrogacy assumed by UNHCR, the less ability it had to influence the state on refugee matters. While UNHCR as a surrogate in the 1990s example garnered more responsibility and authority at the local level, it was not able to sway government perspectives (in policies, rhetoric or other ways) toward refugees. If anything, it was further entrapped in its C&M response, unable to speak out freely or transfer blame or responsibility back to the state. On the other hand, UNHCR found itself as more influential in helping the 1972 Burundians gain citizenship. As a non-surrogate state, it served as a partner, informer, advisor and advocate, helping to facilitate and lobby the government to make good on its promise to naturalize this group. Tanzania's behavior toward the 1972 cases happened at the same time it was behaving completely differently toward the 1990s cases. In other words, UNHCR's role as a surrogate/nonsurrogate can be seen as having an effect on the state because all other possible explanations were held constant (the context was the same—it was the same time period, the same leader, the same public perception of refugees etc.). This is not to say that surrogacy was the only factor affecting how well UNHCR could influence the state—this chapter has highlighted a number of important explanations contributing to the outcomes observed—but that it is part of the combination of variables affecting state behavior toward refugees.

Certainly, a range of factors also explain UNHCR's ability to influence the state, as well as the policy outcomes; some of these were discussed in the historical overview and context and some in the analysis sections. It will be interesting to see how Tanzania's LI of the 1972 cases finishes and to continue further historical comparisons between the two. Moreover, the solidification of the EAC might alter the political landscape and subsequently the role of UNHCR in further refugee situations. Regardless of whether Tanzania is the "humanitarian superpower" that one interviewee called it, UNHCR's surrogacy in Tanzania provides an interesting lens through which to study an IO operating domestically and by comparison further demonstrates that "less is more" when considering IO surrogate states and influence on the state.

Notes

1 This chapter often refers to these groups as "Tanzania (1972)" and "Tanzania (1990s)" to compare the two.

2 Barbara Harrell-Bond, *Imposing Aid: Emergency Assistance to Refugees* (Oxford: Oxford University Press, 1986), 91.

Simon Turner, *Politics of Innocence: Hutu Identity, Conflict and Camp Life* (New York: Berghahn Books, 2010), 132.

3 Jeffrey Herbst, *States and Power in Africa: Comparative Lessons in Authority and Control* (Princeton, NJ: Princeton University Press, 2000), 151.

4 Herbst, *States and Power in Africa: Comparative Lessons in Authority and Control*, 175.

5 Loren B. Landau, *The Humanitarian Hangover: Displacement, Aid and Transformation in Western Tanzania* (Johannesburg: Wits University Press, 2008), 39.

6 Landau, *The Humanitarian Hangover: Displacement, Aid and Transformation in Western Tanzania*, 31.

7 Cranford Pratt, "Julius Nyerere: Reflections on the Legacy of his Socialism," *Canadian Journal of African Studies* 33, no. 1 (1999): 137–152.

8 Landau, *The Humanitarian Hangover: Displacement, Aid and Transformation in Western Tanzania*, 31.

9 Landau, *The Humanitarian Hangover: Displacement, Aid and Transformation in Western Tanzania*, 39.

10 Landau, *The Humanitarian Hangover: Displacement, Aid and Transformation in Western Tanzania*, 39.

11 Landau, *The Humanitarian Hangover: Displacement, Aid and Transformation in Western Tanzania*, 60.
12 UNHCR Official T 2012.
13 UNHCR Official T 2012.
14 Monica Kathina Juma and Astri Suhrke, "Introduction," in *Eroding Local Capacity: International Humanitarian Action in Africa*, ed. Monica Kathina Juma and Astri Suhrke (Uppsala: Nordiska AfrikaInstitutet, 2002), 170.
15 James Milner, *Refugees, the State and the Politics of Asylum in Africa* (Basingstoke, UK: Palgrave Macmillan, 2009), 108.
16 Bonaventure Rutinwa, "The Marginalisation of Local Relief Capacity in Tanzania," in *Eroding Local Capacity: International Humanitarian Action in Africa*, ed. Monica Kathina Juma and Astri Suhrke (Uppsala: Nordiska AfrikaInstitutet, 2002); Milner, *Refugees, the State and the Politics of Asylum in Africa*; Landau, *The Humanitarian Hangover: Displacement, Aid and Transformation in Western Tanzania.*
17 The Tripartite Approach (also known as the Tripartite Model or Tripartite Agreement) is a key component to understanding Tanzania's response to refugees and UNHCR's ability to influence policy. In 1964 Tanzania entered a tripartite agreement with UNHCR and the TCRS to manage the Mwesi settlement of Rwandans from Congo. Tanzania agreed to provide the land for settlement, staff support, basic tools, access to community services and a waiver on import duty goods related to the settlement. TCRS was to manage the settlement, and UNHCR provided the funding and technical advice (Milner, *Refugees, the State and the Politics of Asylum in Africa*, 112). This agreement became the model used for subsequent years with other refugee influxes. When it was conceived, the Tripartite Agreement was based on the idea of a refugee situation having an emergency phase, a self-support phase and an integrated settlement phase (Rutinwa, "The Marginalisation of Local Relief Capacity in Tanzania," 82, citing Neldner 1981, 167). External actors like UNHCR were expected to leave as refugees became integrated in their communities (Rutinwa, "The Marginalisation of Local Relief Capacity in Tanzania," 83). Obviously, this was not the case.
18 Gasarasi 1987; Charles Gasarasi, "The Tripartite Approach to the Resettlement and Integration of Rural Refugees in Tanzania," Research Report No. 71 (Uppsala: The Scandinavian Institute of African Studies, 1984).

Charles Gasarasi, "The Tripartite Approach to the Resettlement and Integration of Refugees in Tanzania," in *Refugees: A Third World Dilemma*, ed. John R. Rogge (Totowa, NJ: Rowman and Littlefield, 1987), 99–114.

Rutinwa 2002 in Milner, *Refugees, the State and the Politics of Asylum in Africa*, 112.

19 Milner, *Refugees, the State and the Politics of Asylum in Africa*, 113.
20 The Tripartite Agreement's effects on the trajectory of Tanzania's refugee policy are staggering. Many have celebrated it as one of the best models of refugee aid management and one that demonstrates cooperation and responsibility sharing (e.g. UNHCR Official I 2012). Others are more critical. Rutinwa, for example, notes that while the Tripartite Approach was only supposed to involve external actors for a fixed period of time, it gave donors more control over the settlements and "marked the end of local initiatives" (Rutinwa, "The

Marginalisation of Local Relief Capacity in Tanzania," 83–84; Patricia Daley, "Refugees and Underdevelopment in Africa: The Case of Barundi Refugees in Tanzania," D.Phil Thesis, Faculty of Anthropology and Geography, University of Oxford, Oxford, United Kingdom, 1989, 214). By extension, this meant the end of LI as it had been carried out in that period. UNHCR was also only supposed to undertake the provision of goods and services "in consultation with the various regional officers and departments," even though in practice it "usurped the responsibility of local authorities and the villages" (Rutinwa, "The Marginalisation of Local Relief Capacity in Tanzania," 84, citing Daley 1989, 233). Rutinwa also emphasizes that the Tripartite Agreement created a hierarchy of subordinate relationships, with donors at the top, followed by IPs, the state and then refugees (84). He argues that the most important negative impact of the Agreement was the erosion of the power and position of local government by international aid agencies (87). He also argues that the other victims of this model were local actors, including refugees, local authorities and churches, "which had to compete with international aid agencies for resources but without the same political clout. Eventually they became as ineffective as some government departments (Daley 257). The demise of local relief capacity was complete" (Rutinwa 87).

21 Rutinwa, "The Marginalisation of Local Relief Capacity in Tanzania," 76.

22 Horace Campbell and Howard Stein, ed., *Tanzania and the IMF: The Dynamics of Liberalization* (Boulder, CO: Westview Press, 1992); Milner, *Refugees, the State and the Politics of Asylum in Africa*, 115.

23 Milner, *Refugees, the State and the Politics of Asylum in Africa*, 115.

24 Milner, *Refugees, the State and the Politics of Asylum in Africa*, 116.

25 Rutinwa, "The Marginalisation of Local Relief Capacity in Tanzania," NGO Official F 2013.

26 Milner, *Refugees, the State and the Politics of Asylum in Africa*, 116.

27 Milner, *Refugees, the State and the Politics of Asylum in Africa*, 116.

28 Landau, *The Humanitarian Hangover: Displacement, Aid and Transformation in Western Tanzania*, 66.

29 Milner, *Refugees, the State and the Politics of Asylum in Africa*, 122.

30 Rutinwa, "The Marginalisation of Local Relief Capacity in Tanzania."

31 Landau, *The Humanitarian Hangover: Displacement, Aid and Transformation in Western Tanzania*, 69.

32 Landau, *The Humanitarian Hangover: Displacement, Aid and Transformation in Western Tanzania*, 69.

33 Landau, *The Humanitarian Hangover: Displacement, Aid and Transformation in Western Tanzania*, 67; Milner, *Refugees, the State and the Politics of Asylum in Africa*, 122.

34 Khoti Kamanga, "The (Tanzania) Refugees Act of 1998: Some Legal and Policy Implications," *Journal of Refugee Studies* 18, no. 1 (2005): 104.

35 Kamanga 2005 in Milner, *Refugees, the State and the Politics of Asylum in Africa*, 122.

36 Rutinwa, "The Marginalisation of Local Relief Capacity in Tanzania," 79, 88.

37 Rutinwa, "The Marginalisation of Local Relief Capacity in Tanzania," 76.

38 UNHCR Official T 2012.

39 UNHCR Official T 2012; GoT Official M 2013.

40 There are currently some hold-ups in the final stages, however, as politicians representing districts where the 1972 newly naturalized Tanzanians (NNTs as UNHCR calls them) are supposed to be relocated are pushing back and resisting integration.

41 UNHCR Official T 2012.

42 Milner, *Refugees, the State and the Politics of Asylum in Africa*, 109; see Appendix B for more.

43 The former MHA went so far as to say that "personal relationships are everything" and that the foundation of trust and frankness between top UNHCR leadership and MHA leadership are what made the policy of LI for the 1972 Burundians possible (GoT Official A 2013).

44 Milner, *Refugees, the State and the Politics of Asylum in Africa*; Landau, *The Humanitarian Hangover: Displacement, Aid and Transformation in Western Tanzania*; Herbst, *States and Power in Africa: Comparative Lessons in Authority and Control.*

45 Landau, *The Humanitarian Hangover: Displacement, Aid and Transformation in Western Tanzania*, 6.

46 Tanzania has been among the top five African asylum countries for as long as asylum statistics have been available (UNHCR, *The State of the World's Refugees: Fifty Years of Humanitarian Action* (Oxford: Oxford University Press, 2000); Milner, *Refugees, the State and the Politics of Asylum in Africa*, 124).

47 Milner, *Refugees, the State and the Politics of Asylum in Africa*, 124.

48 Other concerns included changes in local practices in light of the refugee influx and arrival of expatriate staff; physical/environmental degradation, including destroyed crops, deforestation for firewood and water depletion; and local markets being affected by the imbalance of aid flooding into the region, driving down prices of some local goods and driving up other costs for locals (Landau, *The Humanitarian Hangover: Displacement, Aid and Transformation in Western Tanzania*, 68; Milner, *Refugees, the State and the Politics of Asylum in Africa*, 119).

49 NGO Official F 2013.

50 UNHCR Official T 2012.

51 Rutinwa, "The Marginalisation of Local Relief Capacity in Tanzania," 77, 86.

52 Rutinwa, "The Marginalisation of Local Relief Capacity in Tanzania," 12.

53 Rutinwa, "The Marginalisation of Local Relief Capacity in Tanzania," 13.

54 Rutinwa, "The Marginalisation of Local Relief Capacity in Tanzania," 90.

55 Rutinwa, "The Marginalisation of Local Relief Capacity in Tanzania," 89–92.

56 Rutinwa, "The Marginalisation of Local Relief Capacity in Tanzania," 89.

57 NGO Official F 2013; UNHCR Official O 2013.

58 NGO Official K 2013.

59 Arguably whether C&M leads to surrogacy or surrogacy leads to C&M is a "chicken/egg" question, but understanding that they are often paired together—regardless of which causes which—is what is important here.

60 Rutinwa, "The Marginalisation of Local Relief Capacity in Tanzania," 85.

61 Landau, *The Humanitarian Hangover: Displacement, Aid and Transformation in Western Tanzania*, 60.

62 Landau, *The Humanitarian Hangover: Displacement, Aid and Transformation in Western Tanzania*, 31.

63 Rutinwa, "The Marginalisation of Local Relief Capacity in Tanzania," 92.

64 Ironically, the same local officials who felt powerless are now exercising immense power by holding the final stages of LI for the 1972 Burundians

hostage. As noted earlier, because they feel they were not properly consulted about integrating these refugees into their districts, they are stalling decisions (NGO Official F 2013; GoT Official A 2013; GoT Official B 2013; UNHCR Official I 2012).

65 Rutinwa, "The Marginalisation of Local Relief Capacity in Tanzania," 88.

66 Rutinwa, "The Marginalisation of Local Relief Capacity in Tanzania," 88.

67 Rutinwa, "The Marginalisation of Local Relief Capacity in Tanzania," 88.

68 Landau, *The Humanitarian Hangover: Displacement, Aid and Transformation in Western Tanzania*, 140. He cites a national-level executive saying, "My impression is the national government liaises with aid agencies, leaving the local authorities as "gasping spectators"' (Landau, *The Humanitarian Hangover: Displacement, Aid and Transformation in Western Tanzania*, 140). He argues that this strange set-up of "spatialised and transnationalised . . . governmental practise represents a hybrid of domestic and international leadership and responsibility, a consequence of globalisation of a kind not normally considered, where Kasulu is at once anchored more firmly to the national while enmeshed in practical and moral logics that extend far beyond the country's borders" (Landau, *The Humanitarian Hangover: Displacement, Aid and Transformation in Western Tanzania*, 145).

69 Landau, *The Humanitarian Hangover: Displacement, Aid and Transformation in Western Tanzania*, 144.

70 Simon Turner, "Negotiating Authority between UNHCR and 'The People'," in *Twilight Institutions: Public Authority and Local Politics in Africa*, ed. Christian Lund (London: Wiley-Blackwell Publishing, 2007), 100. Turner continues to unpack the ways in which UNHCR confers power on individuals from "above," in some ways upsetting traditional balances and culture, something that others, like Harrell-Bond, have also examined. It is interesting to note that he rarely mentions the government in any of his analysis, giving the impression that they were largely irrelevant ("Negotiating Authority between UNHCR and 'The People'," 99–100).

71 Turner, "Negotiating Authority between UNHCR and 'The People,'" 100. Refugee women are quoted as saying that "UNHCR is a better husband" than their own husbands (Simon Turner, *Politics of Innocence: Hutu Identity, Conflict and Camp Life* (New York: Berghahn Books, 2010), 132).

72 Rutinwa, "The Marginalisation of Local Relief Capacity in Tanzania," 91.

73 Rutinwa, "The Marginalisation of Local Relief Capacity in Tanzania," 89.

74 Landau, *The Humanitarian Hangover: Displacement, Aid and Transformation in Western Tanzania*, 140.

75 Landau, *The Humanitarian Hangover: Displacement, Aid and Transformation in Western Tanzania*, 140.

76 Rutinwa, "The Marginalisation of Local Relief Capacity in Tanzania," 90.

77 Rutinwa, "The Marginalisation of Local Relief Capacity in Tanzania," 76.

78 Landau, *The Humanitarian Hangover: Displacement, Aid and Transformation in Western Tanzania*, 142.

79 Landau, *The Humanitarian Hangover: Displacement, Aid and Transformation in Western Tanzania*, 1.

80 See Milner, *Refugees, the State and the Politics of Asylum in Africa*, for more on the positive and negative effects of hosting refugees experienced by Tanzania.

81 Landau in Milner 2009, 126.

82 Landau, *The Humanitarian Hangover: Displacement, Aid and Transformation in Western Tanzania*, 143.
83 Landau, *The Humanitarian Hangover: Displacement, Aid and Transformation in Western Tanzania*, 144.
84 Such perceptions also flow from the fact that UNHCR has funded much of MHA's needs: "A good part of our MHA refugee department comes from UNHCR in terms of vehicles, project staff are paid by UNHCR" (GoT Official B 2013). An MHA interviewee directly linked this working relationship to success in dealing with refugee matters: "to be honest, it is those relations that have enabled us to do so much in trying to find durable solutions" (GoT Official B 2013).
85 Landau, *The Humanitarian Hangover: Displacement, Aid and Transformation in Western Tanzania*.
86 (E.g. UNHCR Official J 2012; also Milner, *Refugees, the State and the Politics of Asylum in Africa*, 113, cites van Hoyweghen 2002, 317; Daley 1989; 1992).
87 NGO Official K 2013.
88 NGO Official F 2013.
89 Milner, *Refugees, the State and the Politics of Asylum in Africa*, 113. "the sudden influx of huge numbers of landless peasants in the form of refugees could be seen as a blessing by the state as it has sought to intensify the productivity of peripheral areas. . . . The presence of refugees also offers the opportunity to attract long-term development aid to remote areas and to fill rural causal labor demands (Daley 1992, 138–9)" (Milner, *Refugees, the State and the Politics of Asylum in Africa*, 113).
90 Rutinwa, "The Marginalisation of Local Relief Capacity in Tanzania," 84.
91 Rutinwa, "The Marginalisation of Local Relief Capacity in Tanzania," 85.
92 UNHCR Official T 2012.
93 Some might argue that UNHCR secretly or subconsciously prefers encampment, but regardless, its stated objectives (which included rhetoric about greater access to refugee rights and protection and less strict encampment policies) were falling on deaf ears at the state level. The state may have listened to some arguments, but in general, as UNHCR Official C (2013) said, UNHCR trades its ability to speak out when it funds and carries out all refugee-related programs.
94 GoT Official M 2013.
95 GoT Official M 2013.
96 UNHCR Official O 2013.
97 GoT Official B 2013.
98 NGO Official F 2013. Yet macho rhetoric dominated the interview with the former MHA. GoT Official A (2013) reiterated that the government had been managing the old settlements (of the 1972 caseload) for some 10 to 15 years without any UNHCR presence. At the same time, mutual respect was apparent. Another MHA official empathized with UNHCR, seeing "how difficult it is for them" to serve so many masters (international donors, governments, other stakeholders and of course the refugees they are to prioritize) (GoT Official B 2013). GoT Official A (2013) also said, "I often feel sorry for UN officials . . . because they have to play quite a bit of high-level politics."
99 NGO Official F 2013, UNHCR Official O 2013, GoT Official M 2013.
100 Landau, *The Humanitarian Hangover: Displacement, Aid and Transformation in Western Tanzania*, 145.

101 Landau, *The Humanitarian Hangover: Displacement, Aid and Transformation in Western Tanzania*, 141.
102 Landau, *The Humanitarian Hangover: Displacement, Aid and Transformation in Western Tanzania*, 141.
103 Landau, *The Humanitarian Hangover: Displacement, Aid and Transformation in Western Tanzania*, 141.
104 Landau, *The Humanitarian Hangover: Displacement, Aid and Transformation in Western Tanzania*, 145. "Whereas representatives of the district or regional administration remain infrequent visitors to Kasulu's villages, residents now witness an almost constant stream of international NGO and UN staff and vehicles. With their presence, new sets of normative expectations are emerging, as many Kasulu residents come to believe that the international relief organizations have a duty to help Tanzanian citizens" (Landau, *The Humanitarian Hangover: Displacement, Aid and Transformation in Western Tanzania*, 10).
105 UNHCR Official C 2013; UNHCR Official E 2013; UNHCR Official N 2012.
106 Rutinwa, "The Marginalisation of Local Relief Capacity in Tanzania," 91.
107 UNHCR Official O 2013.
108 NGO Official F 2013. One example he provides is that of a new building for the Ministry of Home Affairs' Refugee Department, funded in large part by UNHCR. The Tanzanian government also gained vehicles, computers, airstrip redevelopment, roads, urban water supply renovation and agricultural development initiatives through multilateral funding (Landau, *The Humanitarian Hangover: Displacement, Aid and Transformation in Western Tanzania*, 72).
109 GoT Official M 2013.
110 GoT Official B 2013; GoT Official M 2013; UNHCR Official J 2012.
111 Rutinwa, "The Marginalisation of Local Relief Capacity in Tanzania," 93.
112 Landau, *The Humanitarian Hangover: Displacement, Aid and Transformation in Western Tanzania*, 69. However, this does not necessarily refute the main point that UNHCR was a surrogate state but that it had little influence on the policies that were made. It simply reinforces the fact that it was a surrogate state and had some authority and power at the local level, which does not contradict the arguments made in this research.
113 Landau, *The Humanitarian Hangover: Displacement, Aid and Transformation in Western Tanzania*, 117.
114 Landau, *The Humanitarian Hangover: Displacement, Aid and Transformation in Western Tanzania*, 1.
115 Landau, *The Humanitarian Hangover: Displacement, Aid and Transformation in Western Tanzania*, 66.
116 Landau, *The Humanitarian Hangover: Displacement, Aid and Transformation in Western Tanzania*, 68.
117 Landau, *The Humanitarian Hangover: Displacement, Aid and Transformation in Western Tanzania*, 155.
118 Landau, *The Humanitarian Hangover: Displacement, Aid and Transformation in Western Tanzania*, 155.

5 Uganda

- **Refugee-hosting policies and history in Uganda**
- **UNHCR's domestication and surrogacy in Uganda**
- **UNHCR's influence on Uganda**
- **Conclusion**

In comparison to Kenya and Tanzania, Uganda provides a case where UNHCR had taken on surrogacy in the past but has since moved away from surrogacy, instead favoring a form of partnership with the government. This chapter will provide a brief background to Uganda's refugee history and policy in order to contextualize the discussion about UNHCR in Uganda. It will then consider how UNHCR domesticated, originally taking on surrogacy with Sudanese refugees but more recently moving away from surrogacy with Congolese refugees. The chapter then focuses on what its surrogacy (or lack thereof) has meant for UNHCR's ability to influence state behavior toward refugees. In line with the framework, it ultimately argues that UNHCR in Uganda has been better positioned to affect decisions about refugees when it does not domesticate as a surrogate state but rather works in partnership with the Ugandan government.

Refugee-hosting policies and history in Uganda

General modern history

A former British colony, Uganda has had a violent history over the past century. It achieved independence in 1962, with Milton Obote as its first prime minister. In 1971 Obote was overthrown by a coup led by army chief Idi Amin, who subsequently expelled Uganda's Asian population and began a period of violence in Uganda. Political instability and violence followed, and an estimated half a million people were killed in state-sponsored violence during a series of coups in the 1970s and 1980s. In 1986 another military coup installed Yoweri Museveni as president, and he and the National Resistance Army implemented "no-party" democracy. A five-year civil war followed, which finally ended with the restoration of political participation.[1] In 1995 a new constitution reintroduced political parties, but in 2000, Ugandans voted to maintain the "no-party" system, rejecting multi-party politics. Simultaneously Uganda conducted interventions in the DRC and Zaire (in 2005 it was accused by the International Criminal Court (ICC) of invading and killing DRC citizens in 1999), faced conflict with Rwanda and became one of the founding members of the EAC in 2001. In 2005 Uganda returned to multiparty politics; however, presidential term limits were also abolished, and Museveni again won elections in 2006, and more recently again in 2011, despite accusations of vote rigging.

Uganda has faced a number of broader security challenges. Recently, it has emerged from a long battle with the violent rebel group, the Lord's Resistance Army (LRA) in northern Uganda. It has also deployed peacekeepers to Somalia as part of an AU mission since 2007 and suffered a bomb attack from Somalia's al-Shabaab in 2010. It has had continuous border disputes with the DRC (in 2012 the UN accused Uganda of sending troops into the DRC to fight alongside the M23 rebel movement, which Uganda denies and, in an angry response, pledged to withdraw its forces from all UN-backed international missions in Somalia, the Central African Republic and the Democratic Republic of the Congo), as well as tensions with neighboring Rwanda.

Things are changing quickly in Uganda, however, particularly as the UK-based company Heritage Oil reported a major oil find. This will likely have a significant impact on the economy and development of Uganda. In addition, Western-backed economic reforms have brought some economic improvements since the 1990s, but Uganda has also been hit hard with the 2008 global fiscal crisis. Socially Uganda has been praised as a "pioneer of liberalization of the media in Africa" and for vigorous campaign efforts against HIV/AIDS. However, it has also been the subject of criticism over its 2010 antihomosexuality bill.[2] New displacement from South Sudan is also creating tensions and challenges to Uganda's response efforts.

An evolution of refugee policies

Uganda has hosted refugees from many of its neighbors, including the Democratic Republic of the Congo (DRC), South Sudan, Somalia, Burundi, Rwanda, Ethiopia and Eritrea. UNHCR reports that in 2012, there were more than 190,000 registered refugees and asylum seekers in Uganda, in addition to nearly 30,000 IDPs. In the past, Uganda was a "warehousing" country that bound refugees to camps based on security concerns. In reference to

Sudanese refugees, for example, Tania Kaiser writes that they were required to stay in "remote, politically marginalized border areas, demonstrating the government's desire to keep them separate and prevent integration."[3]

In the last decade, this has shifted significantly, and Uganda no longer requires refugees to stay in closed settlements or camps. Now, the majority are spread across settlements in the north and southwest of the country,[4] though there are many more thousands in Ugandan towns and cities who are not receiving any assistance.[5] UNHCR also reports that Uganda's IDPs and refugees are increasingly found in urban areas, many living in Kampala.[6] Congolese and Rwandans make up the longest-staying population of refugees in Uganda, and the Congolese have the highest numbers. UNHCR reports that many either do not want to, or are unable to, return home and claims to be seeking LI prospects for them.[7] The protracted nature of Uganda's displaced populations is also notable: Uganda has hosted high numbers of refugees for protracted periods of time, in many cases for decades on end.[8]

Yet in spite of its history of hosting refugees, its violent past has also made it a refugee-producing country for decades.[9] Indeed, most interviewees stated that Uganda has a long history of sending and receiving refugees and recognizes that it is in a "difficult neighborhood" of war-torn neighbors.[10] This historical view of being a refugee-producing and -receiving country has thus informed Uganda's approach toward refugees. Many interviewees for this research stressed that Ugandans themselves understood what it meant to be displaced, as many government officials (e.g. Refugee Minister Stephen Malinga) had themselves been refugees.[11] Moreover, during World War II, Uganda received displaced Europeans,[12] and in the 1950s and 1960s, Uganda received refugees from Sudan, Kenya, Rwanda, Congo, Ethiopia and Somalia.[13]

During all of this, Uganda was also generating its own IDPs and refugees, first under Obote and then under Idi Amin.[14] Zachary Lomo, Angela Naggaga and Lucy Hovil report that Uganda received refugees throughout the 1970s and 1980s as well and that, by 1985, refugees made up some seven percent of the population.[15] Amidst a troubled economy, continued internal violence and little state capacity, Uganda continued to host more refugees—by 1995 it hosted over 300,000 refugees, with more arriving every day.[16] In spite of this, many interviewees from the government, UNHCR and NGOs stated that Uganda generally treated refugees well and that it rarely *refouled* them. They argued that hospitality was inherent to Ugandan culture, that Ugandans saw refugees as an asset more than a burden and that because they shared the same tribal roots, they were like brothers and sisters.[17] It is perhaps a result of these characteristics that Uganda in general has a number of strong refugee-advocating civil society groups, institutions and organizations (e.g. the Refugee Law Project in Kampala).

Accordingly, Uganda's refugee policy has evolved over time and, like the other case studies, has been largely contingent on social, economic, political and security contexts. In addition, different responses to major refugee influxes like Sudanese and Congolese help illustrate some shifts in policy. As examined here in comparison to Tanzania and Kenya, Uganda sees itself as having more open and progressive policies toward refugees. Kaiser writes:

> The language used by officials of central government with reference to refugees in Uganda is one of solidarity and brotherhood. . . . [T]heir humanitarian response is based on the kind of understanding which is not evident in the international agencies and in many of the NGO staff. Government policy towards refugees is described by UNHCR as "progressive and liberal" and is generally accepted to be generous and sympathetic.[18]

Uganda has practiced refugee integration alongside high numbers of IDPs of its own. One interviewee also spoke extensively about the fact that Uganda has not had a national identity card system (though they plan to create one this year). He stated that this meant that "if you can blend in"—as so many Congolese who flee to Uganda are able to do, speaking local dialects and having similar physical features—"you can become Ugandan."[19]

What is perhaps most progressive is that the 2006 Refugee Bill in Uganda allows refugees the choice of where they would like to live. FMO writes "It is one of the few countries of asylum to allow refugees to either settle themselves within the national population, or to live in a UNHCR-sponsored refugee settlement."[20] The 2006 Refugee Act (originally proposed in 2000 and passed in 2006) also harmonized municipal law with international obligations and created a department of refugees, an independent appeals body and various other refugee rights.[21] It was also meant to encourage self-sufficiency.

However, Kaiser and other scholars are quick to note that Uganda's refugee policy still needs improvement and that it is greatly affected by regional political and security concerns. Past research, for example, has called for clarity in the law.[22] The 2006 Refugee Act is also still awaiting some legal clarification and would benefit from continued improvements.[23] Moreover, like most states, Uganda is prone to viewing refugees as temporary and counting on their returning, rather than considering that their displacement may be long and that many may never go home or gain resettlement. It also tends to view refugees through a political and security lens, as Lomo et al. write that refugees' "presence is as much a political issue as a humanitarian one."[24] For example, some Rwandan refugees have been implicated in using Uganda as a base for cross-border attacks into Rwanda.[25] Sudan has made similar accusations, and Kaiser notes that Uganda's own "'war in the North' has been inextricably interconnected with the Sudanese conflict."[26] Likewise, transit camps that were supposed to be temporary have become long term, and their proximity to the border has also exacerbated political tensions.[27] IDPs are another complex piece of the PRS, and government concern about IDPs, rebel movements and border areas have contributed to a security-focused response. If Uganda begins to feel as though refugees are a security problem—either exacerbating tensions with neighbors or causing insecurity themselves—future policies may shift.

Economically speaking, refugees in Uganda have had both positive and negative impacts on the country, which also lend context to Uganda's refugee policy choices. Kaiser writes that Sudanese refugees in Uganda have positively affected local economies where they have been able to contribute to agriculture or business and thus increase economic activity around the settlements.[28] She attributes negative effects on the economy to government policies of restricting refugees to camps in poor conditions.[29] She also writes that some Ugandan local politicians have benefited from being able to channel refugee aid to their areas.[30] In addition, growing concerns over land distribution might have negative future effects on refugee policy, particularly as Congolese continue to arrive. Interviewees stated that if Uganda starts feeling like it does not have enough land (which it appears to be starting to, with population growth and discoveries of oil), it will likely begin policies of encampment, rather than provide land to refugees.

The Settlement Policy (SP)

The SP (closely linked to the SRS discussed on p. 145ff) of Uganda has generated global praise and has been viewed as relatively progressive and open. Put simply, the SP requires refugees to live in settlements if they are going to receive assistance from UNHCR but allows them to choose if they prefer to live elsewhere and survive without assistance. Consequently, many have chosen to move to Kampala or other cities. Those who have stayed in the settlements continue to receive some assistance but also have plots of land to farm (generally 50 meters by 100 meters of land, owned by the government and given to them) and for the most part are able to move freely. Indeed, when visiting the settlements, it is very different than visiting a camp: it is very difficult to tell where the settlement ends and a village begins, and in some cases, the road through a settlement alternates from village to settlement, and back again.[31] In other words, the settlement and village already appear integrated from an outsider's perspective.[32]

In conjunction with the SRS/DAR (see p. 145ff), the SP purports to provide refugees with the option of living away from camps and achieving self-reliance. The government and UNHCR's idea of the settlements was to provide land to those who did not plan to repatriate in the near future as an attempt to promote self-sufficiency.[33] Another expected benefit of the SP was to work toward integrating services provided to refugees with the host population as a "win-win" situation, whereby refugees and locals would both benefit. They were supposed to offer a more permanent departure from temporary transit camps[34] and were also to move from emergency relief to long-term development.[35]

Interviewees said that settlements generally resulted in less scapegoating,[36] particularly as they are owned by the government rather than locals (meaning locals are not trying to regain their land). Even though settlements are spread out and tend to be on large, isolated pieces of land, interviewees generally thought that settlements were quite good and encouraged *de facto* integration.[37] After all, refugees are free to intermarry, work, move freely and make many choices more freely. One mentioned that refugees could "blend in and take the identity" they needed,[38] and another argued that settlements enabled refugees to have better relations with local communities.[39] Another UNHCR employee stated that settlements offer better services (as opposed to going to a city) and that some people leave for Kampala to see what it is like but then decide to return to settlements in order to receive services.[40] Another stated that refugees in Uganda are "free to work, go to school and access health care" and mentioned that locals make use of these services as well (indeed, while conducting interviews, the researcher observed many locals waiting in line at the clinic in the settlement).[41] Overall, then, the SP has won tempered praise, as scholars like Michela Machiavello (2003); Richard Black (1998); Tania Kaiser (2008); and Lucy Hovil, Tania Kaiser and Zachary Lomo (2005) agree that it provides far more opportunities for self-reliance and better access to human rights than confinement to local settlements or camps and that local communities look far more favorably upon refugees that are self-settled.

However, there are also a number of criticisms of the SP. Some report terrible conditions for refugees, including overcrowding and inadequate food, water and shelter.[42] Others note that the land given to refugees is undesirable land in isolated areas that are difficult to cultivate or that plots are too small for self-reliance.[43] Hovil also argues that refugees are less secure in camps and settlements because they are easy targets,[44] and Lomo et al. also write that their insecurities and poor conditions make them prime targets for rebel recruitment.[45] Others have voiced concerns over whether refugees are really being able to make a choice about their own futures with assistance only available to those who stay in settlements,[46] or whether the SP is more about controlling what the state sees as economic and security threats.[47]

Still other scholars raise concerns about the SP perpetuating a view that refugees are temporary and should be contained and the view that only refugees in settlements are the "true" refugees because they are the only ones receiving assistance from international actors.[48] Hovil et al. write, "In stark opposition to international refugee law, the implementation of the SP in Uganda has effectively redefined the category 'refugee' so that it has come to refer to a person who is in receipt of assistance and living in a physical space defined by the government of Uganda."[49] Finally, some scholars argue that the SP has not produced the self-reliance envisioned and limit refugees in what they can choose to do.[50]

UNHCR's domestication and surrogacy in Uganda

Recalling the spectrum of domestication, shown in Figure 5.1, UNHCR has taken on various domestic roles at different times in Uganda. Research and interviews point to past UNHCR surrogacy with Sudanese refugees and more recently less UNHCR surrogacy with Congolese refugees. UNHCR has been involved with refugees in Uganda for decades. Contrary to Tanzania or Kenya, UNHCR today tends to frame its involvement with refugees as a partnership with and complementary to responsibilities taken on by the government of Uganda (GoU). It works through the Office of the Prime Minister (OPM), which provides land for housing and agriculture and oversees security, law and order in the settlements. UNHCR partners with national and international NGOs to provide technical, financial and material support and manages the settlements in conjunction with OPM.[51] This is quite different than the government abdication and full surrogate state role seen in Kenya or with the 1990s Tanzania example. Indeed, interviewees strongly argued that Uganda has progressed in recent years to a state where refugee self-sufficiency has been achieved in some cases, thus disagreeing with any notion that UNHCR in Uganda is acting as a surrogate state by providing for refugees in every manner of life.[52] Many settlement refugees now enjoy freedom of movement, the right to work, participation in political processes and choice on whether to move to the cities or remain in the settlements to receive assistance, all signs that they are less dependent on UNHCR to be their surrogate state from a C&M or governance perspective.

Figure 5.1 Spectrum of UNHCR's domestication in Uganda, comparing roles with Congolese and Sudanese refugees

Past surrogacy (examples, motives, conditions)

In its earliest days in Uganda, UNHCR was not a surrogate state and arguably was not even domesticated. It did not have a presence on the ground and only served as an advisor on refugee issues. It was not until its involvement with Sudanese refugees that it assumed surrogacy, the height of which was in the 1990s. At this time, the GoU abdicated refugee responsibilities to UNHCR. Kaiser, for example, writes that during this phase, refugees'

> understanding of what it is to be a refugee . . . did not allow for the absence of the international community, represented by UNHCR. The organisation had gained a *fictive kinship status in the everyday discourse*, often being referred to as the "mother and father" of the refugees, on the basis of the provision of assistance in extremis which it offered.[53]

This demonstrates various indicators of surrogacy, including forms of governance, service provision and the perception that it is an authority in charge.

In another example, Hovil et al. describe district officials complaining about difficulties in getting UNHCR to invest in their areas.[54] The fact that the official was frustrated about not receiving development funding from UNHCR—not his or her own government—makes the point well. Kaiser also reports that many Sudanese refugees looked to UNHCR as the provider of their security and protection, not even considering local or central authorities as having a role in their safety.[55] This, too, points to the perception that UNHCR, not the state, is the authority in charge.

Other literature outlines additional examples of UNHCR's surrogacy and Uganda's abdication. In one case, Kaiser (2002) discusses the tensions between UNHCR and OPM regarding handing over refugee camp responsibilities to the government. In this case, UNHCR and the GoU/OPM had agreed on the goals of self-sufficiency and integration in theory but defined them differently and had different priorities:

> While UNHCR looks towards a future when they have little to do with the settlement, the refugees having achieved self-sufficiency and been integrated for the short term into the local population, the central government maintains that as the representative of the international community, UNHCR has no option but to remain centrally involved.[56]

In this respect, Kaiser asserts that UNHCR and GoU had an "implicit working arrangement whereby UNHCR, rather than the host state, is ultimately seen as responsible for refugees' well-being."[57] She continues to say that Uganda had refused to take over financial responsibility for refugees as envisaged under SRS and that it still depended on UNHCR to carry out basic refugee-related functions.[58] Moreover, she concludes that Uganda saw refugees as an "international and not a national concern" and that by allowing refugees on their territory, Uganda felt "they have done their duty and the rest is on other international actors."[59] Even amidst district and local budgets that include some refugee-related aspects, GoU expected UNHCR to cover these costs.[60] In Kaiser's view, Uganda at this time sought all the decision-making power with none of the responsibility (although since her writing in 2002, GoU has taken more ownership of refugee matters, as indicated in the next section).

This abdicationist approach is not unlike the other UNHCR surrogate state examples in Tanzania and Kenya. As outlined in the framework and other case studies, the adoption of surrogacy tends to happen when there is a void left by the state and UNHCR steps in because it feels it has little choice but to do so if it is going to care for refugees and carry out its work. Indeed, when UNHCR was a surrogate state in Uganda, officials expressed reluctance at taking on such a role and emphasized that it had never been the intention of staff or the organization. Rather, UNHCR's surrogacy at this time resulted from the "slippery slope" of aid and protection and a response to the GoU's abdication from its responsibilities. UNHCR's Uganda Representative recalled that "at the end of the day it comes down to saving a life," and thus protection becomes operational in many different ways, ways that can easily snowball into state-like activities beyond the mandate of refugee protection.[61] Another UNHCR employee stated:

> We live in the house that we build [regarding UNHCR in Uganda]. . . . Sometimes when you see the government doesn't have the capacity, you cannot pretend. . . . The problem is that emergency status is taking forever . . . we keep the mindset of emergency response when it has passed, and then you let the government step back because you are doing it. . . . We need to remember that we cannot do everything ourselves.[62]

The shift from abdication to partnership

In the last decade or so, UNHCR has shifted away from surrogacy to more of a partnership model with the government, as shown in Figure 5.2. Some interviewees even gave the impression that UNHCR was almost thought of as a department within the government (though not an instrument, as it still has its own autonomy).[63]

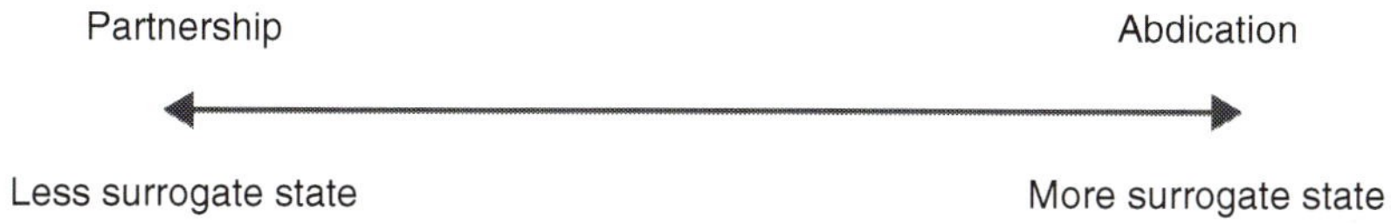

Figure 5.2 Subview of the "surrogate state" end of the spectrum paired with state disposition

In general, interviewees described the relationship between UNHCR and OPM as quite good—one that is relatively honest and communicative and where both actors are on the same page. One UNHCR official emphasized the closeness of UNHCR and OPM: "we have a desk in the government department and work together on a daily basis . . . the power still lies with the government, but we have clear marked responsibilities."[64] In addition, the 2006 Refugee Act even mentions UNHCR several times and is also meant to be a part of the SRS/DAR, further emphasizing the partnership and formality of roles the government and UNHCR share with one another.

OPM and UNHCR officials interviewed in the settlements and field offices stressed this partnership even further. They discussed working closely on nearly every refugee-related project (even raising criticism from NGOs and scholars who viewed their closeness as detrimental to UNHCR's ability to hold the government to strict refugee protection standards; e.g. Chris Dolan and Lucy Hovil 2006). Moreover, the UNHCR Uganda Representative stated, "Here, we are fortunate that the GoU is both involved and willing to consider new ideas . . . it is so rare to have this."[65] The Representative also focused on the various places where "interests converge" between donors, the government and UNHCR, paving the way for a productive relationship and emphasizing cooperation.[66]

Moreover, an OPM Assistant Commander in the Kyaka II settlement even spoke of UNHCR as if it were one of its fellow government departments, indicating that UNHCR would sit in on RSD meetings with OPM and funded primary schools that were used by both the local and refugee children.[67] He still began each sentence with the reminder that the government was in charge ("It is us who introduce UNHCR to the community" or "The government asked UNHCR to help") but also stated that UNHCR funded "programs, salaries, vehicles . . . office furniture . . . even non-food items. We work very closely."[68] Indeed, UNHCR still funds a number of refugee projects, though OPM staff have greater presence and ownership. While some of these interviewees may have felt obliged to paint OPM as the authority and UNHCR as a mere assistant (when the reality may be different than the rhetoric), there was general consensus and consistency in interviews and literature that partnership was at the core of UNHCR and OPM's working relationship.

UNHCR's influence on Uganda

The variance within the Uganda case—differences between UNHCR's role as a surrogate state with Sudanese refugees versus UNHCR's role as a partner to the GoU with Congolese refugees more recently—demonstrates that surrogacy does not translate to more influence on the state. Measuring influence follows from the framework, which uses both material and nonmaterial indicators to understand influence vis-à-vis IO surrogacy. While any number of variables affect UNHCR's ability to influence the state,[69] careful analysis of material policies (in particular the SRS/DAR), perception of authority and its ability to influence individual leaders helps demonstrate that "less is more"—or in other words, UNHCR is less able to influence the state when acting as a surrogate state. Most of the focus in this chapter has been on UNHCR's role with Congolese refugees, which is more recent than with the Sudanese (whose presence has decreased in recent years). However, the next section briefly considers UNHCR's surrogacy with Sudanese refugees and its subsequent lessened influence on the state.

Past: UNHCR's surrogacy and less influence

Past research outlines that UNHCR acted as a surrogate state, carrying out all facets of refugee protection and assistance. In turn, as argued by the framework, this made it less able to speak out in attempts to influence Uganda. While UNHCR certainly demonstrated the authority and responsibility in a given locale that comes with surrogacy, it was quite limited in how it could leverage the state. The GoU could override UNHCR's surrogate state authority and power in the name of security at virtually any time,[70] and thus UNHCR could not influence concrete decision-making at its own will. Furthermore, humanitarian actors like UNHCR and its IPs rely on the Ugandan army for security and thus are in a difficult position: "We are caught between denouncing them and needing them."[71] Security concerns, for example, have always trumped UNHCR's preferences in the eyes of the Ugandan state and muzzled any potential for UNHCR to speak out in the past. Kaiser writes that at times the government has ignored UNHCR and marched refugees to the border at gunpoint and with tear gas.[72] For these reasons, it is easier to understand why UNHCR has had to settle for a largely humanitarian, rather than protection-oriented agenda in Uganda. Dolan and Hovil refer to this as "soft" protection (using humanitarian assistance) instead of "hard" protection (directly confronting governments on human rights issues).[73] It ultimately constrains UNHCR's actions.[74]

UNHCR as a surrogate was also constrained by the political balance it had to strike. It needed to maintain a good working relationship, respecting Ugandan sovereignty and authority so that it could continue to carry out its work in the field. Dolan and Hovil write that in the past situation in northern Uganda,

> Both NGOs and UN bodies [were] reluctant to speak out against the government for fear of being ejected, and as a result few international NGOs have used their presence as a starting point for putting pressure on other actors—the government or their own or other donor governments—to address the wider issues.[75]

An example of this is the 2003 expulsion of the UNHCR representative who spoke out against the government's moving of Sudanese refugees to an unsafe settlement and was characterized as taking "measures to undermine its policy."[76] Dolan and Hovil continue to write that those who have spoken out have been intimidated, whether at the local or national level, and they cite one interviewee saying, "The problem of the country is that it's a development success story. And this has been supported by the UN RC. . . . You can't be with them and criticize them. You can't do both."[77] In another interview, Dolan and Hovil write:

> The Country Director of a large INGO summed up the dilemma . . . : "We are prepared [to raise difficult issues], but I am not authorised to have [my organization] closed down. . . . It is rarely better for us to leave". A field-worker reiterated this point, saying: "On the ground we want to do a good job, but there is an element of real compromise. We are always thinking, what will the state do?" . . . In Uganda, the government told NGOs to remain silent on issues of government responsibility.[78]

Kaiser (2002) also discusses the constraints UNHCR felt when it could not influence district, local or central authorities to create a budget for taking over the settlements it was trying to hand over. While she outlines some places where UNHCR had leverage, the organization was essentially stuck in its position. Thus, when UNHCR acted as a surrogate state in Uganda, it was less able to speak up about refugee issues and subsequently less influential on the state.

Present: SRS/DAR as a material policy example of more influence coming out of partnership

In contrast to the past, UNHCR's more recent role with Congolese refugees—one that embraces partnership over surrogacy—demonstrates the organization's increased ability to influence the state. The SRS/DAR policy is one example of UNHCR's ability to influence GoU when it has fewer surrogate state properties and works instead via partnership. While SRS was meant for Sudanese refugees as well, it can currently be most easily seen among Congolese refugees. Building on the SP, SRS intended to move refugees toward self-sufficiency and, in doing this, to contribute to Uganda's long-term development.[79] This was meant to create a win-win dynamic: refugees are not encamped and have greater access to their rights, and Ugandans benefit from their presence by developing remote parts of the country.[80] Thus, it was an attempt at linking a policy of LI with a national development plan. When it was written, it was envisaged that by 2003:

> refugees would be able to grow or buy their own food, access and pay for basic services, and maintain self-sustaining community structures. The SRS was designed to be implemented at a district level, with OPM and UNHCR playing coordinating roles, and "[ensuring] harmonisation of policy."[81]

It was formally launched at UNHCR's 2004 ExCom meetings in Geneva and has been considered part of UNHCR's wider global strategy of DAR.[82] Its goal was to reduce aid dependency and to integrate refugee and local government services, including things like agricultural production, water and sanitation, education, infrastructure development, health and nutrition and the environment, thus eliminating parallel service delivery systems and benefiting both refugees and locals.[83]

In this case, UNHCR helped to write the policy and implement it—a clear sign of influence. Indeed, UNHCR took part in all major meetings with government officials, and the policy would not have been passed without its partnership with OPM.[84] In reference to the related SP, Gottschalk et al. write, "Although in legal terms the Settlement Policy is founded in national legislation, UNHCR cannot disavow its own responsibility for the policy. Not only did the agency play a significant role in the policy's establishment, but it continues to actively endorse it."[85] Again, this research does not seek to measure the success or failure of such policies—for OPM, UNHCR or refugees—but rather to outline instances where UNHCR was able to influence outcomes via its role, still maintaining a lot of responsibility, but working in partnership with OPM rather than as a substitute. Moreover, it is clear that the policy cannot be entirely attributed to UNHCR, but UNHCR was certainly instrumental in bringing it about and lobbying the government.[86]

In addition to UNHCR's influence via material policies like SRS, more recent examples of UNHCR's role with Congolese refugees also demonstrates more influence via its perception as an authority in partnership with the government. Indeed, interviewees noted some of the ways UNHCR was able to influence OPM's refugee decisions or areas where they made decisions on their own. While one NGO official stated that there were many things that only the government could do, he stated that UNHCR is "in on everything," even though the authority in the "camp" (interviewees constantly made the mistake of interchanging "camp" and "settlement") lies with the camp commander.[87]

Another NGO senior leader stated that OPM acted more like UNHCR's IP and that while it still had the final say in refugee matters, many day-to-day issues were overseen by UNHCR. He gave one example of drilling boreholes, noting that they (the NGO) had to get UNHCR's permission, even though it was technically OPM's role to approve borehole drilling. He stated that they included OPM in the decision "just to make them feel good" but that it was really UNHCR that signed off.[88] Likewise, Lomo et al. write that, while in theory UNHCR was only supposed to make recommendations to the GoU's Directorate of Refugees regarding prima facie status refugees from Sudan and Congo, "in practice, this recommendation is as good as a final decision."[89] While UNHCR in Tanzania (1990s) and Kenya may have had similar levels of influence in their given locales, the difference in the Ugandan case is that there was a perception that UNHCR was an authority in *partnership* with the government, not usurping power or marginalizing the state to the extent seen in the others. In response, the state was more receptive to UNHCR's input.

Finally, UNHCR was better positioned to use its "moral tool" of influence when it was less of a surrogate state. As one senior UNHCR official put it, the GoU may still have the sovereignty, power and final say, but they are constrained in how they exercise it because UNHCR brings both funding[90] and a close, watchful eye over how refugees are treated—a type of soft power all its own: "We are . . . a witness for what is going on 'on the ground' and they will be very careful not to abuse."[91] This is not to say that moral authority necessarily trumps other types of authority (e.g. decisions based on security concerns of the state)—indeed, as one field UNHCR staff said, people look up to UNHCR, but they know that the camp commander from OPM is still in charge[92]—but simply that there are ways in which UNHCR holds other "types" of authority, influence or power and that UNHCR is more free to exercise these forms of leverage or influence when it is not a surrogate state. Cases like Kenya or Tanzania (1990s), on the other hand, show UNHCR having a more difficult time applying its "moral authority." This is not solely reflective of surrogacy but in part displays how surrogacy can limit or entrap UNHCR's ability to speak out. When it is a surrogate state and relies on the government for access to continue its programs, it is less able to criticize and influence the authorities.[93]

In sum, these examples of influence from UNHCR's more recent role amongst Congolese refugees are rooted in the view that UNHCR is a partner to the government, not an opponent or substitute. Interviewees from the government and UNHCR expressed that the two worked well together and that UNHCR was influential and heard when the government made policy decisions.[94] This was especially evident in the SRS policy, which UNHCR helped write and implement. The relationship is far from perfect but presents a very different picture than UNHCR's earlier surrogate state role with Sudanese refugees and its role in Tanzania (1990s) and Kenya.

Mechanisms of marginalization of the state and responsibility shifting

Why does the "less is more" relationship of IO surrogacy and influence work in Uganda? In the previous chapters, the mechanisms of the framework (marginalization of the state and responsibility/blame shifting) helped explain why this was the case. In this example, because UNHCR was less of a surrogate state, less marginalization of the state and less responsibility shifting—thus more "ownership of the refugee issue" on the part of the state—helps explain why this relationship of influence occurred.

Unlike in Tanzania, more of the responsibility and blame stays on GoU in the current context of Congolese refugee assistance. This keeps the state more involved and more engaged in refugee matters and hence the relationship of partnership rather than abdication. As Dolan and Hovil (2006) write, UNHCR is better able to address protection needs when it is more focused on human rights protection than meeting humanitarian need (which arguably leads to surrogacy). Indeed, UNHCR has played an instrumental role in encouraging Uganda to adopt policies that are better for refugee rights, such as SRS/DAR and SP, which more closely resemble LI with freedom of movement and the right to work. Access to these rights is touted as a major goal in almost any PRS where UNHCR is working. They are usually something the state is against and UNHCR is for. In other words, UNHCR's ability to help persuade Uganda indicates more influence in this case.[95]

Less marginalization of the state means a more engaged state: a state with more expertise and a state that feels more "ownership" of refugee issues. This again means less of a void, less abdication and less of a need for surrogacy in the first place.[96] Uganda has also trended toward managing refugees from the center (despite some broader governance trends of decentralization of power).[97] This has also meant that GoU feels a greater sense of "ownership" over refugee issues than the other cases of abdication, such as Kenya or Tanzania (1990s). While this has meant that local officials have not always felt their opinions are heard,[98] it also means that the GoU has seen the benefits of cooperating with UNHCR in order to reap benefits from the presence of refugees (e.g. the development of rural areas with UNHCR funds). Unlike in Tanzania (1990s), where UNHCR's surrogacy was benefiting the state and absorbing blame that should have gone to the state, the GoU's image was partially tied to refugee issues, and partnering with UNHCR helped to find solutions to refugee problems. GoU therefore had incentive to solve refugee problems and thus incentive to listen to UNHCR's input.

Another reason less state marginalization and less responsibility shifting (in other words, more state "ownership") grants UNHCR more influence is that GoU sees how partnering with UNHCR (rather than abdicating all responsibilities to it) helps it to broadcast power to remote border areas and subsequently to have more power over refugee issues and refugee-hosting areas.[99] In this sense, UNHCR's assistance to refugees is a mode through which the government—seen as UNHCR's partner—can reach areas it would otherwise not have the capacity to reach. Having a more hands-on approach in tandem with UNHCR (rather than letting UNHCR do everything) also enabled Ugandan authorities to build up more expertise on refugee issues, thus having the capacity and knowledge to respond and work with UNHCR, rather than simply ceding refugee affairs to UNHCR and ignoring any input from UNHCR.

In sum, unlike in Kenya or Tanzania (1990s), UNHCR's role with the Congolese has not forced it to trade its moral authority or ability to speak out for access. Because it is not a surrogate state dependent on keeping the government happy in order to maintain access, it has been able to lobby the state more, advocating for better policies when necessary.[100]

Further reflections on partnership

Partnership (instead of abdication and surrogacy) is at the core of why UNHCR has more influence with the state (with respect to the Congolese refugee situation). And while partnership and less surrogacy translates into greater UNHCR influence on the state than abdication and more surrogacy, this does not meant that positive results always emerge for the actors involved, not least the refugees. Nor is it the case that UNHCR has unlimited influence. Indeed, UNHCR officials interviewed continually stated that they did not see themselves as having hard "power," but that they had "advisory" roles.[101] The UNHCR Representative stated, "We don't have the power . . . the government looks at us as providers of funding and mobilizing the international community . . . we are the international solidarity [helping them comply with their international obligations]. . . . We can give them best practices, we can transfer funding and support and knowledge . . . but decisions have to be made by the government."[102] Some NGOs even argue that UNHCR's partnership has made it corrupt. Regardless, when compared to Kenya and Tanzania (1990s), it is certainly able to have more influence.

The implications for sovereignty, authority, influence and power (including zero-sum power relations) are important in this partnership scenario. Certainly, interviewees all professed Uganda's sovereignty and control over its own territory, but in reality, its partnership with UNHCR demonstrates a shared power story—one where Uganda still holds the material power of decision-making and "veto" power, but where UNHCR holds other forms of power via perception, rhetoric and financial underwriting. In the past with Sudanese refugees, the surrogate state UNHCR may have appeared more powerful,[103] and Uganda's refugee program depended on UNHCR more than it does now. One interviewee noted that in the past, when UNHCR as a surrogate state "ran" camps, it would have been a "disaster" if UNHCR had left; but with the settlement model where there is partnership, there is less dependence on UNHCR.[104] This is a step in the direction of appearing as though Uganda is in control of these territories, even as UNHCR is able to influence the policies more than it had been in the past, as summarized in Tables 5.1 and 5.2.

Table 5.1 Summary of UNHCR in Uganda (Sudanese): IO surrogacy, state abdication, low influence

UNHCR in Uganda (Sudanese): IO surrogacy/state abdication			
Indicator of influence			
Is UNHCR perceived (by locals, refugees or other actors) as a power or authority in the locale in which it is working?	Yes	Are state policies toward refugees in line with UNHCR's priorities?	No
Does UNHCR receive blame when services are not provided? Is it seen (by locals, refugees or other actors) as responsible for things generally attributed to the state?	Yes	Does the GoK feel a sense of "ownership" over the refugee "issue"?	No
Has UNHCR been able to change leader's minds on decisions?	No		
Has UNHCR changed the rhetoric of the issue?	No		
Has UNHCR affected other actors' behavior (local authorities, refugees, locals, other NGOs?)	Yes	= Low influence	
Does UNHCR participate in forms of local governance?	Yes		
Has UNHCR participated in directly writing and/or shaping policy?	No		

Table 5.2 Summary of UNHCR in Uganda (Congolese): less IO surrogacy, partnership, high influence

UNHCR in Uganda (Congolese): less IO surrogacy/partnership			
Indicator of influence			
Is UNHCR perceived (by locals, refugees or other actors) as a power or authority in the locale in which it is working?	Yes	Are state policies toward refugees in line with UNHCR's priorities?	Yes
Does UNHCR receive blame when services are not provided? Is it seen (by locals, refugees or other actors) as responsible for things generally attributed to the state?	No	Does the GoK feel a sense of "ownership" over the refugee "issue"?	Yes
Has UNHCR been able to change leader's minds on decisions?	Yes		
Has UNHCR changed the rhetoric of the issue?	Yes		
Has UNHCR affected other actors' behavior (local authorities, refugees, locals, other NGOs?)	Yes	= High influence	
Does UNHCR participate in forms of local governance?	No		
Has UNHCR participated in directly writing and/or shaping policy?	Yes		

Conclusion

This chapter has explored the role of UNHCR in Uganda. It was a surrogate state in its response to Sudanese refugees but has taken on less surrogacy in favor of partnership more recently with Congolese refugees. Unlike in Kenya, where the state abdicated nearly all refugee matters to UNHCR, Uganda now maintains some degree of "ownership" over refugee affairs and therefore has not left a void that UNHCR has felt compelled to fill in terms of taking on surrogate state properties. In turn, this has meant that UNHCR has been better able to advocate and lobby the state.

From a material, policy perspective, the best evidence of UNHCR's ability to influence Uganda has been its helping to design and implement the SRS policy, in tandem with the SP and UNHCR's DAR. While Uganda adopted the policy for a number of reasons, primary and secondary research in this chapter demonstrate that UNHCR's partnership, rather than surrogacy, has helped make this possible. This is because the state was less marginalized and less of the responsibility was placed on UNHCR. Rather, the government holds more active ownership of the refugee situation and hence is more willing to work with and listen to UNHCR in order to find solutions. OPM and UNHCR have a very close relationship (perhaps too close, according to some critics) that makes this possible.

How Uganda moves forward in partnership with UNHCR and as it continues to absorb increasing numbers of Congolese refugees is difficult to predict and makes it an interesting and important case to watch. As politics shift (the EAC, for example, will have interesting implications for how citizenship and the movement of individuals across borders takes place in East Africa), demographics change, land is contested and a national identity initiative comes into fruition, it is unclear whether Uganda will continue to include UNHCR as a vital partner that it listens to or whether it will adopt strict policies like those of its neighbors (e.g. Kenya). This will also depend on whether settlement or camp models are employed in the future.

From an IR perspective, however, UNHCR's role as a domesticated IO in Uganda demonstrates interesting shifts from surrogacy to partnership. This alone reveals insights about IO behavior "on the ground" and, taken a step further, has implications for how well the IO can influence the state. Indeed, as posited by the framework in Chapter 1, UNHCR has ironically had more influence when it has taken on less of a surrogate state role, as demonstrated here. The next chapter relates some of these findings back to the theory.

Notes

1 Giovanni Carbone, *No-Party Democracy? Ugandan Politics in Comparative Perspective* (Boulder, CO: Lynne Rienner Publishers, 2008), 1.
2 BBC, "Uganda Profile Timeline," 2013. Available from www.bbc.co.uk/news/world-africa-14112446.
3 Tania Kaiser, "Sudanese Refugees in Uganda and Kenya," in *Protracted Refugee Situations: Political, Human Rights and Security Implications*, ed. Gil Loescher, James Milner, Edward Newman and Gary Troeller, 248–276 (New York: United Nations University Press, 2008), 258.
4 UNHCR, "Displacement: The New 21st Century Challenge," *UNHCR Global Trends 2012*. Available from www.unhcr.org/51bacb0f9.html.
5 Michela Michiavello, "Forced Migrants as an Under-Utilized Asset: Refugee Skills, Livelihoods, and Achievements in Kampala, Uganda," UNHCR, New Issues in Refugee Research, Working Paper No. 95, 2003, p. 3, citing Ibutu 1999.
6 UNHCR, "Uganda," 2013. Available from www.unhcr.org/pages/49e483c06.html.
7 UNHCR, "Uganda Country Operations Profile Page." Available from www.unhcr.org/cgi-bin/texis/vtx/page?page=49e483c06&submit=GO.

8 Sarah Dryden-Peterson and Lucy Hovil, "A Remaining Hope for Durable Solutions: Local Integration of Refugees and Their Hosts in the Case of Uganda," *Refuge* 22, no. 1 (2004): 28.

9 Zachary Lomo, Angela Naggaga and Lucy Hovil, "The Phenomenon of Forced Migration in Uganda: An Overview of Policy and Practice in an Historical Context," Refugee Law Project Working Paper No. 1, 2001. Available from www.refugeelawproject.org/working_papers/RLP.WP01.pdf.

10 NGO Official K 2013; USG Official G 2013; UNHCR Official F 2013; NGO Official G 2013; UNHCR Official E 2013.

11 UNHCR Official L 2013; UNHCR Official E 2013; NGO Official G 2013; GoU Official A 2013; USG Official G 2013; UNHCR Official F 2013.

12 Lomo et al., "The Phenomenon of Forced Migration in Uganda: An Overview of Policy and Practice in an Historical Context," citing Gingyera-Pinycwa 1998, 5 on p. 3; USG Official G 2013.

13 Lomo et al., "The Phenomenon of Forced Migration in Uganda: An Overview of Policy and Practice in an Historical Context," 3.

14 Lomo et al., "The Phenomenon of Forced Migration in Uganda: An Overview of Policy and Practice in an Historical Context," 3.

15 Lomo et al., "The Phenomenon of Forced Migration in Uganda: An Overview of Policy and Practice in an Historical Context," 4.

16 Lomo et al., "The Phenomenon of Forced Migration in Uganda: An Overview of Policy and Practice in an Historical Context," 4.

17 USG Official G 2013; NGO Official G 2013; UNHCR Official E 2013; NGO Official K 2013; UNHCR Official L 2013; UNHCR Official F 2013. However, some scholars disagree. Michela Machiavello reports that refugees are often seen as unwelcome, with some seeing refugees as economic burdens who "depend on charity and begging," especially in urban areas. Some even see them as collaborators with former governments against Ugandan nationals ("Forced Migrants as an Under-Utilized Asset: Refugee Skills, Livelihoods, and Achievements in Kampala, Uganda," 4). At the same time, Machiavello (2003) and Kaiser (2002) both outline that there are mixed opinions of how welcome refugees are, and other scholars also note that Uganda has more mixed reactions toward refugees (Tania Kaiser, "The UNHCR and Withdrawal from Kiryandongo: Anatomy of a Handover," *Refugee Survey Quarterly* 21, nos. 1&2 (2002): 201–227).

18 Kaiser, "The UNHCR and Withdrawal from Kiryandongo: Anatomy of a Handover," 8.

19 NGO Official G 2013.

20 Forced Migration Online, "Oruchinga Refugee Camp," 2011. Available from www.forcedmigration.org/podcasts-videos-photos/photos/uganda.

21 Uganda, "The Refugee Act," 2006. Available from www.refworld.org/type,LEGISLATION,NATLEGBOD,UGA,4b7baba52,0.html.

Lomo et al., "The Phenomenon of Forced Migration in Uganda: An Overview of Policy and Practice in an Historical Context," 10.

22 E.g. Lomo et al. write that the system has been largely *ad hoc*, as a result of the lack of written law and transparent policy, and many refugees did not have access to their most basic rights ("The Phenomenon of Forced Migration in Uganda: An Overview of Policy and Practice in an Historical Context," 9). They draw out the tensions between Uganda's obligations as a signatory to CSR51 and the 1967 Protocol, as well as the 1969 OAU Convention, and its

own struggles in recovering from a prolonged civil war and preoccupations with reviving the economy and infrastructure ("The Phenomenon of Forced Migration in Uganda: An Overview of Policy and Practice in an Historical Context," 9).

23 UNHCR Official E 2013; Chris Dolan and Lucy Hovil, "Humanitarian Protection in Uganda? A Trojan Horse?," *Humanitarian Policy Group Background Paper, Overseas Development Institute*, 2006, p. 9. Available from www.odi.org.uk/sites/odi.org.uk/files/odi-assets/publications-opinion-files/381.pdf.

24 Lomo et al., "The Phenomenon of Forced Migration in Uganda: An Overview of Policy and Practice in an Historical Context," 9; Kaiser, "Sudanese Refugees in Uganda and Kenya," 262.

25 Lomo et al., "The Phenomenon of Forced Migration in Uganda: An Overview of Policy and Practice in an Historical Context," 5. Regarding Rwanda, refugees have been coming to Uganda since the 1950s, many Tutsi joining the Ugandan NRA military under Museveni, but turning their efforts toward Rwanda and invading using Uganda as a base. As of 2001, there were some 10,000 Rwandese refugees in Uganda, many of whom are Hutu having fled the 1994 genocide and Tutsi-dominated government (Lomo et al., "The Phenomenon of Forced Migration in Uganda: An Overview of Policy and Practice in an Historical Context," 5). Regarding Congo, the ongoing war is between the DRC government and troops supported by Zimbabwe, Namibia and Angola and rebels backed by Uganda and Rwanda.

26 Kaiser, "Sudanese Refugees in Uganda and Kenya," 253.

27 Lomo et al., "The Phenomenon of Forced Migration in Uganda: An Overview of Policy and Practice in an Historical Context," 5.

28 Kaiser, "Sudanese Refugees in Uganda and Kenya," 256.

29 Kaiser, "Sudanese Refugees in Uganda and Kenya," 257.

30 Kaiser, "Sudanese Refugees in Uganda and Kenya," 257.

31 USG Official G 2013; see Appendix C for more. The main difference between a camp and settlement is that settlements have more freedom of movement, the right to work and, in this case, are a less demarcated area than a camp (see Karen Jacobsen, "Local Integration: The Forgotten Solution," *Migration Information Source*, 2003. Available from www.migrationinformation.org/feature/display.cfm?ID=166; or Anna Schmidt, "FMO Research Guide: Camps Versus Settlements," *Forced Migration Online*, 2003. Available from www.forcedmigration.org/research-resources/expert-guides/camps-versus-settlements/fmo021.pdf for more). It is worth noting, however, that numerous officials made the mistake of using "camp" and "settlement" interchangeably, an interesting issue in and of itself, pointing to the subtle differences, and confusion even among those working there (UNHCR Official F 2013; UNHCR Official L 2013; GoU Official A 2013).

32 UNHCR Official L 2013; UNHCR Official F 2013; GoU Official A 2013.

33 Lomo et al., "The Phenomenon of Forced Migration in Uganda: An Overview of Policy and Practice in an Historical Context," 7; Sarah Dryden-Peterson and Lucy Hovil, "Local Integration as a Durable Solution: Refugees, Host Populations and Education in Uganda," New Issues in Refugee Research, Working Paper No. 93, 2003. Available from www.unhcr.org/3f8189ec4.html.

34 Dryden-Peterson and Hovil, "A Remaining Hope for Durable Solutions: Local Integration of Refugees and Their Hosts in the Case of Uganda," 29.

35 Lucy Hovil, "Free to Stay, Free to Go? Movement, Seclusion and Integration of Refugees in Moyo District," Refugee Law Project Working Paper No. 4, 2002, p. 13. Available from www.refugeelawproject.org/working_papers/RLP.WP04.pdf.
36 USG Official G 2013.
37 Dryden-Peterson and Hovil, "Local Integration as a Durable Solution: Refugees, Host Populations and Education in Uganda," Kaiser, "Sudanese Refugees in Uganda and Kenya," 257; USG Official G 2013; UNHCR Official C 2013.
38 UNHCR Official C 2013.
39 USG Official G 2013.
40 UNHCR Official C 2013.
41 UNHCR Official E 2013.
42 Hovil, "Free to Stay, Free to Go? Movement, Seclusion and Integration of Refugees in Moyo District," Lomo et al., "The Phenomenon of Forced Migration in Uganda: An Overview of Policy and Practice in an Historical Context," 6.
43 Lomo et al., "The Phenomenon of Forced Migration in Uganda: An Overview of Policy and Practice in an Historical Context," 7; Lucy Hovil, Tania Kaiser and Zachary Lomo, "We Are All Stranded Here Together: The Local Settlement System, Freedom of Movement, and Livelihood Opportunities in Arua and Moyo Districts," Refugee Law Project Working Paper No. 14, 2005, p. 22. Available from www.refugeelawproject.org/working_papers/RLP.WP14.pdf.
44 Hovil, "Free to Stay, Free to Go? Movement, Seclusion and Integration of Refugees in Moyo District," 17, 23.
45 Lomo et al., "The Phenomenon of Forced Migration in Uganda: An Overview of Policy and Practice in an Historical Context," 6.
46 Hovil, "Free to Stay, Free to Go? Movement, Seclusion and Integration of Refugees in Moyo District," Hovil et al., "We Are All Stranded Here Together: The Local Settlement System, Freedom of Movement, and Livelihood Opportunities in Arua and Moyo Districts," 4.
47 Lomo et al., "The Phenomenon of Forced Migration in Uganda: An Overview of Policy and Practice in an Historical Context," 7; Noah Gottschalk, Moses Chrispus Okello and Katinka Ridderbos, "There Are No Refugees in This Area: Self-Settled Refugees in Koboko," Refugee Law Project Working Paper No. 18, 2005, p. 3. Available from www.refugeelawproject.org/working_papers/RLP.WP18.pdf.

Machiavello, "Forced Migrants as an Under-Utilized Asset: Refugee Skills, Livelihoods, and Achievements in Kampala, Uganda," 1.

48 Lomo et al., "The Phenomenon of Forced Migration in Uganda: An Overview of Policy and Practice in an Historical Context," Gottschalk et al., "There Are No Refugees in This Area: Self-Settled Refugees in Koboko," 21.
49 Hovil et al., "We Are All Stranded Here Together: The Local Settlement System, Freedom of Movement, and Livelihood Opportunities in Arua and Moyo Districts," 4; see also Machiavello, "Forced Migrants as an Under-Utilized Asset: Refugee Skills, Livelihoods, and Achievements in Kampala, Uganda," 28.
50 Hovil, "Free to Stay, Free to Go? Movement, Seclusion and Integration of Refugees in Moyo District," 13; Machiavello, "Forced Migrants as an Under-Utilized Asset: Refugee Skills, Livelihoods, and Achievements in Kampala, Uganda," Hovil, "Free to Stay, Free to Go? Movement, Seclusion and Integration of

Refugees in Moyo District," 23; Gottschalk et al., "There Are No Refugees in This Area: Self-Settled Refugees in Koboko," 14ff; Dryden-Peterson and Hovil, "Local Integration as a Durable Solution: Refugees, Host Populations and Education in Uganda." Note: many of these were written between 2000 and 2005, and as demonstrated here, there have been a few more positive views since.

51 UNHCR has also been involved with IDP operations since the implementation of the cluster approach but has been phasing out of its operations given the relative restoration of calm in northern Uganda. UNHCR reports that its refugee and IDP budget grew between 2006 and 2008 but dropped in 2009 as Sudanese refugees and Ugandan IDPs were returning. They report an increase in 2010 and 2011 with some arrivals from the DRC ($54.5M in 2010 to $81M in 2011) and reported plans to phase out of IDP operations in 2012, with a $66M budget reported. Generally, however, those working on refugees in Uganda say there is now little overlap with IDP issues, which have largely subsided in recent years (UNHCR, "Uganda Country Operations Profile Page," 2013. Available from www.unhcr.org/cgi-bin/texis/vtx/page?page=49e483c06&submit=GO).

52 Hovil, "Free to Stay, Free to Go? Movement, Seclusion and Integration of Refugees in Moyo District," 3; UNHCR Official L 2013; UNHCR Official F 2013.

53 Kaiser, "The UNHCR and Withdrawal from Kiryandongo: Anatomy of a Handover," 15, emphasis added.

54 Hovil et al., "We Are All Stranded Here Together: The Local Settlement System, Freedom of Movement, and Livelihood Opportunities in Arua and Moyo Districts," 31.

55 Kaiser, "The UNHCR and Withdrawal from Kiryandongo: Anatomy of a Handover," 16.

56 Kaiser, "The UNHCR and Withdrawal from Kiryandongo: Anatomy of a Handover," 10.

57 Kaiser, "Sudanese Refugees in Uganda and Kenya," 262.

58 Kaiser, "Sudanese Refugees in Uganda and Kenya," 262.

59 Kaiser, "The UNHCR and Withdrawal from Kiryandongo: Anatomy of a Handover," 9.

60 Kaiser, "The UNHCR and Withdrawal from Kiryandongo: Anatomy of a Handover," 9.

61 UNHCR Official C 2013. He stressed the desire to find better ways to pass off refugee responsibilities to government actors and the never-ending need to engage development actors. He also talked about the struggle with local capacity when trying to hand over service delivery and how, when they do, the quality often goes down: "Skilled NGO workers leave and they can't provide high quality salaries to maintain high quality people" (UNHCR Official C 2013). This also contributes indirectly to UNHCR staying and maintaining state-like functions.

62 UNHCR Official E 2013.

63 This is not to say that this is always a positive or negative for the refugees. There have been times when the teamwork between UNHCR and OPM has not always resulted in positive outcomes for refugees, according to several NGO workers and various studies from previous years. Kaiser's study, for example, discusses UNHCR and GoU joint attempts to pressure unregistered refugees to leave, giving an impression that they were colluding ("The UNHCR and Withdrawal from Kiryandongo: Anatomy of a Handover," 4). Indeed, several

NGO workers (both African and expatriate) emphasized how corrupt the government and UNHCR were in Uganda, particularly in comparison to Tanzania and Kenya (NGO Official D 2013). These were solely impressions—direct evidence was not provided at the time of conversation—but it was mentioned often and described as if it were fact, something that "everybody who works here just knows." In addition, Kaiser points out that the close working relationship between UNHCR and OPM, particularly at the field level (interviewees also confirmed a close working relationship between OPM and UNHCR in the field) can make it difficult for UNHCR to pressure the GoU in refugee protection issues ("Sudanese Refugees in Uganda and Kenya," 262).

64 UNHCR Official L 2013.

65 UNHCR Official C 2013.

66 UNHCR Official C 2013.

67 GoU Official A 2013.

68 GoU Official A 2013.

69 In terms of the material, SRS example, some additional explanations for why Uganda was more open to adopt the policy at the urging of UNHCR include: individual leadership; empathy for refugees (e.g. Stephen Malinga, the Minister for Disaster Preparedness and Refugees, was himself a refugee in the United States (USG Official G 2013)). One UNHCR official stated, "[it] is quite open . . . many [OPM staff] say 'we have been refugees ourselves, so we understand' . . . the element of empathy is very important" to working as a team (UNHCR Official E 2013)); pan-Africanist sentiments leading to expressions of unity with refugees; and less securitization of refugees (than Kenya or Tanzania). Others might argue the simple calculation that UNHCR in Uganda has more influence because it pays for things. Kaiser, for example, writes that the GoU only considered SRS and SP because UNHCR was willing to pay for them ("Sudanese Refugees in Uganda and Kenya," 260; Hovil et al., "We Are All Stranded Here Together: The Local Settlement System, Freedom of Movement, and Livelihood Opportunities in Arua and Moyo Districts," 4). Still others argue that UNHCR's strategy with SRS did not have the best interests of refugees at heart (see Machiavello, "Forced Migrants as an Under-Utilized Asset: Refugee Skills, Livelihoods, and Achievements in Kampala, Uganda") or that SP and SRS have only made refugees more dependent on UNHCR's assistance and thus further in the direction of surrogacy than partnership. Other factors affecting state behavior and how well UNHCR can influence Uganda on refugee issues include the availability of land, how the emergency is dealt with from the start (e.g. camps versus settlements), development goals, population growth, natural resource discovery and the perception of refugee permanence/temporariness (UNHCR Official C 2013; UNHCR Official E 2013; UNHCR Official O 2013; NGO Official G 2013; NGO Official D 2013). Thus, surrogacy is one of a range of factors combining to determine UNHCR's ability to influence Uganda's behavior toward refugees.

70 Although this is arguably true in any case, whether UNHCR is a surrogate state or not.

71 Interviewee in Chris Dolan and Lucy Hovil, "Humanitarian Protection in Uganda? A Trojan Horse?," *Humanitarian Policy Group Background Paper, Overseas Development Institute*, 2006, p. 12. Available from www.odi.org.uk/sites/odi.org.uk/files/odi-assets/publications-opinion-files/381.pdf.

72 Kaiser, "Sudanese Refugees in Uganda and Kenya," 264.

73 Dolan and Hovil, "Humanitarian Protection in Uganda? A Trojan Horse?," 18.
74 It is also worth remembering that UNHCR is always constrained by its top-down hierarchical organization. Dolan and Hovil, for example, cite the frustration on the part of humanitarian workers on the ground that have to carry out an inflexible agenda planned at headquarters ("Humanitarian Protection in Uganda? A Trojan Horse?," 12).
75 Dolan and Hovil, "Humanitarian Protection in Uganda? A Trojan Horse?," 12.
76 Refugee Law Project, "The Plight of Achol-Pii Refugees and Refugee Policy in Uganda," 2003. Available from www.refugeelawproject.org/archives.php.
77 Dolan and Hovil, "Humanitarian Protection in Uganda? A Trojan Horse?," 12.
78 Dolan and Hovil, "Humanitarian Protection in Uganda? A Trojan Horse?," 12.
79 Hovil, "Free to Stay, Free to Go? Movement, Seclusion and Integration of Refugees in Moyo District."
80 Dryden-Peterson and Hovil, "A Remaining Hope for Durable Solutions: Local Integration of Refugees and Their Hosts in the Case of Uganda," 29.
81 Dryden-Peterson and Hovil, "A Remaining Hope for Durable Solutions: Local Integration of Refugees and Their Hosts in the Case of Uganda," 30.
82 Hovil et al., "We Are All Stranded Here Together: The Local Settlement System, Freedom of Movement, and Livelihood Opportunities in Arua and Moyo Districts," 10.
83 Dryden-Peterson and Hovil, "A Remaining Hope for Durable Solutions: Local Integration of Refugees and Their Hosts in the Case of Uganda," 30; see also Kaiser, "The UNHCR and Withdrawal from Kiryandongo: Anatomy of a Handover," 11; Gottschalk et al., "There Are No Refugees in This Area: Self-Settled Refugees in Koboko," 17ff. Similar to the SP (as noted earlier), a number of scholars have been critical of the SRS/DAR policies, arguing that it has not helped to socially integrate refugees into their host societies (Dryden-Peterson and Hovil, "A Remaining Hope for Durable Solutions: Local Integration of Refugees and Their Hosts in the Case of Uganda," 30; Hovil et al., "We Are All Stranded Here Together: The Local Settlement System, Freedom of Movement, and Livelihood Opportunities in Arua and Moyo Districts," 11; Gottschalk et al., "There Are No Refugees in This Area: Self-Settled Refugees in Koboko," Kaiser, "The UNHCR and Withdrawal from Kiryandongo: Anatomy of a Handover," 20; Peter Nabuguzi, "Refugees and Politics in Uganda," in *Uganda and the Problem of the Refugees*, ed. Anthony Ginyera-Pinycwa (Kampala: Makerere University Press, 1995), 99). Many argue that SRS does not give refugees "full" choice and that it implies that the only "true" refugees are those receiving assistance in the settlements. Security, economic, environmental and political concerns also emerge in their critiques, as well as concerns about parallel delivery systems. Others, like Machiavello (2003) argue that UNHCR and OPM may say that they want to integrate refugees but actually sabotage self-sufficiency prospects and possible integration.
84 UNHCR 2003.
85 Gottschalk et al., "There Are No Refugees in This Area: Self-Settled Refugees in Koboko," 24.
86 UNHCR, "Development Assistance for Refugees (DAR) for Uganda Self Reliance Strategy: Way Forward," RLSS/DOS Mission Report 03/11, 2003. Available from www.unhcr.org/41c6a19b4.html.
87 NGO Official G 2013.
88 NGO Official K 2013.

89 Lomo et al., "The Phenomenon of Forced Migration in Uganda: An Overview of Policy and Practice in an Historical Context," 9. This can even be seen in the way the Refugee Law Project talks about the refugee situation, outlining the responsibilities of GoU and UNHCR in tandem, a telling thing in and of itself (Refugee Law Project, "The Migration of Refugees from Tanzania to Uganda: Whose Responsibility?" 2003. Available from www.refugeelawproject.org/archives.php).

90 Financially speaking, UNHCR does fund most of Uganda's refugee activities, but interviewees expressed that the government takes a more active role in ownership and oversight of how funds are spent as well. This more active role enables UNHCR to use its expertise and funds to work with the state, potentially influencing its decisions more.

91 UNHCR Official C 2013.

92 UNHCR Official F 2013.

93 Scholars like Dolan and Hovil ("Humanitarian Protection in Uganda? A Trojan Horse?") would say that Uganda struggles with this, too. As noted earlier, the UNHCR Representative to Uganda was even expelled in 2003, demonstrating the need for UNHCR to balance speaking out with keeping good relations to maintain access. However, this study would argue that this struggle was greater when UNHCR was involved as a surrogate state and is less of an issue now that it works in partnership with the government. The partnership is not perfect but arguably gives UNHCR more input because it is not the only actor "doing everything, paying for everything, and unable to expect anything from the government" while the government simply chooses to maintain the status quo and ignore any suggested changes from UNHCR.

94 UNHCR Official E 2013; UNHCR Official F 2013.

95 Again, this is not to say that UNHCR's role was the sole reason these policies were adopted but that it did play a part.

96 Again, the framework does not argue causality of abdication/surrogacy and partnership/nonsurrogacy. In some cases, abdication may cause surrogacy, and in others, surrogacy may lead to abdication (the same is true with partnership). For the purposes of this argument, it is only necessary to know that they are paired, not that one necessarily causes the other.

97 Kaiser, "The UNHCR and Withdrawal from Kiryandongo: Anatomy of a Handover," 7.

98 For example, one Assistant Camp Commander stated that while OPM tried to have good relations with local authorities, they had little influence on decisions (GoU Official A 2013); local officials demand that 30 percent of UNHCR funds go to local needs, but interviews from NGOs stated that OPM continues to overshadow local government needs and desires, leaving them constantly dissatisfied (NGO Official G 2013).

99 Kaiser, "Sudanese Refugees in Uganda and Kenya"; Karen Jacobsen, "The Forgotten Solution: Local Integration for Refugees in Developing Countries," Working Paper No. 45, 2001. *New Issues in Refugee Research*, Geneva: UNHCR; Jeffrey Herbst, *States and Power in Africa: Comparative Lessons in Authority and Control* (Princeton, NJ: Princeton University Press, 2000); Christopher Clapham, *Africa in the International System: The Politics of State Survival* (Cambridge: Cambridge University Press, 1996).

100 Again, scholarship from earlier in the decade argues that UNHCR has had to remain silent when it should speak out, perhaps because it is too much "in

cahoots" with the GoU. However, this research found that UNHCR's partnership relationship with the government gave it more input in the state's decisions about refugees, not less.

101 NGO Official G 2013; UNHCR Official E 2013.

102 UNHCR Official C 2013.

103 For example, Kaiser's (2002) discussion of the handing over of the Sudanese Kiryandongo settlement demonstrates this. She writes that UNHCR "told" the government they were giving the settlement back to them—requiring the government to fund it but also implying that UNHCR had been "in charge" of that land by handing it back over, when authorities, as Kaiser notes, may have thought they were always in charge of it. She writes, "This attempt to hand over responsibility for Kiryandongo was understood as a precedent for other settlements in northern Uganda and was entirely unwelcome. Furthermore, the government rejected the vocabulary of UNHCR, asking how a settlement which, by virtue of it being in Uganda, has been 'owned' by it throughout its existence, could be 'handed over'" (Kaiser, "The UNHCR and Withdrawal from Kiryandongo: Anatomy of a Handover," 13).

104 UNHCR Official L 2013.

6 Conclusions

- **Summarizing the framework and methods**
- **Practical reflections for UNHCR**
- **Theoretical implications**
- **Calls for further research and concluding thoughts**

There are now a record number of displaced persons in the world—some 65 million.[1] Most are in protracted situations, with the length of time in displacement averaging 26 years.[2] Refugees and other forced migrants are now front and center on the international agenda, relating to a host of security and economic concerns. From President Trump's antirefugee policies, to Europe's response to Syrian refugees and the UN's attempt to respond to forced migration in a more comprehensive way with the New York Declaration, the world recognizes that forced migration is no longer a side issue. It is a major part of the global conversation between states, the UN, NGOs, civil society and the general public.

In light of this, UNHCR, the largest actor tasked with refugee protection and often the global leader on refugee issues, seems poised to expand its portfolio. This is not an inherently "good" or "bad" thing—how UNHCR adapts remains to be seen. What is clear is that there are a range of roles it has assumed in the past, and these varied roles can affect its ability to influence states on refugee matters. Now is a critical time to examine how UNHCR can/should manage its heightened role in the face of mass displacement.

This book, therefore, has sought to contribute to this critical analysis of UNHCR's role as a surrogate state in PRS through a broader framework posited about international organizations. It has examined the relationship between an IO's ability to influence the state and its role at the domestic level—analysis that is very relevant to understanding IOs working on multiple levels (from headquarter down to field level). While no two IOs are identical—indeed, UNHCR is unique in many ways: it is normative (its mandate is based on refugee protection as enshrined in the 1951

Convention Relating to the Status of Refugees and the subsequent 1967 Protocol); it serves mainly noncitizens (refugees); it works on multiple levels (globally/internationally, nationally and locally); and it plays multiple roles (donor, negotiator/liaison between states, lawyer of refugees, humanitarian relief organization etc.)—there are some traits of IOs working "on the ground" that are generalizable across cases. In the same way scholars like Michael Barnett and Martha Finnemore (1999) have compared across IOs, one might consider how conclusions about UNHCR here relate to IOs like IOM, UNDP, WFP or ICRC, for example, which may have different mandates, structures, methods and systems but do work on multiple levels and interface with the host state. They must serve local populations while also maintaining politically advantageous relations with the host state. They also work operationally on the ground but also work through a number of partners and subcontracted organizations. (Some literature even discusses surrogacy in relation to NGOs, as examined in the case study chapters.[3])

The book created a framework of "domestication" to understand first when and how surrogacy occurs and what it looks like and second, what it means for an IO's ability to influence the state in which it is working. UNHCR was an excellent IO to study because of its multileveled presence, working at headquarter, regional and field levels. In the East African examples studied here, UNHCR, though focused on refugee protection, did everything from providing water, paying police salaries, paving roads and even distributing land in some cases—tasks far beyond their original intent. Some of these tasks took on the form of state substitution. As noted earlier, Crisp and Slaughter (2008) write that UNHCR's C&M model "created a widespread perception that the organization was a surrogate state, complete with its own territory (refugee camps), citizens (refugees), public services (education, health care, water, sanitation, etc.), and even ideology (community participation, gender equality)."[4] In turn, refugees in Africa have arguably been "effectively governed by the UNHCR, rather than by any state administration."[5]

The framework considered how IO surrogacy is met with state abdication or partnership, and examined how state marginalization and responsibility shifting help to explain the counterintuitive finding that surrogate state IOs like UNHCR tend to have less influence over state policy; their influence is greater when they work in partnership with the state. Indeed, UNHCR interviewees lamented at UNHCR's "taking over" state responsibilities and funding departments or projects that "should" be funded by the state. They expressed frustration at trading access to their work with their ability to speak out, thus losing the ability to "responsibilize" the government and instead doing everything themselves.[6]

The notion that UNHCR is substituting for the state at all is itself an interesting debate at both the empirical and theoretical levels. But taken a step further—considering how UNHCR's surrogacy affects its ability to influence the state—also has important theoretical implications for broader questions about "how IOs matter" and how they can impact state behavior.

Comparing and contrasting the case studies

The case studies of Kenya, Tanzania and Uganda demonstrate variance in UNHCR's role and relationship with the state and subsequently its ability to influence the state. As noted in Chapter 1, they demonstrate variance in both material (policy-related) and nonmaterial indicators of influence and varying degrees of surrogacy. At face value, they are somewhat easy to compare: Uganda, Tanzania and Kenya are in the same region; have hosted large numbers of refugees for long periods of time; and have had UNHCR involved in refugee assistance as a surrogate state and otherwise. Moreover, they are all developing countries, former colonies, and have authorities that struggle to broadcast power to remote areas, thus leaving them ripe for IO involvement and potential IO surrogacy.[7]

However, there are significant differences between each case as well as within cases when comparing different points in history. The case studies demonstrate variation on UNHCR's role and level of surrogacy and its ability to influence state policies on refugees. Uganda (Congolese) and Tanzania (1972) represent higher levels of partnership, lower levels of surrogacy and higher levels of influence, whilst Tanzania (1990s), Uganda (Sudanese) and Kenya demonstrate state abdication, high levels of surrogacy and low levels of influence. Process tracing and secondary literature reviews have helped uncover the conditions under which UNHCR assumed surrogacy and how/why it was maintained, and the mechanisms of marginalization of the state and responsibility shifting help unpack why these relationships of influence are true in conjunction with other explanations. This variance points to the relationships posited in the framework, as shown in Figure 6.1.

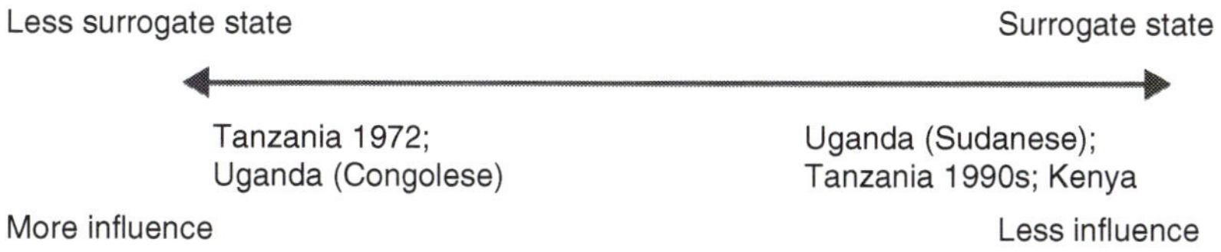

Figure 6.1 Relationship between UNHCR's surrogacy and influence on the state in Kenya, Tanzania and Uganda

Kenya

Kenya demonstrates a case where UNHCR has taken on a higher degree of surrogacy and the state practices abdication of its responsibilities toward refugees (and arguably toward locals in the region as well). Thus, by comparison, it is more extreme than the other two cases. UNHCR in Kenya assumed surrogacy to fill a void left by the state in refugee protection and assistance to Somali refugees in the NEP. It has been largely responsible for service provision and has taken on a range of governance functions. For its part, the authorities have had little incentive to change this set-up, content to focus solely on the security issues associated with refugees, letting UNHCR pay for and carry out all other activities and responsibilities.

Interestingly, this has meant that UNHCR has little influence on state decisions toward refugees. Certainly, a number of factors explain this counterintuitive relationship (including securitization, historical context, international pressures and regional dynamics), but UNHCR's surrogacy, the focus of this inquiry, also sabotages the organization's ability to "responsibilize" the government or argue for refugees' increased access to their rights. While there are some changes on the horizon, UNHCR remains limited in how much it can affect policy or be heard on refugee-related issues, and refugees remain largely encamped or in the shadows in urban slums.

Tanzania

Tanzania offers a "double-case study," with two distinctly different cases in one. Burundian refugees that fled in 1972 were treated very differently than Burundian refugees that fled in the 1990s. The former experienced very little assistance from UNHCR or the state until recently, while the latter experienced a surrogate state UNHCR. It is not a coincidence that UNHCR's ability to influence in both cases varied as well. Despite its small role, UNHCR was able to encourage the GoT to consider LI for the 1972 cases of Burundians. This was in part due to historical factors (former President Nyerere had "promised" this, and this caseload was already largely integrated into Tanzanian society, self-sufficient and contributing to society) but also due to UNHCR's role as a resource and "sharer of information." It was not a surrogate state among this group and thus was able to speak out and advocate in a different way than it was with the 1990s caseload, for whom it substituted for the state. Indeed, the state practiced partnership with UNHCR for the 1972 caseload and abdication for the 1990s caseload. UNHCR's surrogacy among the 1990s caseload was extensive, to the point where people expected little to nothing from the government and held UNHCR responsible for public services and functions of governance.[8] In turn, the government had no incentive to change the status quo, and UNHCR subsequently had lower levels of influence on policies and decisions about refugees. It certainly had increased responsibility and some forms of local authority with the 1990s cases, but this did not translate to greater influence. Thus, UNHCR had greater influence on the government with the 1972 caseload but not with the 1990s caseload.

Uganda

The third case, Congolese refugees in Uganda, offers one of the clearest views of partnership with the state. In this case, UNHCR took on some surrogate state properties but not nearly to the extent as seen in Kenya or in Tanzania in the 1990s. There is some variance within this case as well (among UNHCR's role with Sudanese—a surrogate state—versus Congolese refugees—not a surrogate state), but broadly speaking, UNHCR's lesser surrogate state role and its partnership with the state have granted it greater influence on state decisions and policies about refugees among both material and nonmaterial indicators of influence. For example, UNHCR was instrumental in bringing about the SRS/DAR in Uganda. While the policy is not perfect, it has received praise for granting refugees greater access to their right to work and freedom of movement (the cornerstones of a policy of LI). The case study traces a number of factors that bring about this outcome and the relationship between the GoU and UNHCR. It also demonstrates how UNHCR's role of partnership, rather than full-out substitution for the state, helped bring about greater influence.

Practical reflections for UNHCR

> [T]he moment we start to act like the state, we lose . . . we cannot just run a camp for 30 years.[9]

As UNHCR takes even more leadership in an international arena increasingly focused on refugees, it is being asked to do many things. It would serve the organization well to do a deeper analysis of its role as a surrogate state vis-à-vis durable solutions, protection, C&M models, programs and staff. While this book does not prescribe policy, there are some UNHCR-specific lessons that can be gleaned from the case studies, as well as some broader themes about UNHCR's domestic role as a surrogate state. First, while UNHCR's overall rhetoric and its staff tend to say that surrogacy is not what the organization wants, nor is it good for any actors involved (especially refugees), it seems to have difficulty resisting surrogacy when the conditions for it are present. After all, whether reluctantly filling a void or aggressively grabbing power, UNHCR officials tend to express a moral obligation to take on projects beyond their mandates in order to protect refugees. And once it is acting as a surrogate state, it struggles to scale back when the situation is winding down. As UNHCR Official J stated in 2012, the familiar patterns of substitution for government are difficult to break.

While this study only looked at UNHCR's surrogacy in Kenya, Tanzania and Uganda, UNHCR acts as a surrogate state in many other PRS around the world, and thus these findings are generalizable to other cases. In particular, UNHCR policies and operational strategies are "top-down" from Geneva and thus relatively uniform across regions. Still, further research should be done on other cases to consider how this complex picture points to UNHCR's need to more critically engage with the scope and scale of its operations, and to deeply question the extent to which surrogacy happens accidentally or on purpose.

More importantly, it would seem that surrogacy does not help UNHCR achieve its larger goals of helping refugees gain fuller access to their rights and protections under international law. Perhaps UNHCR should consider how to avoid surrogacy in situations where the state leaves a void and what some alternatives to surrogacy might be that still enable refugee protections and needs to be addressed. At the same time, UNHCR may find that it may have little choice to maintain surrogacy in cases where refugees are in dire need and the state is nowhere to be found. In these cases, there may be value in finding ways to minimize the length of time that it acts as a surrogate state and to maximize its influence on the state by other means, perhaps finding new areas of leverage or agreement on other durable solutions that move away from confinement, encampment and C&M that tend to be found with surrogacy and PRS. Development actors are an important part of this conversation.

To that end, UNHCR may also want to investigate whether its role as a surrogate state in some PRS inadvertently leads states to directly choose more restrictive policies, including encampment and confinement. Certainly, UNHCR would argue that this is the opposite of its goal in such situations, but the case studies point to this as a possibility. In these cases, does UNHCR's surrogacy water down the ways in which UNHCR can protect refugees (e.g. Dolan and Hovil 2006)? Does this mean that it should scale back some of its field operations in favor of returning to a greater focus on legal protection? Or might there be a way to instead channel surrogacy into improvements for refugees instead?

On the other hand, UNHCR might also want to consider when its surrogacy is a benefit to refugees, the host state and the organization's interests.

After all, while surrogacy may lead to less influence, it does not necessarily point to a bad relationship with the authorities. Even where state abdication is present in tandem with UNHCR's surrogacy, the government-UNHCR relationship may not necessarily be negative. Other research might also include how this study on UNHCR as a surrogate state in PRS might contribute to understandings of UNHCR's role with IDPs. In addition, broader studies might also consider the role and effects of UNHCR's IPs "on the ground," who are often subcontracted to carry out day-to-day activities. Their influence on the state and the broader relationship of UNHCR's surrogacy with the state is also important.

Theoretical reflections

A number of theoretical reflections follow from this study. Specific to UNHCR—and likely many other NGOs with similar structures—the passing of time affects how the IO operates and its relationship with the state and other actors, not least those it seeks to serve. Surrogacy also tends to occur where states leave a gap (abdication); in contrast, when states feel a stronger sense of ownership and thus take a more active role, surrogacy is less likely (partnership). Likewise, the research has shown that influence at the local level does not necessarily translate to influence at a national or international level. At the very least, it has also shown that money alone (i.e. a very wealthy IO) does not translate to influence.

This research also has implications for the broader concepts of sovereignty and power in international relations. This book has shown that an IO substituting for the state does not necessarily equate to more power. African states in particular, which have hosted many international actors intervening in their territory, are often viewed as weak or "at the bottom of any conventional ordering of global power, importance and prestige."[10] In addition, as their economies have lagged, many African states had to cede some sovereign decision-making power to international bodies offering to help, thus making them subject to "a comprehensive superstructure of international accountability (Young 1999, 34–5)."[11] Furthermore. there is a general conclusion among scholars that "African post-colonial states have been strong on juridical sovereignty and weak on empirical sovereignty (Jackson 1990)."[12] Indeed, these issues have been at the core of many of the conditions listed for UNHCR's surrogacy: the weakness or even absence of a state presence in a given locale opens the door for IO surrogacy, even if the state still claims power over national decisions.[13] This implies that an IO surrogate state is absorbing power or authority where the sovereign state has not been able to or did not desire to.

The effects of IO surrogacy within a "weak" sovereign state, then, are profound, even if the IO cannot ultimately influence the state's decisions. As noted in the Tanzania case, for example, Landau writes,

> Even after the aid dollars dry up and the refugees return home, these dynamics will have changed how citizens relate to one another, the state, the territory they inhabit, and a set of processes—displacement and humanitarianism—that are an under-explored form of globalization."[14]

In the Tanzanian context, he argues that UNHCR's absorption of the blame for areas where the state is lacking enables the state to shirk its responsibilities, which in turn transforms the social contract between citizens and their leaders. As noted in Chapter 4, an international actor working as a surrogate state "challenges the territorial basis for domestic politics and the classical Weberian state."[15]

IO surrogacy also affects state sovereignty in Africa by uninvolving the state in certain aspects of governance, an important facet of the mechanisms proffered in this book. Semboja and Therkildsen (1992), for example, refer to this as "state contraction" and focus on the privatization of service provision—now carried out by nonstate actors instead of the state. They argue that the proliferation of nonstate actors in some states (especially in Africa) has transferred decision-making power to other actors and further maintained an absence of central authorities from remote areas, leading to questions about the state's sovereignty.[16] Clapham, for example, writes that, by privatizing many services normally carried out by the state, NGOs, not the state, liaised with foreign donor states.[17] This, then, excludes the state from decisions it may have otherwise been a part of. Case studies have also shown that the state may find itself in a position where its only option is to leverage refugee aid for more international development assistance.[18] While the refugee-hosting area may be bringing attention to a remote area that might otherwise be ignored by international and domestic actors, it can also create the perception that the state is not entirely in control of certain areas, thus looking less "viable" as a sovereign state.[19]

Calls for further research and concluding thoughts

Inevitably, this book has prompted a host of other areas for further research, both in terms of the theoretical ideas and empirical cases examined here. Theoretically, the idea that "less is more" in terms of IO involvement and its influence on the state in which it is working prompts questions about how far such assertions can go. Where does one draw the line? Surrogacy might mean less influence, but surely the opposite—an IO with hardly any or no domestic-level involvement—is not likely to have maximum influence. So where might the greatest point of influence be, if it can be identified at all? And how can IOs alter their levels of influence based on their roles on the ground? Further studies should consider this.

Moreover, further research should not only look at other IOs' domesticated presence "on the ground," but also the inverse of a domesticated IO: the "internationalization of the local." Some IR scholarship already points to this (including some of the UNHCR surrogate state scholarship), but further investigation of this topic would naturally follow from this research. Globalization literature may also shed light on this. Further research might also analyze other variables affecting the levels of influence an IO has on a state, including the role of leaders and individuals, a variable frequently mentioned in the interviews conducted here. Literature on capacity building is also complementary to this study and could benefit from some of the framework's analytical tools. Finally, additional scholarship might examine the extent to which surrogacy is "good" or "bad"—that is, the extent to which it benefits the actors involved, and the refugees in particular. This study has not made normative judgments on whether UNHCR's surrogacy was positive or negative (though it has identified drawbacks and ways it has been useful in some of the cases), but further research might provide guidance on these issues, be it with international relief actors, multinational corporations (MNCs) or other types of IOs working domestically.

The ever-changing political landscapes of each case study also makes them fertile ground for further research in the areas of IO surrogacy and influence on state decisions about refugees. Evolving displacement and political changes are happening quickly. In Kenya, the DRA has been disbanded, and UNHCR is still very active amidst ongoing government attempts to close Dadaab. Tanzania and Uganda are also facing fresh new groups of refugees and other migrants, and it is unclear whether policies will shift significantly as UNHCR continues its work. Uganda has also been working on a national identification program to document all Ugandans, which may make it more difficult for refugees to "slip in under the radar." This, too, will affect UNHCR and the state's relationship, roles and policies. Thus, there are many issues to continue to research on the theoretical and empirical levels.

In conclusion, this book has examined IOs working at the domestic level. It focused specifically on IOs that take on surrogate state properties, considering when and how surrogacy occurs. While this part of the argument was descriptive, it demonstrates not only that an IO can act autonomously, but also as a substitute for the state when there is a void. States tend to respond with either abdication—letting the IO "do everything"—or partnership—joining the IO in its work. It then considered what this means for the IO's relationship with the state and in particular its ability to influence its behavior. Surprisingly, the study found that there was an inverse relationship between IO surrogacy and its ability to influence the state: the more an IO takes on surrogacy, the less influence it has. The mechanisms of marginalization of the state and responsibility shifting helped explain these outcomes. The empirical focus of the book examined the presence of UNHCR as a surrogate state (to varying extents) in PRS in Kenya, Tanzania and Uganda. These cases showed variation in surrogacy and across levels of influence on the state, as well as in policy outcomes and nonmaterial indicators of influence.

In addition to demonstrating the conditions for IO surrogacy, the relationship between an IO surrogate and the state and the ways in which surrogacy affects an IO's ability to influence the state, the case studies pointed out important differences between IO behavior on different levels. Indeed, the domesticated presence of UNHCR as a surrogate state brought new questions to the forefront about its role within the state with which it is working. These questions generated insights that were very different from the international-level inquiries that tend to dominate IR studies of IOs.

In one way, then, this study has moved away from statist ontologies in IR, as Barnett (2001) and others would call for, by considering other forms of authority besides the traditional sovereign state and its recognized borders.[20] It has engaged with the messy and overlapping layers of "international," "national" and "local" and considered where IOs assume authority and power, without subsequent influence on state decisions. On the other hand, the "so what?" portion of the research—that which tried to understand how IO surrogacy affected its ability to influence the state—took the questions back to IR's traditional stomping grounds of the state.

The counterintuitive findings on the relationship between IOs domesticated as surrogate states and their influence on the state are provocative. In one sense, the findings seem to demonstrate that there are few limits as to how much responsibility a domesticated, surrogate state IO can take on, but there remain limits on its influence and power. It is possible that claims like this uphold notions of the sovereign state, highlighting that no matter how much an IO takes on in terms of responsibilities or authority, the sovereign state (no matter how "weak") is still "in charge." Or, it is possible that these new axes of "power," though they may not translate into influence over broader state policy decisions or general behavior, are radically reshaping the way governance takes place, particularly in remote, rural areas where a traditional central state presence is not felt. Either way, these themes about domestication and influence certainly add to bigger IR questions about "how IOs matter" and how they are understood in the literature.

Certainly, applying the framework to other IO case studies will help uncover additional insights about IO surrogate states and further confirm the claims argued here. However, the central arguments of this book—that an IO can become a surrogate state at the domestic level but that the increased responsibility and localized authority that come with surrogacy do not grant it greater influence on the state—pose challenges to the theoretical ways IR considers IOs and empirical understandings of UNHCR's approaches to refugee assistance.

Ultimately, the counterintuitive claim addresses a gap in the literature on IOs working domestically and proves that IO influence and its presence within a state might have an inverse relationship. Cases where the IO takes on expansive projects "on the ground" going so far as to substitute for the state, resulted in less, not more influence on the state overall. Thus, it might just be the case that less is actually more.

Notes

1 UNHCR, "Global Forced Displacement Hits Record High." Available from www.unhcr.org/afr/news/latest/2016/6/5763b65a4/global-forced-displacement-hits-record-high.html.
2 US Department of State, "Protracted Refugee Situations." Available from www.state.gov/j/prm/policyissues/issues/protracted/.
3 In Kibondo, Tanzania, for example, the TCRS carried out many of the governance and service provision functions on behalf of UNHCR.
4 Jeff Crisp and Amy Slaughter, "A Surrogate State? The Role of UNHCR in Protracted Refugee Situations," in *Protracted Refugee Situations: Political, Human Rights and Security Implications*, ed. Gil Loescher, James Milner, Edward Newman and Gary Troeller (New York: United Nations University Press, 2008), 131–132.
5 Christopher Clapham, *Africa in the International System: The Politics of State Survival* (Cambridge: Cambridge University Press, 1996), 257.
6 NGO Official K 2013; UNHCR Official C 2013; UNHCR Official E 2013; UNHCR Official N 2012.
7 Clapham, *Africa in the International System: The Politics of State Survival*; Jeffrey Herbst, *States and Power in Africa: Comparative Lessons in Authority and Control* (Princeton, NJ: Princeton University Press, 2000).
8 Loren B. Landau, *The Humanitarian Hangover: Displacement, Aid and Transformation in Western Tanzania* (Johannesburg: Wits University Press, 2008).
9 UNHCR Official J 2012.
10 Clapham 1996, 3 in James Milner, *Refugees, the State and the Politics of Asylum in Africa* (Basingstoke, UK: Palgrave Macmillan, 2009), 11.
11 Milner, *Refugees, the State and the Politics of Asylum in Africa*, 13.
12 Thomas Callaghy, Ronald Kassimir and Robert Latham, "Introduction: Transboundary Formations, Intervention, Order, and Authority," in *Intervention and Transnationalism in Africa: Global-Local Networks of Power*, ed. Thomas Callaghy, Ronald Kassimir and Robert Latham (Cambridge: Cambridge University Press, 2001), 12.
13 See also Milner's (2009) discussion, which draws on Buzan's three components of state sovereignty, noting that, while in theory all states are sovereign and

equal, there are weaker states such as many in Africa. He discusses Jackson's (1990) "quasi-states" that were given "sovereign equality with decolonization but in reality are far from equal with other states in their capacity to provide "concrete benefits which have historically justified . . . sovereign statehood" (Jackson 1990, 21 in Milner, *Refugees, the State and the Politics of Asylum in Africa*, 10).

14 Landau, *The Humanitarian Hangover: Displacement, Aid and Transformation in Western Tanzania*, 1.

15 Landau, *The Humanitarian Hangover: Displacement, Aid and Transformation in Western Tanzania*, 155.

16 Milner notes that they have further shared the experience of state contraction, or rather, of central state withdrawal from what were earlier depicted as some of its key responsibilities. This was most spectacularly seen in Uganda, where the government even withdrew from the basic function of providing minimal physical security but was also evident in Tanzania and to a lesser extent Kenya with regard to the provision and maintenance of infrastructure and basic social services (Milner, *Refugees, the State and the Politics of Asylum in Africa*, 12).

17 Clapham, *Africa in the International System: The Politics of State Survival*, 264.

18 Milner cites Clapham (1996: 193), noting that this "metamorphosis" resulted from a number of pressures "which made it extremely difficult for them to cling to their previous insistence on unfettered sovereignty in the international arena combined with monopoly statehood in the internal one" (Milner, *Refugees, the State and the Politics of Asylum in Africa*, 180).

19 To be fair, however, one might argue that African states have never been close to the model of the Weberian, "modern" state assumed by much of the IR literature, especially in international relations (see Chapter 3, Robert H. Jackson, *Quasi-States: Sovereignty, International Relations, and the Third World* (Cambridge: Cambridge University Press, 1990); Callaghy et al., *Intervention and Transnationalism in Africa: Global-Local Networks of Power*, 13, 197. However, it is also arguable that many developing states around the world have similar properties. Thus, one must use caution not to imply that IO surrogacy completely erases state sovereignty all together.

Herbst 2000, 3 in Milner, *Refugees, the State and the Politics of Asylum in Africa*, 79.

20 Michael Barnett, "Authority, Intervention, and the Outer Limits on International Relations Theory," in *Intervention and Transnationalism in Africa: Global-Local Networks of Power*, ed. Thomas Callaghy, Ronald Kassimir and Robert Latham, 47–68 (Cambridge: Cambridge University Press, 2001), 47.

Index

Note: Page numbers in italic indicate a figure and page numbers in bold indicate a table on the corresponding page. Entries referring to endnote content are indicated by a page number, an "n", and the note number.